.edu

PETER LANG

New York • Washington, D.C./Baltimore • Bern
Frankfurt am Main • Berlin • Brussels • Vienna • Oxford

Dr. Tracey Wilen-Daugenti

.edu

TECHNOLOGY AND LEARNING
ENVIRONMENTS IN HIGHER EDUCATION

PETER LANG
New York • Washington, D.C./Baltimore • Bern
Frankfurt am Main • Berlin • Brussels • Vienna • Oxford

Library of Congress Cataloging-in-Publication Data

Wilen-Daugenti, Tracey.
.edu: technology and learning environments in higher education /
Tracey Wilen-Daugenti.
p. cm.
Includes bibliographical references.
1. Education, Higher—Computer-assisted instruction.
2. Educational Technology.
I. Title: Technology and learning environments in higher education.
LB2395.7.E338   378.1'734—dc22   2008039381
ISBN 978-1-4331-0318-6

Bibliographic information published by **Die Deutsche Bibliothek**.
Die Deutsche Bibliothek lists this publication in the "Deutsche
Nationalbibliografie"; detailed bibliographic data is available
on the Internet at http://dnb.ddb.de/.

Cover design by Clear Point Designs

The paper in this book meets the guidelines for permanence and durability
of the Committee on Production Guidelines for Book Longevity
of the Council of Library Resources.

To Gary,

$$\frac{n(V+D)^{(E+T)}}{P} = \infty \ (S)$$

Thanks for sharing your formula for business success.

$$N = \text{Number of years}$$
$$V = \text{Vision}$$
$$D = \text{Drive}$$
$$E = \text{Education}$$
$$T = \text{Technology}$$
$$P = \text{People}$$
$$\infty = \text{Infinite}$$
$$S = \text{Sucess}$$

Contents

Acknowledgments

Special thanks to my friend Lev Gonick, Ph.D. Thank you for continuing to create a vision for tertiary education leaders on new possibilities and paths for innovative education on campus and in the community. I appreciate your willingness to share some of your vision in this book and to support me in my interest in exploring the potential of technology in education.

Thank you to my academic ally Joe Cevetello, Ed.D. Your interest in higher education and your passion to change the status quo by envisioning the next-generation opportunities for K-20 are admirable and inspiring. Your generosity in sharing your vision in this book is greatly appreciated.

Special thanks to my mother and mentor Patricia D. Wilen, Ph.D., who has supported me through my entire educational journey. Thank you for encouraging me to continue to pursue advanced degrees even when it seemed impossible. Thank you also for spending countless hours reviewing, editing, and contributing to all of my papers and books. I appreciate your excitement and willingness to investigate the uses of newer technologies in education as well as your ability to grasp new concepts and explore them in depth. Thank you for your multiple contributions to this book.

I offer my sincere gratitude to my associate Alva Grace R. McKee—a truly dedicated and successful woman with admirable educational goals in the sciences and a profound interest in improving the education opportunities for students worldwide. Thank you for your time and interest in reviewing, validating, and guiding many of the ideas in this book. Thank you also for taking a leadership role in organizing the glossary for this book, which I know will be a key resource for many readers.

Special thanks to Michael Adams, my creative and patient IBSG colleague at Cisco. Your enthusiasm in exploring the use of creative technologies with me and your encouragement for me to articulate my vision for higher education institutions have been invaluable.

Introduction

At the end of their graduating year, students often ask me if I can leave them with any words of advice. And every year my response has been the same: Set your sights on obtaining 5 degrees, take as much technology training as your university and workplace will offer, and stay flexible and relevant in your career. My advice usually provokes a stimulating question about what is required today and what will be required in the future to remain relevant, productive, and employed participants in a vastly changing world. While continuous learning would be my first recommendation to all individuals, today's employers tend to place more value on the number and level of degrees that individuals secure. Second, careers are complex and often require a number of interdisciplinary areas of studies that for many may mean intersecting a variety of degrees in the sciences, business, psychology, law, and other specialized areas. Third, no one can take your degrees away from you; these go with you anywhere.

In today's environment, a student can expect to have more than 5 jobs, and many jobs are yet to be defined. Being prepared to participate in or create the next genre of employment is a critical part of what each of us faces on our paths to learning and employment. Education is a key factor in helping you define who you are, your strengths, likes and dislikes.

Technology is here to stay—it leaves a lasting impact on each of our lives and is a core requirement in today's working world. My view is that technology literacy should be integrated into our learning lives at an early stage, just as a foreign language would be. In this way, fluency in technology may be achieved and the difficulty in applying it to all areas of life may be eliminated or minimized. Shockingly, many students do not have their first experience with technology until they reach higher education, and there are still some who do not have experience until they enter the workforce. These individuals are placed at a disadvantage, having "to learn" later in their careers what could have been integrated early on.

At the same time, I meet many faculty members who have mixed viewpoints. Many are concerned that the universities are not aggressively pursuing a technology strategy, soliciting faculty input, or offering a plan on how to integrate and support technology. These faculty members come from all disciplines and all ages and truly want to create the best environment for their students, themselves, and their institution.

I also meet many faculty members who have difficulty understanding the value of technology as they did not have it themselves as students. They are smart and successful and have educated many successful students the "traditional" way, so they question why the current model may not continue to be appropriate for students.

I have empathy for faculty members, as I am aware of the tremendous workloads that many carry with their research and teaching requirements leaving little time for learning new technologies. Many do use technology once they have had the opportunity to find its value in research computations, writing, or collaborations. I also empathize with their students who might enter the workforce as I did, initially unprepared and unable to cope in high-tech companies until I took the initiative to train myself to avoid career setbacks.

Fortunately, many institutions have placed their technology leaders in the university cabinet, thus emphasizing that technology is important. There are chief technology officers (CTO) and chief information officers (CIO) of institutions that have a clear vision and strategy for their campus and have had success in using technology to enhance teaching, learning, administration, and research. I have made it a point to include some of these strategists in this book so that we can learn how and what they have done successfully. And globally, I have respectfully spent ample time with university presidents and vice chancellors who have increasingly broad and complex roles. Although many do not understand technology in its entirety, they have the vision to set strategy and empower their key technology leaders (CTOs and CIOs) to deploy a technology vision for the institution. They do this through the organization structure and budget policies that ensures that their faculty and students have the best technology capabilities to achieve success in a rapidly moving world— capabilities that enhance the profile and desirability of their universities. I feel that these unique leaders are doing a tremendous service to all of us in higher education.

The Internet has already transformed higher education by streamlining campus administrative processes, enhancing facilities such as dorms and classrooms, enabling digital libraries, expanding access to distance learning, and creating engaging learning environments through video and computer simulations. Even so, many Higher Education Institutions are trying to understand how the next generation of Internet and virtual-reality technologies will impact their students and campuses. These technologies include Web 2.0, multimedia, virtual presence, gaming, and the proliferation of next-generation mobile devices.

In this book, I will discuss how higher-education institutions can use these technologies to enable next-generation learning environments on and off campus. In a learning environment, students have complete access to any higher-education resource, including experts, lectures, content, courseware, collaborative dialogs, information exchanges, hands-on learning, and research—no matter where they are located. If fully enabled, the learning environment will blur the line between on- and off-campus experiences and remove barriers to learning and research—thereby greatly improving access and the quality of education for students globally.

Drivers of change in higher education

Institutions seeking to understand how the next generation of Internet technologies will make an impact on their students and schools need to be aware of current trends:

- College-aged students are rapid adopters of new technologies, devices, and applications.
- Web 2.0 and social networking technologies enable easier access to increasingly available education content and online expertise, offering a venue for contributing and sharing knowledge regardless of location.
- Students are taking more responsibility for their own learning.
- Credible content is continually available on the Web.

- Video has high-adoption rates and is a key medium in higher education.
- M-learning (mobile learning) is on the rise in higher education.
- Gaming will be a key medium used in higher education in the near future.
- Evergreen students—those who bring in newer technology and learning expectations—are already evolving from Generation Y to Generation V (visual, versatile, virtual).
- Information and technical literacy are critical to remain relevant in the working world.

Learning environments are a way for higher-education institutions to address the ever-growing number of technology trends that are rapidly becoming available to and used by students. In addition, a learning environment gives students a range of educational resources from which to choose, while not hampering the education system already established. This book discusses the current key trends in higher education and offers suggestions on how to address evolving trends and learning environments, as well as a method (Centers of Excellence) for getting started on campus. This book also includes strategies that key education leaders are using to address technology in higher education.

Technology Trends Impacting Higher Education Today

CHAPTER ONE

Web 2.0 and Social Networking Technologies

Web 2.0 and social networking technologies enable real-time participation and collaboration

Web 2.0, a term coined by Tom O'Reilly in 2004, describes the latest advances in collaborative Internet technologies. It opens the Internet on a social level where individuals are able to edit and add to the online information space.[1] With Web 2.0, users participate in creating knowledge and sharing expertise rather than acting as passive recipients, making the Web an environment for sharing, collaborating, and exchanging thoughts and ideas.

Web 2.0 and social networking technologies are experiencing rapid growth:

- MySpace adds about 230,000 new accounts every day.[2]
- Two new blogs are created every second.[3]
- The English version of Wikipedia contains more than 2 million user-generated articles.[4]

- YouTube hosts more than 6 million videos, growing at about 20% every month.[5]
- The photo-hosting site Flickr has more than 2 billion images and 20 million unique tags.[6]
- The Digg homepage received 13,283 unique visitors and 2,527,056 hits as of January 2007.[7]
- Twitter has almost 1 million users.[8]

These technologies are important because they enable active participation in the creation and sharing of knowledge. Students between the ages of 18 and 24 spend 6.5 hours per week on social networking sites: 70% use message boards to communicate with friends; 61% talk online to people whom they have never met in person, and 56% send email messages or use instant messaging to ask their professors for help with assignments. Students today actively participate and collaborate using social networking technologies.[9] "Pervasive use of these tools is evident among students, and this will only grow in the coming months. The social aspects of these audience-centered technologies, firmly established as powerful tools for creative expression, offer great potential for building a community in the context of teaching and learning."[10]

Wikis, blogs, and RSS in higher education

Over the past 15 years there has been such a significant increase in technology in higher education that many professors find it difficult to teach without the use of the Internet. Many of the applications (learning management systems, e-learning), however, were developed to deliver content in a one-way format—from professors to students. Web 2.0 technologies create new possibilities for teaching and learning because they require very little technical knowledge to use them. Some of the promising technologies for higher education are mashups, blogs, wikis, tagging, social communities, and social networking sites. People are using these technologies to look at problems in many different ways, form relationships with pieces of information, and create new ideas that are shared with others. This poses a challenge of how to integrate these "paradigm-altering" technologies into higher-education teaching and learning.[11]

Blogs, wikis, and RSS (Really Simple Syndication) feeds have quickly been adopted in classroom environments. This feverish adoption has been characterized as a new wave of teaching:. For example, blogs are different from books—a book is predicated on micro content whereas blogs are about posts, not pages.[12] Larry Lessig, founder and CEO of Creative Commons and a Stanford law professor, maintains a blog[13] where students can respond to views posted by Lessig on topics ranging from politics to copyright laws. Dickinson College, in Carlisle, Pennsylvania hosts blogs for campus community members to enable students to create journals of their volunteer activities, internships, and activities abroad.[14]

Administrators are using blogs as a means to introduce new or prospective students. Blogs represent a powerful tool for engaging people in larger public conversations. Henry Jenkins noted that at MIT, a number of students were developing blogs focused on their thesis research. By doing this, many of them made valuable, professional contacts and gained visibility for their work. Some even received high-level job offers based on the professional connections they made on their blogs. Other benefits of blogging include deepening research, providing feedback mechanisms on their arguments, connecting students to previously unknown authorities, and pushing students forward in a way that a thesis committee would not be able to accomplish. Jenkins notes that at MIT research teams are blogging not only about their own work but also about key developments in their fields.[15]

Major educational benefits of blogs in higher education:

- Promote critical and analytical thinking
- Promote creative, intuitive, and associational thinking
- Promote analogical thinking
- Provide potential for increased access
- Provide exposure to quality information and to a combination of solitary and social interactions.[16]

RSS is a Web feed format that enables the user to subscribe to online content using an RSS reader or aggregator.[17] Through these readers, the user automatically receives new content from a variety of Web sites to which they have subscribed. A number of institutions have incorporated RSS feeds into their online offerings. Peterson's, a leading internet search provider of colleges and universities, graduate schools, online degrees, private schools and study guides to students, maintains a college and university feed directory that catalogs hundreds of higher-education RSS feeds organized by topics such as admissions, libraries, research centers, and technology.[18]

Wikis have been likened to streams of conversations that are revised, truncated, and amended[19] and are used by institutions as a way to facilitate collaborative writing or group projects involving multimedia. Wikipedia.com, for example, has more than 10,000 users who regularly edit or contribute content, making wikis ideal for facilitating collaborative content in classrooms.[20] At the global education department at Dickinson College, students can publish and edit newsletters using wikis with ease and with the benefit of built-in trace-ability for grading and feedback.[21] Faculty at Oberlin College, Oberlin, Ohio and Columbia University, among others, have developed assignments where students create or edit Wikipedia articles to learn how to write neutral, exposi-tory text and experience the process of peer review and revision.[22]

Web 2.0 networking and sharing in higher education

Social networking sites such as Facebook, MySpace, and Bebo have been ad-opted by a large percentage of college students. As of 2005, 85% of students at supported colleges use Facebook in the United States alone.[23] Facebook allows them to join virtual groups based on common interests, see which classes they have in common, and learn about each other's hobbies and interests through their profiles.[24] In addition to Facebook, other social communities such as StudiVZ help students find other students who are participating in the same classes or lectures through the sharing of common interests. An example is a third-year agrology student who used his university agrology club's Facebook site to connect with other members to learn more about graduate schools and options. Through the site, the student was able to connect to 2 institutions, as well as several of the faculty who taught graduate programs.[25]

Web-sharing applications such as "del.icio.us" enable users to share book-marks and tag Web sites; this kind of bookmarking has become popular par-ticularly with educators who work from different computers and want to have their bookmark readily available. Users have the benefit of browsing their own bookmarks as well as "friends" sites. The College of William and Mary, in Wil-liamsburg, Virginia uses del.icio.us to enable students to share and comment on readings from a government course and create a personal bank of related sites.[26]

Flickr is a Web site that enables anyone to upload, tag, browse, and com-ment on photos. One of its many uses in the classroom is as a resource for an upper-level course on residential architecture. As part of the course, students were instructed to photograph homes representative of the architectural styles the class was discussing using digital cameras or cell phones. Students up-loaded photos to a private group on Flickr that the professor created and used the tools to provide captions, prompt discussions, and converse with other stu-dents about their photos, thus adding to the collective knowledge of the group. Flickr has value in teaching and learning because it allows students studying photography or other art-related subjects to receive feedback and engage with a community of experts and amateurs, exposing students to the realities of the field. Flickr also exposes students to participatory learning by capitalizing on the ubiquity of digital cameras and students' desire to share their work in a learning community using a comfortable platform.[27]

Mapping mashups have become popular in higher education for both administrative and informational purposes. A mashup combines separate, stand-alone technology into a novel application. The most widely known mashups are real estate or geography maps that have pop-up markers on which users can click to find points of interest or more information and details. Universities are using mashups as an orientation tool for the campus; students can locate available housing or alumni addresses. A professor at Mansfield University of Pennsylvania uses a mapping mashup to help students learn about plate tectonics; students view a map of the world, and pushpins indicate evidence of tectonic plates. Another professor uses mapping mashups in a history class on World War II. The mashup represents major events that led up to and took place during the war. The map covers the world, and users can zoom in and out—seeing superimposed images of maps, dates, and events. The maps also have flags that pop up, and when clicked on, each flag opens a pop-up box that names the location, shows a photograph, and lists important events.[28]

The ever-popular video-sharing site YouTube is being used by students and faculty alike to post and discuss videos. A spin-off called TeacherTube provides a venue for educational content. The Web site has the largest number of registered users among college-focused sites. The site BigThink is dedicated to video clips for intellectual content and discussions.

Summary

Web 2.0 has already redefined the ways in which students and researchers collaborate, connect, and learn. Web 2.0 has also changed how universities deliver content. Many institutions have made blogs, wikis, RSS feeds, and social bookmarking integral parts of course delivery and collaborative learning. Finally, university libraries are making use of Web 2.0 technologies to distribute information and interact with students and faculty. Tim O'Reilly, founder and CEO of O'Reilly Media, predicted that by 2008, Web 2.0 will have become mainstream.[29] In many respects, we are already there.

CHAPTER TWO

Video

Video, particularly video on the Internet, has become a key medium for delivering both consumer and education content. A 2007 research study conducted by the Pew Research Center indicates that 76% of the people who view online videos are adults ages 18–29, a group that Pew refers to as "contagious carriers" in the viral spread of online video[1]; many of these viewers are students. In addition to consuming video content, students are also producing their own content. The term "prosumer," derived from an amalgamation of the words producer and consumer, is often used when referring to college students or other participants using Web 2.0 technologies.[2]

A 2007 paper published by Cisco Systems Inc. projects that Internet Protocol (IP) traffic will double every 2 years through 2011.[3] The primary cause for this is the increase of high-definition (HD) video data usage and production by consumers and the expansion of high-speed broadband penetration worldwide. Cisco projects that consumer IP traffic will grow at a compound annual growth rate of 52% from 2006 to 2011, versus a 29% growth rate for business IP traffic. Today most of the data exchanged are in peer-to-peer (P2P) traffic; with video files being a substantial portion of the exchanged material, Internet video streaming and downloads are expected to become an even larger share of the bandwidth.[4]

These findings come as no surprise as video has made its way into college education systems and students' lives. Some uses in education include broadcasting lectures, recording classroom sessions as video on demand (VOD), distributing content via podcasts, hosting instructional clips on YouTube (www.youtube.com)—a popular Internet video Web site—as well as student assignments, video blogs (vlogs), high-definition videoconferencing, and broadband education channels.

Video in higher education through the airwaves

mtvU

MtvU is a popular medium that students use for video. MtvU (www.mtvU.com) is a 24-hour college network channel for college students. The channel's core offering is music, but it also offers college news, health, and original content produced by students. It reaches over 750 U.S. college campuses, or more than 7.5 million college students.[5] The content is delivered on the air, online, and on mobile devices. All programming is no longer than the length of a music video (4–5 minutes). The site features celebrities teaching a one-day college course—such as Elie Wiesel, Madonna, John McCain, Sting, and Kanye West. Each week the show *The Dean's List* gives a different college student the chance to be an mtvU "VJ-for-the-day," running their top 10 music video picks for the national college audience.

In a move indicating its interest and commitment to higher education, MTV Networks, the parent company of mtvU, acquired RateMyProfessors.com, a popular site where students provide feedback on professors and courses.[6]

Video use in education

Videos sourced from the Internet, or any network, are categorized into 3 groups: live streaming, on-demand streaming, and videoconferencing.[7] All 3 have uses in higher education:

- Streaming video is a sequence of "moving images" sent in compressed form over the Internet. With streaming video or streaming media (i.e., streaming video with sound), a Web user does not have to wait to download a large file before seeing the video or hearing the sound because the media is sent in a continuous stream and is played as it arrives. The user needs a player, which is typically a special program that decompresses the streamed data, sending video data to the display and audio data to the speakers. A player can be either an integral part of a browser or downloaded from the software maker's Web site.[8]

- VOD is short for *Video-on-Demand*, an umbrella term for a wide set of technologies and cpmpanies whose common goal is to enable individuals to select videos fiom a central server for viewing on a television or computer screen. *VoD* can be used for entertainment (ordering movies transmitted digitally), education (viewing training videos), and *videoconferencing* (enhancing presentations with video clips). Although VoD is being used somewhat in all these areas, it is not yet widely implemented. VoD's biggest obstacle is the lack of a network *infrastructure* that can handle the large amounts of data required by video..[9]

- A videoconference is a live connection between people in separate locations for the purpose of two-way communication, usually involving audio and often text and video. In its simplest form, videoconferencing provides transmission of static images and text between 2 locations. Sophisticated videoconferencing systems provide transmission of full-motion video images and high-quality audio between multiple locations.[10]

Podcasts

Podcasting is one of the more popular trends in higher education today.[11] Podcasting is a means of publishing audio and video content on the Web as a series of episodes with a common theme. These episodes are accompanied by a file called a "feed" that allows listeners to subscribe to the series and receive new episodes automatically.[12] New content can be automatically downloaded to subscribers as soon as it is available. Unlike video- or Web-streaming content, podcasts are not designed for real-time broadcasting. The content is prerecorded so that users can download and play the material at their leisure, independent of network connectivity.[13]

In a university setting, a podcast is typically audio or visual content that is automatically delivered over the university's network through a subscription process. Once a student subscribes to the podcast feed, the media can be regularly distributed over the Internet or within the school network and accessed with an iPod, notebook, or desktop computer.[14]

The use of podcasting by colleges falls into 3 categories:[15]

- Audio or video archiving of classroom lectures and/or university events
- Delivery of supplemental course materials such as prerecorded lectures before class, video reviews of homework problems, and third-party podcasts that relate to the coursework or class summaries that highlight important information
- As part of a course assignment where students develop their own podcast

A number of Boston-based colleges have adopted podcasting in teaching and learning environments.[16] The technology is being used primarily to record class lectures, which students can download at a later date. Events outside the classroom are also being podcasted and made available for downloading; an environmental group at Emerson has published podcasts of speeches by Senator John Kerry and other campus guests. Emerson also records alumni career guidance talks for students.

Northeastern University finds podcasting valuable for students who commute or may miss a class due to their work schedule. Podcasting for these students provides a convenient way to listen to lectures while mobile. Podcasting also is popular among Northeastern University professors who prefer to use class time for collaboration and discussion instead of lectures; they record their lectures in advance and expect their students to watch the lectures before coming to class. Some professors at MIT not only videotape their lectures but also homework "help sessions" facilitated by a teaching assistant.

Many colleges also use podcasts to showcase research findings as well as in athletics to review training programs, college broadcasts, review college campus athletic sites etc.

On May 30, 2007, Apple announced the launch of iTunes U, a substore in the iTunes Store (www.itunes.com). This site hosts podcasts including course lectures, language lessons, lab demonstrations, sports highlights, and campus tours provided by leading U.S. colleges and universities including Stanford University, UC Berkeley, Duke University, and MIT.

Podcasts from iTunes can be loaded onto an iPod with a single click of a mouse. Users can experience the podcast on-the-go, anytime, making learning from a lecture as simple as enjoying music. The Apple iTunes store currently reports more than 2 million downloads of music, movies, and TV shows per week, and through the iTunes U framework, the same audience who download mainstream content—an audience not limited to students—are now easily able to obtain content developed and distributed by educational communities.

iTunes U makes it easy for students to search thousands of audio and video files from schools across the country, while giving educational institutions an effective way to distribute audio and video content to students. With downloadable presentations, performances, lectures, demonstrations, debates, tours, and archival footage, higher education has many more resources available to students and faculty. To participate, colleges and universities build their own iTunes U sites and then link these sites to the iTunes Store. Faculty can easily post content created for their classes, while students can download what they need when they need it—empowering them to learn any place, any time.[17]

Because of its simplicity, ease of use, and wide distribution, many universities have adopted this framework to make and deliver college course content. More than half of the nation's top 500 schools use iTunes U to distribute their digital content to students—and to the world. Each participating school can open all or part of its site to the public—through the iTunes U framework—making it accessible to anyone who wants to learn.

Benefits of podcasting

A 2007 paper published by researchers at Carnegie Mellon University consolidated findings from a number of higher-education institutions that studied podcasting in the college environment.[18] Some of the studies included in the paper indicated how students used educational podcasts:

- At the University of Washington, only 20% of the students listened to more than 75% of the recorded lectures. Many students have also been known to fast-forward the recordings to specific points in the lectures, and most students perceived the podcast as a review tool rather than as a lecture replacement. The paper indicates that there was no significant impact on attendance due to podcasting classes. Most of the students viewed the recorded lectures as study tools that had a positive impact on their performance.[19]
- Researchers from the University of Michigan School of Dentistry noted that 85% of the students surveyed believed that the lecture archives had a positive impact on exam grades. The university found that when offering a course in 3 formats—video, audio with slide presen-

tations, and audio only—audio was twice as popular as the other 2 formats combined. One of the more surprising finds was that more students reported listening to lecture podcasts at home and on a computer rather than in a mobile environment on a portable device.[20]

- In a study of software engineering students at Appalachian State University, a performance comparison was done between those who attended a standard lecture in the classroom and those who reviewed the podcast lecture in advance and used classroom time for hands-on activities and problem solving. Results indicated no difference in test performance; however, the project grades for the podcast group were 10% higher, indicating that spending time in the classroom performing hands-on activities instead of just listening to lecture gave students more skills and practice to apply their knowledge to their projects.[21]

- A professor noted in a spring 2006 study at Bentley College that students were not using the recorded podcasts because of their length (average length was 60 minutes) and asked students to produce abbreviated lecture podcasts between 6–10 minutes for extra credit. The review concluded that, apart from enjoying the benefits from the shorter podcasts, students learned and shared a variety of multimedia features as well as a desire to show off their creativity.[22]

While the Carnegie Mellon project reviewed early podcasting applications, the use and growth of this medium continues on global college campuses.

Many professors agree that a key benefit of podcasting is its instant popularity outside academic circles; many professors now post their materials on iTunes U for free viewing. Material posted by MIT Physics Professor Walter Lewin, 71, was a "top download" by learners mainly because of Lewin's creativity and showmanship. He does physics experiments on himself, rides tricycles, and performs a number of stunts to prove the laws of physics. In addition to top scores he also receives fan mail. Other top podcasts include a philosophy lecture on existentialism by UC Berkeley Professor Hubert Dreyfus and a lecture titled "Contemplation of Quantum Mechanics" by Leonard Susskind of Stanford University.[23]

Podcasting tools

Podcast Producer.   In October 2007, Apple released OS 10.X—a new operating system that includes a feature called Podcast Producer. Podcast Producer simplifies the process of creating a podcast to just a single mouse click.

Trinity College in Dublin, Ireland, uses Podcast Producer to capture voice and presentation slides in several auditoriums, and to record and assess microteaching.[24] UC Berkeley has integrated Podcast Producer as a part of its "open cast" delivery system.[25] The university anticipates that Podcast Producer will help simplify the process of creating podcasts and enable more individuals with the flexibility to create rich multimedia podcasts.

YouTube. YouTube is the leading online video community that allows people to discover, watch, and share originally created videos online. The video-sharing site allows people to "Broadcast Yourself"; users can easily upload and share video clips that are hosted on YouTube.com. These video clips can be embedded into Web sites, blogs, and emails. The company was started in 2005 and was later acquired by Google in October 2006.

Today, users can watch most videos on the site for free, and registered users are permitted to upload an unlimited number of videos, which are typically filmed from an individual's cell phone camera or digital camera, or portable movie camera in their home or other local environment. The posted videos are rated using a star system based on popularity. Related videos, determined by title and tags, are posted to the right of a selected video. YouTube has a number of functions that help the user flag, tag, and share videos with others.

The growth and adoption of YouTube has been significant. In July 2006, the company noted that more than 100 million videos were being watched every day, and 2.5 billion videos were watched during the month of June 2006. Fifty thousand videos were being added every day as of May 2006, increasing to 65,000 by July of the same year. A *Wall Street Journal* article, published in August 2006, reported that YouTube hosted more than 6 million videos (requiring about 45 terabytes of storage space) and had about 500,000 user accounts.[26] As of December 2007, YouTube hosted nearly 59 million videos.

YouTube use in college classrooms. YouTube is being used by college instructors in a variety of ways. Professors have become overnight "rock stars"; gaining popularity on YouTube and other video sites would help extend learning beyond the physical confines of the classroom and make teaching more accessible.[27] Like iTunes U, YouTube has created exposure to educational research and thought leadership by professors. YouTube academia stars include Marian C. Diamond, world renowned professor of anatomy and neuroscience, UC Berkeley. Diamond, who has taught for 40 years and has published more than 5 books, receives global fan mail for her YouTube lectures. A thought-provoking video commentary on students today by Michael L. Welsh, a professor at Kansas State and 200 students in his cultural anthropology class garnered more than 1 million hits and more than 6,000 comments.[28]

In line with the growing popularity of professors positing videos to social networking sites, a new site called BigThink (www.bigthink.com) was developed in January 2008. BigThink is a niche site that offers video interviews with academics, authors, politicians, and other thought leaders using video. According to cofounder Victoria R. M. Brown, "People like to learn and be informed of things by looking, watching, and learning." Learners can browse the site by experts, expertise, and ideas. Participants can also engage in online debates and discussions.

YouTube has become an instructional tool for not only teaching standard academia, but also for integrating artistic components into the course work. Christopher Conway says he uses YouTube in his classes to show film excerpts of key historical moments in Latin history, as well as Latin poetry and music videos.[29] Alexandra Juhasz teaches a class titled "Learning from YouTube" at Pfizer College in California. She videotapes her classes, posts the videos on YouTube, and encourages students to post video responses to communicate with each other.[30] Bucks Country Community College, in Newton, Pennsylvania, uses YouTube clips to teach culinary lessons.

In October 2007, UC Berkeley announced that it was the first university to offer video classes through YouTube.com/ucberkeley, an education channel on YouTube with more than 300 hours of free video classes.[31] Since then, other universities such as the University of Southern California, the University of New South Wales in Australia, and Vanderbilt University in Nashville, Tennessee, have also created education channels to deliver course content.

Doing homework using YouTube.   Students are also using YouTube as a way to produce multimedia assignments. As noted in the Cisco 2007 study, the majority of IP traffic is consumer-created video. Consumer devices such as cell phones, digital cameras and handy cams have made video production affordable—almost free. Thus, students, in addition to being consumers of video content, have become producers of video content. As a result, it is becoming the norm to include video in class assignments and presentations. In some cases, students are rendering their entire assignments as video projects. Many of these assignments are created for use in the classroom or posted to the university's own education channel on YouTube.

In addition to YouTube, which previously was Google's largest video community competitor, Google also has its own video community service. Called Google Video, the service is geared toward providing a large archive of searchable videos for free. Besides amateur media, Internet videos, advertising, and movie trailers, the service also aims to distribute commercial, professional media, such as televised content, movies, and university lectures.

TelePresence

Another technology worth noting is Cisco's TelePresence system, a highly advanced, videoconferencing solution that creates an "in-person meeting" experience. In the past, videoconferencing systems have been difficult to set up, a challenge to use, and have failed to provide quality resolution and sound to replicate face-to-face interaction. TelePresence delivers real-time, face-to-face interactions between people in dispersed geographical locations, both at work and at home using advanced visual, audio, and collaboration technologies. The technology transmits life-size, high-definition images and spatial discrete audio. TelePresence makes it easier than ever to discern facial expressions during crucial business discussions and negotiations across the "virtual conference table."[32]

The academic community has expressed great interest in the TelePresence system. Many see it as an opportunity to reduce travel and related expenses, as well as enhance collaboration. Possible uses for TelePresence in higher education include providing distance-learning programs and connecting researchers to one another on campus, to other research institutions and to corporations. Ph.D. students and committees can use TelePresence to review dissertations, present oral exams, and dissertation defense in a conference-like setting. Other uses include student and faculty interviews and meetings between graduate students, student and professors, and administrative and cabinet staff.

In the third quarter of 2007, an MBA class at Arizona State University conducted a TelePresence experiment. Cisco systems hosted the class (18 students) on site in their Arizona office. The professor divided the group into three smaller groups of 6 students each. One group toured the firm and met with sales executives to learn about Cisco's core business; the second group were with a professor in a small group discussion about their projects in a meeting room at Cisco Systems; and the third group used TelePresence to connect with a business author who was at Cisco's Bangalore office to discuss International business and high technology firms. Every 15 minutes the groups rotated, so that they could experience each learning event. When asked which experience the students enjoyed the most the students noted that the TelePresence experience was "extremely enjoyable" because it felt "real" and "lifelike' and yet connected them to a foreign country without having to travel. They could not believe they were interacting with someone thousands of miles away. Presently, Georgia Tech, in Atlanta, and Maharishi Vedic University, in The Netherlands, have deployed TelePresence systems.

Summary

Video has become a key medium in higher education, both for educators and students. It is expected that video will continue to grow in use and popularity, providing a variety of uses in education. Online video in particular has become a key medium for many educators and students, mainly in the area of teaching and learning. Multiple distribution channels such as iTunes U, YouTube, and mtvU have been adopted by higher education as a way to provide content to students and also as a venue for them to express themselves. In addition, faculty members have reaped an added benefit of exposure and distribution of their thought leadership—not to mention stardom. New technologies such as TelePresence offer another innovative way to connect people and close the distance between campuses.

CHAPTER THREE

Mobile Devices

Mobile learning, or M-learning, is another trend under exploration in higher education. Nearly all college students in most developed and many developing countries own a mobile device and use it frequently, both on and off campus. New product models are released every few weeks by many manufacturers. These gadgets contain multimedia functionality, are typically feature-rich, and are equipped not only for phone calls and text messages but also for connecting to Web sites and playing games online. The adoption of mobile devices in higher education, however, has been slow. Some educators do not understand how to use these devices in learning, and others are uncomfortable with technology, despite research studies documenting positive input from students about mobile learning. Technology limitations and concerns about security and privacy are also factors to slow adoption. Despite these obstacles, mobile devices continue to receive positive evaluations by researchers from academic institutions for their use in education.

The growth of mobile devices

Students and their families in the United States spent about $12.8 billion on electronics in 2007, up about 22% from 2006. Much of this spending was on cell phones and newer mobile devices such as the Apple iPhone.[1] The growth and adoption of mobile devices are astounding and continue to increase. More than 50% of all U.S. households own at least one digital camera, mobile phone, and PC and have Internet access. By 2010, mobile phones will reach 19 million more households; MP3 players will reach 26 million more households, and personal digital assistants (PDAs) will reach 4 million more households in the United States.[2]

The trend in consumer devices is impacting college campuses. While 77% of U.S. college students ages 18–26 already own a PC, an astounding 93% own a cell phone and 58% have an MP3 player.[3] Adults between the ages of 18 and 26 are often first to adopt new technologies and use them in their daily lives, whether at home, at play, or at school.[4]

Mobile device use in Europe exceeds that of the United States. In the United Kingdom, 75% of the general population and 90% of young adults have mobile phones.[5] By the end of 2003, 82% of the population of The Netherlands was estimated to use mobile devices, compared to 54% of the population in the United States.[6] Research also indicates that when children in The Netherlands reach 14 years of age, 98% are connected using mobile devices, and 100% of young adults ages 16–22 have a mobile device.[7]

Mobile phones are also prevalent in Asia-Pacific. There were nearly 678 million subscribers in the region in 2005; it was predicted that this number would reach almost 827 million by 2006.[8] Korea has the world's highest percentage of users of third-generation mobile phones and is the second largest mobile market in Asia-Pacific in terms of penetration (93%).[9]

Impact of mobile devices on higher education

Students' engagement on college campuses is different today than it was a decade ago. In the past, engagement was defined as the time and effort spent in-person on activities such as academics, student organization, and communicating with faculty and friends. With the introduction of technology, the methods by which students communicate, interact, and manage these activities have changed. Campus learning environments now include intelligent whiteboards, chat tools, videoconferencing systems, digitized movies, electronic libraries, and mobile devices. These devices help today's students experience the material in myriad ways that are different from previous generations.[10]

The shift from a wired to a wireless campus

Many higher-education institutions have become wireless in the past few years to support the use of mobile devices.[11] More than 90% of public universities and 80% of private universities in the United States have employed some degree of mobile wireless technology.[12] Furthermore, 57% of U.S. campus libraries had wireless networks in 2001, increasing to 88% by 2003. The projection at that time was that all campus locations such as parking lots, football stadiums, and coliseums will be equipped with wireless networks.[13] In 2005, prospective students attending campus tours at Brown University, in Providence, Rhode Island, requested that the school implement wireless coverage across the entire campus. This sentiment was mirrored in annual student surveys among many U.S. universities.[14]

A key reason for this shift from a wired to a wireless campus is that wired technology limits the ability of users to access the network 24/7 and prohibits mobility. The benefits of using mobile, wireless technologies (handheld devices, PDAs, cell phones) over wired or tethered computers include improved efficiency and effectiveness in teaching and learning.[15] In addition to being convenient, wireless technology is also economically efficient and will become more efficient as the costs decrease and wireless services improve.[16] Installing a wireless network is more cost effective than a wired network because it is simpler to set up and manage, and it improves productivity because it supports mobile devices.[17] Other benefits include collaboration among students and students and teachers, and among faculty. Wireless networks also enhance the learning environment and improve productivity,[18] creating an M-learning model.

M-learning defined

M-learning is defined as the intersection of mobile computing with e-learning.[19] It is also defined as "any activity that allows individuals to be more productive when consuming, interacting, or creating information mediated through a compact, digital portable device that the individual carries on a regular basis. Such a device also has reliable connectivity and fits in a pocket or purse."[20] M-learning is all about "learning on the move."[21] Devices such as mobile phones, PDAs, and MP3 players enable this learning regardless of geographical or temporal restrictions.

"Mobile" in the context of this paper is defined as "portable and personal."[22] PDAs, multifunction devices, and cell phones are the most frequently used in m-learning studies.

Mobile technology and learning uses are classified into 4 quadrants:[23]

- Quadrant 1 is defined as personal and portable. This includes commonly thought of devices such as mobile phones, PDAs, game consoles, tablet PCs, and laptops. These devices support a single user and are perceived as personal.
- Quadrant 2 is defined as personal and static; the technology is static because it can be used only in one location. The technology is personal because a single user can interact with the system. Classroom response systems would be an example of this technology: students in a class respond to questions provided centrally, and usually anonymously, using a device such as a mobile phone, laptop, or a "clicker," which is a device similar to a remote control that students use to answer simple in-class questions or polls.
- Quadrant 3 is defined as portable and shared. Examples are learning kiosks and museum displays. In this case, the learner is mobile but the delivery mechanism is fixed. These devices are less personal and shared by many users, possibly at the same time.
- Quadrant 4 is defined as static and shared. Examples are videoconferencing and electronic whiteboards. These devices are not mobile due to size; they provide shareable interactions.

Most researchers consider quadrants 1, 2, and 3 relevant to m-learning because the devices are mobile and in quadrant 4 the devices are fixed.

Benefits of m-learning in higher education

A study of the use of 3 types of mobile devices—laptop computers, PDAs, and cell phones using Short Message Service (SMS) and Multimedia Messaging Service (MMS)—evaluated the ability of mobile devices to access network resources and their benefits in higher education. Wireless PCs when evaluated in the higher-education environment were found to offer more benefits than wired PCs. What gave the former an edge were additional benefits such as mobility, relaxed fit, strategic deployment, low profile, flexibility, cleanliness, convenience, ease of use because the devices are mobile and not fixed in one location, and fast connection speeds.[24] As expected, smaller laptops were found to be more convenient than larger ones.[25]

Another study found the following benefits of using PDAs in education:[26]

1. Mobility: the devices created the ability for professors and students to work in more places than they could using wired technologies.
2. Information-management capacity: the PDAs replaced pen-and-paper-based management processes with electronic management systems to support data such as students' grades and lecture materials.
3. Beaming capability: PDA-beaming capabilities let teachers and students send and receive documents, spreadsheets, applications, questions, assignments, quizzes, emails, and other types of data.

Portability (small size and weight), social interactivity (collaboration occurs face to face), context sensitivity (mobile devices gather and respond to date in real time, regardless of environment, location, or time), connectivity (devices can be connected and enable data sharing), and individuality (tasks can be customized for individual learners) are other characteristics of PDAs that are unique and conducive to educational use.[27]

Other benefits that mobile connectivity provides for learning include features that allow users to filter and individualize information on their mobile devices; improve collaboration via real-time or instant interactivity, regardless of time and location (leading to better decision making); and help learners do a better job in balancing their work and personal life. For example, a number of studies show that these devices give commuter students the ability to use spare time wisely to finish homework and prepare for lessons.[28]

Three Dutch universities—Wageningen University and Research Centre, Raboud University Nijmeen, and Vrije Universiteit Amsterdam—collaborated on a project called GIPSY (Geo-Information for Integrating Personal Learning Environments), where wireless devices were used extensively in classes that required students to collect data outside the classroom. One advantage of GIPSY was the convenience of email access—anywhere, anytime. Another was assurance that the Internet was always with students, keeping them from having to go to a physical location to log on to the Internet. A third benefit was that the devices were useful for downloading e-books, taking notes, and highlighting text. Furthermore, the study indicated that the devices were easy to use and compact in terms of having applications such as the agenda, email, Internet, and contacts in one place. Disadvantages included slow connection speeds, nonuser-friendly keypad (a keyboard was preferred), small display screen (which resulted in constant scrolling), limited storage for applications, high costs, and risks (including theft, exposure to weather, and loss or breakage).[29]

In a comprehensive paper that evaluated a number of research studies on using handheld devices in learning, applications were divided into 6 categories with subcategories:

1. educational (pushing content, messaging, responding and feedback, exchanging files, posting content, and communicating in the classroom)
2. managing (personal management, administrative work)
3. seeking and handling information (references, revisions)
4. games and simulations
5. data collection
6. context awareness (personalization, active and passive context awareness)

It was concluded, that a majority of the applications for educational use were developed by researchers and tested by students in a practiced or controlled environment. These uses were primarily developed to support teachers' goals, and not those of learners. A majority of the handheld-device research experiments were used to accomplish prescribed tasks that limit the learners' ability to explore other uses for the devices. While the outcome of the research was positive, there were no research projects that allowed students to fully explore the potential of the handheld devices for their own learning purposes.[30]

It was noted in the same study that a majority of the research replicated the practices of learning to use a desktop or laptop computer, rather than find a unique way to fully take advantage of the convenience and portability of the mobile device form factor which differed significantly from a PC.[31] While the innovative use of handheld technology in education, such as data collection, does exist and there are many context-aware applications that take advantage of portability and connectivity, there still is room for more exploration. For instance, handhelds may be studied in a learning environment rather than in isolated situations, allowing students to explore a number of possible uses in an uncontrolled and non-predictive manner. This way, the full potential of these devices and their constraints may be established.

M-learning on college campuses

The following examples show m-learning applications and their benefits in U.S. colleges:

- Students at the University of Connecticut School of Medicine use PDAs during clinical rotations to find quick answers to treatment issues, such as possible drug interactions or best practices in patient care. They also track patient encounters and keep a student log with the PDAs.[32]

- Quinnipiac University, in Hamden, Connecticut, is developing a program to provide students with preloaded smart phones and pocket PCs for college communications, academic tools, and course work. In their Physician Assistant Program, for example, the devices have applications that are used in both clinical and classroom settings (e.g., Merck Manual, Tarascon, InfoRetriever, E*Value Clinical Suite).[33]

- A professor at the University of Texas at Dallas found Twitter (www.twitter.com) beneficial for his graduate classes to send quick blogs and receive comments and feedback from students through their devices. A Twitter user is limited to a 140-character text message on a cell phone.[34]

- The University of Cincinnati deployed "Bearcat Phones" that provide faculty, administration, and students instant access to academic information, as well as links to services such as the campus police and shuttle bus.[35]

- Wake Forest University, in North Carolina, uses pocket PC devices in classrooms for teaching and learning. The university created a custom program called ClassInHand that turns the pocket PC with a wireless card into a Web server, presentation controller, and feedback or quizzing/polling device for classroom instruction.[36]

Outside the United States, mobile devices are slowly penetrating college campuses as well. Some campuses have deployed pilots exploring the use of mobile devices in teaching and learning.

- Bishop Burton College (East Riding, Yorkshire, England) uses mobile devices for learning activities in and outside the classroom. The devices are used to collect data in the field or at workshops for later analysis. The operating systems were compatible with the college's desktop computers, so data could be uploaded and worked on in class, as well as in the field.

- Dewsbury College (West Yorkshire, England) customizes class Web pages in smaller sizes that still contain hyperlinks to video and audio files to support various learning preferences. The customization allows students to download content to their handhelds faster.

- Leeds Thomas Danby College (West Yorkshire, England) uses PDAs as a way to deliver formative assessments, also referred to as "drill-for-skill assignments" for learners, and has integrated audio in some cases. This method enabled immediate feedback from educators.[37]

- Monash Medical Centre (Victoria, Australia) is a major teaching, research, and referral hospital. Students use mobile devices to record patient information instead of using paper-based bed charts that they found were more prone to human error.[38]
- Researchers at Kinjo Gakuin University (Nagoya, Japan) studied Japanese college students and m-learning. They found that students used cell phones and PDAs to view study materials and answer quizzes. The university conducted additional research on how quickly students could type class notes on a cell phone, and their preference to do so. The college found that students preferred typing on desktop computers and cell phone keypads, suggesting that Japanese students could take class notes and write reports on their mobile phones.[39]

Although the above-mentioned university pilots have enjoyed some success, M-learning on campus is still in its infancy.

M-learning and learning theory

Researchers have evaluated M-learning practices against existing learning theories. They found applicability with the following theories:[40]

- Behaviorist: This theory suggests that learning is facilitated through the reinforcement of an association of a stimulus with a response. M-learning examples that proved applicability of this theory are classroom response systems such as ClassTalk (*http://Web.mit.edu/etg/www/related%20work/classtalk.htm*) and Qwizdom (www.quizdom.com), as well as examples of text messages to mobile phones.
- Constructivist: This theory suggests that learning is an active process in which learners construct new ideas based on their current and past knowledge. Relevant examples noted included (1) Virus Simulation Game, where learners observe the spread of a virus by moving around the classroom and interacting with others to learn how diseases start and spread; and (2) Environmental Detective, where students use mobile devices equipped with GPS to navigate physical spaces to determine the source of an environmental contamination and prepare a remediation plan.
- Situated Learning: This theory suggests that learning is enhanced

when it takes place in an authentic context. Examples include museum and gallery exhibit displays, learning kiosks, and multimedia tours.

- Collaborative Theory: This theory suggests that learning is promoted through social interactions. These learning experiences include mobile devices to support social interactions as another means of collaboration, without replacing any other mode such as human-to-human interaction and online discussion.

- Informal and Lifelong Learning: This theory suggests that learning happens all the time outside of the classroom through other means, such as large projects, conversations, television programs, newspaper articles, and more. In one application, breast cancer patients use mobile devices to track their condition, access sources of information, and connect with other patients to learn more about their situation.

Considerations

Many researchers agree that when studying the applicability of mobile devices in higher education and learning theory, it is important to understand the context in which the devices are being evaluated. They noted that many initial studies have been evaluating mobile devices in the same way they did a personal computer, rather than taking into consideration the form, fit, and function of the device.[41]

In a study at the University of Massachusetts in Lowell, students' use of e-learning applications in the classroom was evaluated, and the participants were invited to provide feedback on the applications deployed. A key finding was that it is important to understand the strengths and weaknesses of a particular technology—in this case, the handheld device—while deploying good pedagogical practices to achieve specific learning goals. The study notes that the granularity of the content delivered is also critical. For example, it is not possible to take a 2-hour course on a wireless handheld device because it is much smaller than a PC or laptop computer.

Researchers propose that the evaluation of handheld mobile devices should include family, institution, and community environments and uses.[42] Due to the convergence of learning and technology, the stage has been set for successful m-learning environments. Learning has become more individualized, learner-centric, situated, and collaborative and so requires technologies that would support advancements in learning by being ubiquitous, mobile, and durable.[43]

It should be noted that although mobile technologies are computer-based, they should not be viewed as portable versions of computers. The form factor is different—size, screen keyboard, and mobility add a new dimension to the activities that can be supported. In a 2006 study, for example, students used handheld devices to collect data in the field and write annotations. Students sent data to a researcher who was not in the field but at a different remote location. This type of work required the use of a handheld device to assist in the learning activity in a way that the laptop or desktop computer could not. To appreciate the full potential of mobile technologies, educators must look beyond the use of individual devices, embedding them in the classroom or as a part of an outside-of-the-classroom learning experience. Unfortunately, not many educators are willing to examine this technology's potential.[44]

Summary

We are already seeing the impact of wireless campuses and the expansion of mobile devices. For example, the Republic Polytechnic of Singapore has a fully wireless and paperless learning campus (*www.rp.edu.sg/*), and Case Western Reserve has played a major role in creating a dynamic wireless community in Cleveland, Ohio (*http://www.onecleveland.org/*), thus expanding learning opportunities for students.

We are also seeing how devices for listening to music, watching videos, and downloading seminars have been deployed—and are increasing in terms of technology—starting with Duke University in 2004. Preloaded tablet computing devices such as the Nokia N800 that come with course-related PDFs, videos, and materials are used by students at Stanford University School of Engineering in the Introduction to Engineering course.[45]

Higher-education institutions are investing money to meet the demands and expectations of this new generation of students.[46] Winona State University in Minnesota has been giving laptops to incoming students for 6 years; now the school is giving them tablet PCs. The University of Maryland in College Park gave students BlackBerry devices.[47] And in November 2007, the Associated Press noted that Cyber University—Japan's first entirely online university, which opened earlier that year—was offering its first course "Mysteries of the Pyramids" to learners via cell phones.[48]

Researchers suggest that in the future, the delivery of higher education will require mobile wireless phones for faculty and students.[49] It is projected that as the technology improves, the use of SMS and MMS on campus will potentially increase—to alert students to important information such as exams and short tutorials.[50] Next-generation devices such as Apple's iPhone, iTouch, and MacBook Air (www.apple.com) enable learners to be mobile and access content with the touch of a finger via a user-friendly interface and wide screen. These next-generation mobile devices show the potential for enhanced, multi-media-enriched, and convenient just-in-time learning.

CHAPTER FOUR

Gaming

Computer game usage has grown considerably over the past 5 years. Games have also become the central focus of college student life: they play games in-between and during classes, and even as part of private contemplation.[1] According to a 2003 Pew Internet and American Life Project survey of college students and gaming, 70% of college students reported playing video, computer, or online games "at least once in a while," and 65% reported being regular or occasional game players.[2]

Growth of gaming

The gaming sector is an ever-growing sector and increasingly complex to define. Datamonitor, in a recent report, describes digital entertainment platforms as "a complex mixture of art and business in constant transformation, as new technologies help the sector break free of traditional boundaries. . . . In addition the games are undergoing a transformation as IP (Internet Protocol) creates dynamic virtual environments."[3]

Online gaming has undergone tremendous growth in the past few years and is driven by increased penetration of broadband and broader availability of PC and console games played over wide-area networks. Global online gaming revenues were estimated between $7–9 billion in 2007.[4] The key markets for gaming include the United States, China, Japan, and Korea. Online gaming sites had almost 217 million unique visits worldwide and have been growing at a yearly rate of 17%.[5]

Gaming types and platforms

Datamonitor, in a December 2006 report, categorized various games and platforms. Video games are generally defined as electronic or computerized games played by manipulating images on a video display or television screen. There are a variety of game types including role playing, action, sports, and party games. Games accommodate two or more players:

- Single-player games—individuals play against a computer-generated opponent.
- Multiplayer games—multiple participants interact in the same virtual environment, playing against and/or with one another.
- Massively multiplayer online (MMO) games—globally deployed games that run 24/7 and support millions of players playing together. *World of Warcraft* (www.worldofwarcraft.com) and Second Life (*www.secondlife.com*) are two examples of MMOs.

These platforms continue to evolve, blend, and overlap as newer forms of entertainment and services are developed.

MMO games are further divided into 4 types:[6]

1. Massive multiplayer online role-playing games (MMORPGs)—reflect traditional gaming techniques and generally take hours to days to play (e.g., *World of Warcraft*)
2. Free-form virtual worlds—not typical gaming environments but places where the player creates not only an avatar and a life in virtual reality—but also requires lots of time to play (e.g., Second Life)
3. Online game worlds—require less time and are played in a traditional gaming format (e.g., *Guild Wars*)
4. Social network worlds—require more time, involve networking, and are not typical gaming environments (e.g., *Habbo Hotel*)

Video games today are played on a variety of platforms. The rapid advancement of technology has allowed the development of very fast computers that can process massive pieces of data needed to render video graphics. Arcade video game booths are still popular, but almost all gaming now falls under the following 3 platforms:

1. PC gaming—playing games, both on and offline, on a PC
2. Console gaming—playing games on a console or box
3. Mobile gaming—playing games on a phone or mobile device such as an MP3 player or a dedicated mobile gaming device (PSP, DS Lite)

By 2010, analysts predict that Sony, Microsoft, and Nintendo, the 3 major console manufacturers, will together have 146 million units globally. The United States will represent the largest market at approximately 71 million installed units; Europe will be the second largest market with 47 million installed units, and Japan will be the third largest market with nearly 29 million installed units. In addition to having standalone consoles, Nintendo and Sony also have handheld consoles. The total combined number of handheld units is expected to be about 60 million by 2010.[7]

Online gaming

Online gaming has also experienced incredible growth and popularity in recent years. One in every 4 Internet users visits a gaming site, and online gamers visit a gaming site an average of 9 times per month.[8]

A broadband connection and server storage space are necessary to host a game among multiple online users. The player can use a device such as a PC or a game console to play the game. A user buys the game in the form of a CD-ROM, a DVD, or a disk specific for the gaming console. The user also pays a monthly subscription fee to cover the cost of developing and updating their virtual world content and maintaining the server. In online gaming performance, speed and timing are critical factors for many of the games' activities. Voice is also an important element of gaming for team communications, which can take place through PC headsets or instant text messaging. Hardware and software developments continue to advance, supporting the newest gaming multimedia-rich features and are announced at major events, such as the Games Developer Annual Conference (www.gdconf.com).

According to the 2003 Pew survey, 71% of college students play computer games that do not require an Internet connection, 59% play video games on video consoles, and 56% play online games on PCs. College students use games as a way to spend more time with friends, with 20% stating that they felt gaming helped them make new friends, as well as improve existing friendships; and 65% said that gaming has little to no influence in taking time away from family and friends.

Students are able to integrate gaming into their day, taking time between classes to play a game, play a game while visiting with friends or instant messaging, or play games as a brief distraction from writing papers or doing other work. In group college settings such as in residence halls, students are able to multitask: they can play games, listen to music, and interact with others in the room. Pew researchers report that college students have a positive feeling about gaming, with 36% stating it was pleasant, 34% said it was exciting, and 45% said gaming was challenging. Forty-eight percent stated that gaming keeps them from studying, while 9% said that they played games to avoid studying; 32% admitted that they played games during classes that did not contain instructional activities. The study also indicated that more women (60%) reported playing computer and online games than men (40%).[9]

A survey of 650 MIT freshmen found that 88% of the students played games before they were 10 years old, and more than 75% were still playing games as least once a month. 60% of the freshmen responded that they spend an hour or more a week playing computer games. Comparatively, only 33% spend an hour or more every week watching TV, and 43% spend an average of an hour every week reading anything other than an assigned text book.[10]

Learning and games

While gaming is relatively new to higher education, research indicates that games are valuable learning mechanisms. Much of the learning occurs through participation in gaming communities, as the most gifted players pass along what they have learned to other players.[11] James Gee, author of *What Video Games Have to Teach Us about Learning and Literacy*, notes that when kids play video games they "experience a much more powerful form of learning than when they are in the classroom."[12] Data suggest that one of the reasons students pursue technical fields is because they are exposed to technology early in their childhood, and many of these students gain this exposure through playing or using games. Some games such as ones in which multiple players work toward a common goal, provide student skills that will benefit them in the workforce.[13]

Games are complex learning systems that involve virtual worlds, communities of practice (social learning that occurs when participating in social learning practices), trade, blogs, and developer communities.[14] The feature-rich virtual worlds of gaming create a powerful context for learning and situated understanding (learning is tied to the situation). Even though research suggests that games are powerful learning mechanisms, they are still largely in the early stages of being used in higher education.

Higher-education games evaluated

This section outlines a variety of games that have been explored in higher education for use in learning. Although many games in higher education are relatively new and somewhat foreign within the context of teaching and learning, research proves their value and use in higher education.

MIT created and tested a number of games that can be used in higher education. A report titled *Harnessing the Power of Games in Education* evaluated the following MIT games. Below is a summary from the report:[15]

- *Civilization III* allows players to lead a civilization from 4000 BC to present. Students can win the game in a variety of ways that include political, scientific, military, cultural, and economic victories. Players seek out geographical resources, manage economies, plan the growth of their civilization, and engage in diplomacy with other nation states. The report found that this game when played in college classroom environments is a powerful way to introduce students to concepts such as a monarchy, as well as tie together segments of history. This open game, notes the reports coauthor K. Squire, allows students to pursue different questions and ideas. One student can pursue Egyptian history and another can pursue various conquests in the world, while others evaluate concepts of social order, geography, strategy, and resources. Squire also notes that students, when engaged in gaming, use maps, online texts, and education films to improve their performance in the game—not to memorize facts but rather to garner the information they needed to achieve success.
- In MIT's *Revolution*, 25 students enter the gaming environment assuming the role of a person who lives in a colonial town during the Revolutionary period in the United States. The students research the town's history as part of the game. As townspeople, they have roles, responsibilities, routines, and political alignments regarding the American Revolution. There is a series of episodes that takes 40 minutes to

play, and each episode is designed so that users can stage a debate and play out the consequences. At the end of each session, the classroom professor debriefs the segment.

The game's authors suggest that unlike visiting Williamsburg, Virginia, for an afternoon, the game experience is such that the player becomes immersed into the life and times of history through this game and becomes a part of the community or town. While a book may tell give students an historical account of the Revolution, a game can directly immerse the player into the evolution of this period, helping students relive the impact the Revolution had on the people involved. The game's multiplayer framework allows the town community to become a real, social community that reflects the opinions and competing interests of the townsfolk.

- *MIT's Prospero's Island* is a single-player game that provides a gateway into Shakespeare's play *The Tempest*. The game, like the play, is about self-discovery. The student chooses a role (servant, sailor, etc.) and, accordingly, picks a costume and goals that determine how other characters respond to him/her. The player is shipwrecked on an island during the Renaissance period. Through a series of interactions with Shakespearian characters, the player reshapes the world and reworks the narrative of the original play. That is, the players perform literary analysis. The game does not displace the play; it enhances the experience of the person who might be watching or reading the play.
- *MIT's Environmental Detective* is a game that can be played anytime, anywhere using a variety of media, such as a PDA. This game motivates players to investigate an event, weigh the evidence, and compare notes. It also lets players test hypotheses and synthesize information as they draw conclusions about what has occurred and why. The student assumes the role of an environmental scientist, representing one of several factions researching a chemical spill on a college campus. Players take virtual readings of the contaminants and soil, interview virtual informants, and access information.

After they complete the game, students prepare a presentation for the university president. The presentation includes a definition of the problem and a course of action for the university. The authors state that research on simulations and microworlds has shown that games can produce deeper conceptual understandings, particularly in physics. Researchers are finding that augmented reality games can be a powerful way to expose students to learning experiences not possible otherwise.

- *BioHazard/ Hot Zone* was originally created to teach college students introductory college biology and environmental science. It has evolved into a game to help emergency first responders deal with toxic spills in public locations. Players race against the clock to save civilians. The game involves scanning and assessing the situation quickly; teaming; and understanding chemicals, viruses, and symptoms. Individuals also learn how unpredictable behaviors can be in high-stress emergency situations.

The MIT report concludes that educational games, in order to be used fully, should have the same quality as commercial console games in terms of graphics, sound, and playability. Overall benefits of these games include engaging in inquiry, developing expertise, participating in a social practice, and developing an identity as a learning community, rather than merely memorizing names or dates for a test. Games encourage collaboration among players and thus provide a context for peer-to-peer teaching and learning communities. It involves metagaming (conversations about strategy that occurs around the actual game), metacognition (the process of reflecting on learning itself), and critical learning (learning how to not only play a game, but also how to play it in a community and share knowledge across players).

Other universities have also explored the use of games in higher education. In 2006, Purdue University developed a college-level chemistry video game titled *Critical Mass*, which was due for trial in the third quarter of 2007. Designed to teach basic concepts in chemistry, the game was developed by Gabriela Weaver, a chemistry professor, and Carlos Morales, a computer graphics technology professor, with the goal of understanding the aspects of video games that make them both engaging and self-learning environments.

The purpose of the game, according to the developers, was not to replace chemistry classes but to lower the anxiety that students have with chemistry and to help students have a more open mind about pursuing chemistry. The story opens with the player's character awaking from a state of cryogenic sleep by human scientists because something has gone awry in the research facility where the game takes place. The antagonists of the game, played by the computer, are robots who have taken over and are threatening the livelihood of the planet. In this manner, chemistry is depicted as a tool for good and evil, demonstrating that these educational games can include many of the key themes or elements that commercial games have.[16]

A team from the University of Tokyo studied the effect of gaming on learning using a popular commercially available history game titled *Uncharted Waters*,[17] from Koei (*www.koei.com*). The test involved three groups of students from the university. The first group, a control group, attended a history class; each student had a textbook for the entire class. The second group played *Uncharted Waters* for the duration of the class. The third group played the same game along with having to complete coordinating assignments. The third group outperformed both the control group and the second group, supporting the researchers' hypothesis that games had a positive effect on the class curriculum but only when used in conjunction with teaching materials.

The U.S. Armed Forces have also explored the use of commercial games in teaching and education. Studies were conducted by a national university to measure the difference in academic achievement between students who used video games in learning and those who did not. The game *Giant II* (*www.jowood.com*) was tested with first year students and *Zapitalism* (www.lavamind.com) and *Virtual U* (*www.virtual-u.org*) with third year business students. The findings from this study indicated that students in the classes using the game scored significantly higher than classes that did not. There appeared to be no difference in performance between genders or ethnicity, but every participant's score improved significantly the longer he/she played. Students 40 years and under scored significantly higher when playing the games, while students 41 and older did not.[18]

Alice (www.alice.org), a popular first-year college game created by Carnegie Mellon University, teaches students programming in a 3-D environment. Carnegie Mellon notes that *Alice* has been in use by 10% of U.S. education institutions that teach computer science. In addition, the game has helped attract women to jobs in computer science, as well as retain them in this field. Carnegie Mellon and Electronic Arts, a game developer, recently announced a collaboration partnership to develop *Alice 3.0*, which will include characters from the top-selling U.S. game *The Sims* (*http://thesims.ea.com*), for a series of games targeted at making science fun for students in middle school, high school, and beyond.[19] This partnership is significant because it has the potential to take education games mainstream.

While educational games are not mainstream yet by top gaming firms, there are a few commercial games that are popular today and used in college classes with success: *Gazillionaire, Zapitalism,* and *Profitania*, all business-strategy simulation games from Lavamind.com. Other games such as Nintendo's *Brain Age* (*www.brainage.com*) are popular in Japan, where more than 8 million units were sold in 2005.[20] Companies such as Koei are making strides in educational gaming for the Japanese market as well.

These are just some games that have been evaluated with success in the higher education environment. In addition, the Serious Games Initiative, an organization focused on the use of games in exploring management and leadership challenges facing the public sector, is ushering in a new series of policy education, exploration, and management tools utilizing state of the art computer game designs, technologies, and development skills. One of its charters is to help forge productive links between the electronic game industry and projects involving the use of games in education, training, health, and public policy.

Why is adoption slow?

With the extensive use and anticipated growth of gaming, why has higher education been slow to adopt games? Reasons include a lack of familiarity and experience with gaming among current educators, coupled with a lack of educational games in the market; and a perception that games are fun rather than educational.[21]

Games can be defined in two ways: simple and complex. Simple games are *Trivial Pursuit, Monopoly*, and *Scrabble*. These are games that many educators have grown up with and associate with the word "game." In these terms the games were short and fun and did not require much strategy. Complex games refer to games such as *The Sims, World of Warcraft*, and even Second Life. Complex games can take more than 25 years to develop, have multiple players, enable or are enabled entirely by computers, and offer an environment for players to create, collaborate, compete and require strategy. A student today when discussing a game is more likely to be discussing a complex game. Time is a key distinguisher between simple games and complex games. A simple game takes up to 2 hours to complete, and a complex game takes up to 100 hours to complete.[22]

Educational video games are not yet mainstream, despite a fair amount of enthusiasm among educators, at least among those who do not see video games as inherently stultifying. Part of the problem is that the industry, which is dominated by players such as Electronic Arts, has not figured out how to make money from education games.[23] "Commercially they basically have a few ideas that they keep repackaging and retooling, with success," says Eric Klopfer, co-director of Education Arcade, a game project run by the MIT and the University of Wisconsin, Madison. "But that strategy doesn't work for educational games," he says. "You have to have the science and the content tightly woven together. And that makes it hard to copycat successful game strategies from one subject area to another."

Whether education games could become mainstream was a topic explored at the annual Games Development Conference (www.gdconf.com) by researchers from a variety of institutions, including Georgia Tech, the University of Wisconsin, the University of Southern California, and Gamelab. The conference speakers noted that educators want quantifiable evidence that games use in education produces data that shows enhanced student performance. Collecting this type of data collection is a lengthy process to test but research is becoming more available. In addition the participants discussed that in order to ensure a well designed education game more collaboration is required between the large gaming firms and the key gaming researchers to ensure success. [24]

Second Life and virtual worlds

By 2011, 80% of active Internet users will participate in virtual worlds. Second Life is a popular virtual world among not only consumers, but also higher education. Second Life (*www.secondlife.com*), a 3-D online virtual world released in 2003 by Linden Labs of San Francisco, is often categorized as a game because it has similarities to *The Sims*, in which players design characters that build, manage, and live in a simulated city.

Second Life, unlike *The Sims* and *World of Warcraft*, does not have conflict or an end objective designed into the product. "Residents"—the term that defines Second Life users—not Linden Labs, create the content within Second Life.

Participants create a personal avatar in whatever likeness they desire. These avatars are referred to as "residents." A resident is presented opportunities to engage with other residents, attend entertainment events, shop, conduct business, or even buy an island. Since the release of Second Life, users have created replicas of real-world locations, art exhibits, music concerts, and orchestra performances—using the medium to socialize or conduct business using a combination of text chat, streaming media, and voice-over-IP technology.[25]

Second Life currently has more than 9 million residents who create products, offer services, and transact as they would in real life using a currency called Linden Dollars. Second Life software is provided by the game's creators as a free download.

Many large corporations such as Reuters, Pontiac, IBM, and Starwood have purchased islands in Second Life. So have educational institutions. From

April 2007 to May 2007, there were more than 170 educational institutions including accredited colleges, universities, and schools in Second Life. Most institutions had one island; some that have multiple islands. The University of Ohio, for instance, occupied 7 islands within Second Life. Many institutions use Second Life to ensure their brand by creating a campus presence using logos, signage, sidewalks, and footpaths; they are also providing residents with links to other campus locations. [26]

Institutions use their island for 3 main reasons:

- Showcase Second Life projects at their college
- Connect residents to the college Web site
- Solicit new student enrollment.

Within the virtual locations, institutions provide space such as classrooms, art galleries, auditorium, living quarters, offices, visiting libraries, visitor centers, bars, beaches, gardens, restaurants, and game rooms. [27]

A number of colleges are posting video demonstrations on YouTube about how they use Second Life:

- Coventry University (United Kingdom), Texas State University (San Marcos Island), and Ohio University: conduct tours around their islands.
- Kent State University: promotes its fashion shows and the work of students in the fashion program.
- Murdoch University Library in Australia: has created a library archipelago along with other university libraries.
- Harvard Law School: conducts a law school classes in Second Life.

Summary

Computer gaming is a popular form of entertainment and will continue to grow in popularity with college students. Gaming applications are being created for a variety of platforms and devices. The success of student performance from educational games gaining acknowledgment through organizations such as *www.seriousgames.com* and wwwigda.org. A number of gaming researchers at key universities are also sharing their findings about the benefits of educational games. Higher education will see more uses for games as major developers such as Electronic Arts and Lavamind develop and effectively commercialize these products. Once this happens, gaming in higher education will become mainstream.

Increased Use of Technology and Its Implications for Higher Education

CHAPTER FIVE

Increase of Credible Content on the Web

Patricia D. Wilen, Ph.D.

How does the general public search for information on solving their problems? The Pew Institute conducted a telephone survey to explore this question, and, not surprisingly, found that in today's high-tech society, people increasingly rely on the Internet to find answers to their problems: 58% of those interviewed said that they used the Internet either at home, at work, or at the public library.[1] An abundance of data is now available on the Web on almost any topic.

This chapter focuses on some of the many available quality-content sources in a variety of areas, including but not limited to government, history, statistics, museums, science, medicine, health, and mathematics.

Credible sources

Credible content is increasingly being made available by universities through open courseware, digital collections, libraries (such as the United States Library of Congress), museums (including the Metropolitan Museum of Art, the Louvre, and the Vatican Museums), research institutes (such as NASA and the National Science Foundation), and even some U.S. zoos (in Cleveland, St. Louis, and Alaska). Data in the form of images, not just text, are now widely available as well. Other notable examples are:

- *The New York Public Library's* new image database provides free and open online access to thousands of images from the original and rare holdings of the library. "The database spans a wide range of visual media and offers digital images of drawings; illuminated manuscripts; maps; photographs; posters; prints; rare, illustrated books; and more" (www.nypl.org/).
- OpenCourseWare is a large-scale initiative by the Massachusetts Institute of Technology (MIT) to provide free, searchable access to course materials for educators, students, and self-learners around the world. The initiative is reported to receive 2 million visits from users a month. Key users include faculty, students, and independent learners (http://ocw.mit.edu).[2]
- The University of California at Berkeley notes that in one year, it received more than 4.3 million views of videos of lectures posted on the Webcast site hosted by the university (http://webcast.berkeley.edu).[3]
- The Library of Congress offers catalog descriptions and images of 130 million items, including prints and photographs, audio broadcasts, music, and other sources relevant to U.S. history (http://catalog.loc. gov).
- The Education Resources Information Center, sponsored in part by the U.S. Department of Education, provides free access to annotated bibliographic records (citations, abstracts, and other pertinent data) for more than 1.2 million items indexed since 1966, including more than 600 journals, books, conference and policy papers, technical reports and other education-related materials (*www.eric.ed.gov/*).

Some other U.S. government agencies and/or offices that publish data, statistics, and records online are:

- The National Archives
- United States Copyright Office
- Census Bureau—United States and international demographic data
- Government Printing Office
- United States Geological Survey (USGS)
- Department of Health and Human Services—Grants database
- Department of Commerce—National Telecommunications and In-

formation Administration
- Central Intelligence Agency (CIA)—declassified documents and other facts

The prevalence of such services allows self-service learners to take responsibility for their education and find learning resources using available technologies.

Google and search engines—visible vs. invisible Web

Google, the most familiar search engine, currently has roughly 8 billion Web pages indexed and is one of the largest, searchable databases in the world. A recent blog by Google indicated that news, blogs, and information are updated within minutes, enabling access to knowledge faster than ever before.[4] Google can only index what is known as the "visible Web," which is what one sees in subject directories and on "results pages" of user queries or searches in standard search engines such as Google and Yahoo. The invisible Web, also called the "deep Web," is comprised of databases and results of specialty search engines such as library catalogs—results that popular search engines are not able to index—and is estimated to be 500 times bigger than the visible Web.[5] Since 2000, search engine "crawlers" and indexing programs have overcome many of the technical barriers that made it impossible for searchers to find invisible Web pages. For example, pages in non-HTML formats such as PDF, Word, and Excel are now translated into HTML in most search engines and can be indexed and viewed in today's search results.

The first and easiest way to access the deep Web is to use a standard search engine such as Google or Yahoo. Then type in the key words of interest plus the word "+database." There will be fewer results reported for this "+database" search query, but they would most likely be links to databases being maintained by academic or accredited institutions,[6] that is, the information from these institutions would almost certainly be much more credible than most results found from the visible Web.

An extensive list of deep-Web search engines is available in the Online Education Database at http://oedb.org/library/college-basics/research-beyond-google. While some of these search engines are fee-based, most of them are free. Examples of search engines are:

- Clusty.com is a mega search engine that combines the results from top search engines and clusters them into topics for easier use. It ranks the results so that the best results move to the top and the "junk" falls to the bottom.

- Intute.ac.uk is a free online service created by a network of universities and partners in the United Kingdom. Subject specialists select and evaluate the Web sites in the database and describe the resources. The database contains 120,606 records.
- Infomine.ucr.edu is a "virtual library of Internet resources" that was built by librarians from major U.S. universities. It contains databases, electronic journals and books, and articles that are useful to researchers at the university level.
- The Librarians Internet Index (www.lii.org) is publicly funded and publishes a weekly newsletter that describes high-quality Web sites reviewed by librarians and categorizes material by topic.

Tens of thousands of books are also available online for free. The Online Books Page (*http://digital.library.upenn.edu/books/search.html*) offers a database of more than 25,000 English books with full text. Bibliomania (www.bibliomania.com), another free resource, includes study guides. Project Gutenberg (www.gutenberg.org), which calls itself the first producer of ebooks, has books in over fifty languages. Google recently started the Google Book Service (http://books.google.com), which catalogs books that are out of copyright and books that publishers have given Google permission to reproduce electronically.

Many scientific journals also choose to make their research papers available over the Internet. The abstracts for the papers are readily accessible, but to access a paper in its entirety usually requires a fee. A good database for scientific journals is the National Academies Press, which publishes reports on important issues in science and health by the National Academy of Sciences, the National Academy of Engineering, the Institute of Medicine, and the National Research Council. In addition to giving material in subject areas, the National Academies Press offers access to reference materials such as dictionaries, almanacs, encyclopedias, magazines, and newspapers in a variety of languages. The site is also available to persons with disabilities.[7]

Evaluating internet information

Today's students are technology literate; they know how to find information on the Internet. The problem they run into is the accuracy, or lack thereof, of the information. Educators complain that their students lack the skills needed to find quality information. Some complain that students often cannot tell the difference between an infomercial and hard facts.[8] Students can be easily overwhelmed with the sheer amount of data available. *The Chronicle of Higher Education* reported that in 1996 there were 10,000 scholarly databases online; today they exceed 18,000. The article also reported that the Web is teeming with more than 100 million sites, up from 18,000 in 1995.[9] Tara Brabazon, professor of media studies at the University of Brighton, in Brighton, England, complained that students come to the university ill equipped to evaluate the quality of the information being presented on the Internet, especially on Google and Wikipedia. She said that she does not blame the students; she believes that today's students are not being taught good research skills. "We need to teach our students the interpretative skills first before we teach them the technological skills," she said. "Students must be trained to be dynamic and critical thinkers rather than drifting to the first site returned through Google."[10]

How do students go about evaluating the data? How do they determine the reliability and accuracy of the data? How do they determine the amount of information needed and how to access it? How do they decide whether what is presented constitutes quality data, biased opinion, or just plain junk?

Increasingly universities are developing tests to measure what they call "information literacy." The Information and Community Technology Literacy Assessment—developed and administered by the Educational Testing Service, a nonprofit group based in Princeton, New Jersey—is a 75-minute test that measures students' ability in 7 areas, including organizing, evaluating, and communicating with electronic data.[11]

The Association of College and Research Libraries recommends that students develop a list of questions pertaining to their research before they begin their search. They need to identify keywords, synonyms, and other related vocabulary so that they can streamline their search to a manageable framework and timeline. Once they have collected their data, the researcher must compare information from various sources to evaluate its accuracy, reliability, point of view or bias, and decide whether it is fact or opinion, before drawing conclusions.[12] Students must become skilled evaluators of the abundance of information available on the Internet. They should remember that the Internet is similar to a giant library, where the librarian can be very helpful in assisting the students find the data sources that they need for their research.

The Pew study, mentioned at the beginning of the chapter, found that, interestingly, 53% of respondents still went to the library for problem solving. Of these library patrons, 40% were from Generation Y, ages 18–30, which demonstrates that libraries have not become obsolete.[13] Libraries must adapt, however, to high-tech methods of getting information, and they must also teach their patrons better information-gathering skills.[14]

Summary

Today's students have a wealth of resources at their fingertips via the Internet. Some of this information is inaccurate, outdated, biased, or unreliable. The sheer volume of information available can be overwhelming. A student must be able to evaluate the source and the content and validate it. This involves finding quality content; there are many sites where such content exists. This chapter attempted to present a number of quality Internet sources in a variety of subject areas. The school librarian can be of great help also in directing students to other sources. In the next chapter, we will look at information literacy with more depth.

CHAPTER SIX

Technology and Information Literacy

Postsecondary education and technology proficiency are required for jobs

In 2003, the Bush administration released a report, "The Higher Growth Job Training Initiative." The goal of this initiative was to help prepare people for high-growth jobs and to make sure that, as the economy changes, people were not left behind due to lack of skills. It is the first step that the U.S. Department of Labor has taken to engage business and educational investment in finding solutions for the challenges facing the American workforce.

The report identified 14 high-growth sectors that were expected to add a substantial number of jobs to the economy either from existing or emerging businesses that have been transformed by technology and innovation and that now need new skills for workers. These sectors are advanced manufacturing, aerospace, automotive, biotechnology, construction, energy, financial services, geospatial design, healthcare, homeland security, hospitality, information technology, retail, and transportation.[1]

The U.S. economy, like those of other developed nations, is fueled by innovation, and employers are using new productivity enhancing technologies to remain competitive. Two-thirds of America's economic growth in the 1990s resulted from the introduction of new technologies. This continuous process of innovation and technological change has resulted in jobs that demand ever higher skill levels. The U.S. Bureau of Labor Statistics (BLS) projections for 2004 through 2014 indicate that 63% of all new jobs of the twenty-first century will require some postsecondary education.[2] In today's global economy, advancements in technology applications extend across multiple industries, creating the demand for transferable, basic IT skills and competencies among new hires and incumbent workers at almost all levels of employment. All this presents a cross-industry workforce challenge that is, simply stated, to prepare an adaptable workforce with the requisite basic IT skills.

Technical literacy definitions

The U.S. Educational Testing Services (ETS) defines information and communication technology (ICT) literacy as "the ability to use digital technology, communication tools, and networks appropriately to solve information problems in order to function in an information society." It includes not only the ability to use technology as a tool to research, organize, evaluate, and communicate information, but also the possession of a "fundamental understanding of the ethical/legal issues surrounding the access and use of information."[3]

The American Library Association defines information technology skills as those that enable an individual to use computers, software, databases, and other technologies to achieve a wide variety of academic, work-related, and personal goals. Information literacy, they note, is a distinct and broader competence that includes the ability to determine the extent of information needed; to access the needed information effectively and efficiently; to evaluate information and the sources critically; to use and incorporate the information effectively; and to understand the economic, legal, social, and ethical ramifications of the information.[4]

Technology literacy also is defined as the set of abilities and skills where aural, visual, and digital literacy overlap. These include the ability to understand the power of images and sounds, to recognize and use that power, to manipulate and transform digital media, to distribute them pervasively, and to easily adapt them to new forms.[5]

Due to the expansion of multimedia in today's society, those "who are truly literate in the twenty-first century will be those who learn to both read and write the multimedia of the screen."[6]

Today's youth need to learn how to quickly integrate knowledge from multiple sources, including music, video, online databases, and other media. They need to think critically about information that can be found nearly instantaneously throughout the world. They need to participate in the kind of collaboration that new communications and information technologies enable and increasingly demand.[7]

To be literate today, students must have textual literacy, which is the ability to read and write as a central skill. They need to expand their literacy to include research skills, technical skills, and other media literacy. A 2006 MacArthur Foundation paper outlines foundation skills (traditional literacy, research skills, technical skills, and critical analysis taught in the classroom) and new skills (play, performance, simulation, appropriation, multitasking, distributed cognition, collective intelligence, judgment, transmedia navigation, networking, and negotiation) as the new media literacy that is defined as "a set of cultural competencies and social skills that young people need in the new media landscape."[8]

Students are technical but are they literate?

The ETS ICT literacy report, iSkills, assessed more than 6,300 students at 63 universities, colleges, community colleges, and high schools. The report found that students lack many basic skills to use technology to solve information problems. The origination of the study came from librarians and professors who found that students can use technology for social purposes and entertainment but have problems finding information, evaluating it, and putting it to use. This lack of ability to find and critically assess information online was found not only among students but among people in the workplace as well.[9]

The ever-increasing availability of information is adding to students' confusion. In 2007 there were 18,000 scholarly databases online, compared to 10,000 in 1996. Also as of 2007, there were 100 million websites compared to 18,000 in 1995. Google and Microsoft, among others, have been digitizing books and archiving journals. In addition to Wikipedia, there are more academic encyclopedias, such as Citizendium and Scholarpedia.[10]

Although students today, having for the most part grown up with the technology, have less fear about computers and more technical software, they appear to have no more critical ability with multimedia than older people. Unlike the text medium of instruction that starts in the second grade or even earlier, children do not receive similar instruction for multimedia. High school and college courses on media and visual literacy emphasize that TV, cinema, and related media are inferior communication forms and may misrepresent reality. They enforce the idea that real education remains in books and that real knowledge is rational and linear.[11]

The American Library Association notes that literacy needs to be incorporated across curricula—in all programs and services and all through the administrative life of the university—and requires collaborative efforts of faculty, libraries, and administration[12] Higher education institutions are increasingly becoming aware of the need for technology literacy in an ever-growing technology environment.[13] EDUCAUSE, a non-profit organization dedicated to the use of IT in education, published 3 white papers on this topic in 2006; UNESCO published a 115-page handbook in 2006 to promote literacy worldwide, and the National Forum on Information Literacy created a group of 16 educators and business leaders to set national standards for information literacy.[14] While some institutions such as Ohio State have information literacy programs and California State University is contemplating a technology proficiency test for all students, the vast majority of colleges are not addressing this issue directly.

Proposed solutions to address technology literacy

In February 2008, a panel of educators approved and released a document, "Setting Standards on the Core and Advanced iSkills Assessments." This establishes passing scores on 2 information literacy exams that Educational Testing Service (ETS) administers to help colleges understand the abilities of their students as they maneuver through electronic data.[15] This is a step in the right direction, but it must be complemented by various solutions to improve technology literacy.

Today's students actively are involved in what has been called a "participatory culture," but schools have been slow to react. Many adults assume that youth can simply acquire these skills on their own without adult intervention or supervision. Much of this assumption is based upon the fact that children are considered more adept with technology than adults. Adult intervention, however, is needed in 3 key problems noted in a paper published by the MacArthur Foundation:[16]

1. **The participation gap** refers to the inequalities in students' access to new media technologies and the opportunity for participation they represent. Researchers note that although many cities, such as Tempe,

Philadelphia, Boston, and Cambridge, have initiatives to increase access to technology, such as computers, the key is free broadband initiatives, coupled with educational initiatives, that will help students and adults use the technology more effectively.

2. **The transparency problem** assumes that students are actively reflecting on their media experience and can articulate what they have learned from their engagement. The researchers cite *Sim City*, a popular game played where students learn how to manipulate the system to increase their scores rather than solving the real-life problems posed in the game. Another example cited is in an MIT-developed game, where students actively play in a historical reenactment of the American Revolution. The researchers note that the students took the facts of the game at face value, without a question, as if all the facts were authentic (similar to how a student accepts textbook data).

3. **The ethical challenge** assumes that children on their own can develop the ethical norm required to deal with various social issues online. For example, should young children be given the opportunity to decide what is and what isn't appropriate to post about themselves in popular online applications, such as Live Journal or MySpace?

To overcome these problems, the paper proposes a framework that addresses how to rethink literacy, which includes core literacy and the ability to develop new research skills, distinguish between fact and opinion, construct arguments and marshal evidence, use technical skills, and understand the ways new media represent perceptions of the world. These can be taught in classroom environments. For example, a teacher could engage students to reflect on alternative history scenarios, focusing on the how's and why's of events rather than memorizing the actual dates of facts and figures. With simulated games such as *Sim City*, student players could learn how to design a city from the bottom up, rather than from top down, so they learn how land, zoning, and a variety of city functions interact.[17]

Role playing is another technique proposed in the paper, with the Model United Nations project being a prime example of a game that brings together students (who role play a country member) through current debates in foreign policy using the actual governmental procedures. Other examples cited include a program at the University of Southern California where students develop an online game that reflects the current situation of youth in Los Angeles. The paper suggests a systematic approach to media and technology education that starts with access to the technologies and is integrated through school activities, after-school activities, and even at home.[18]

In 1999, the National Research Council (NRC) proposed a framework for computer literacy. Although the report noted that computer literacy is achievable for most people regardless of grade level or experience, the report's framework is focused on college students because "institutions of higher learning have the most experience creating courses about computers and related information systems. Colleges also serve a large constituency with a broad range of interests and specializations to which information technology can be applied." The framework proposes that a serious rethinking of the entire college curriculum is required; in particular, it suggests that academic departments examine how their students can obtain the necessary capability by the time they graduate.[19]

The report outlines 3 key components for educators to build a curriculum to help students become fluent in information technology:

1. Intellectual capabilities: the application and interpretation of computer concepts and skills used in problem solving. This involved the basics of using computers and problem solving computer issues.
2. Concepts: the fundamental ideas and processes that support information technology, a basic understanding of information technology.
3. Skills: abilities that are associated with particular hardware and software systems. Skills would include how to use word processors, email, the Internet, and other appropriate information technology tools effectively.[20]

In August 2006, the National Academies of Sciences proposed that the federal government, state governments, and the private sector should develop tests and surveys to measure Americans' knowledge of technology, how they use it in their daily lives, and their ability to make informed decisions on issues involving technology. The committee reviewed nearly 30 surveys and tests that included questions about technology. They found that none had adequately assessed people's knowledge and use of technology. Data regarding technology use generated from these surveys potentially could allow policymakers to better respond to people's concerns about technology and help educators improve technology-related curricula and teachers' education.[21]

To promote the value and interest in information technology skills for students, it should be done in a manner that resonates with administration, students, and faculty, de-emphasizing information technology jargon. This is the responsibility of the faculty and curriculum committees. Students, it has been found, do create ample digital content, but they are not doing so with faculty guidance and not in a classroom environment. Mostly, it's only for recreational use. Even more concerning is that when students integrate multimedia into their assignments, they sometimes are ridiculed by faculty as not presenting something academically rigorous.[22]

Instead of categorizing the skills, one solution proposes a framework that prepares students to become content creators within their professional or disciplinary specialties. For example, an advertising student can create an advertisement as a class assignment. To do this, the student must learn how to use a video camera, the relevant software, and various technologies to integrate the script using software, audio, lighting, and special effects. The student also must learn about intellectual property rights. The activity would help students understand and use technologies while developing the necessary computer skills to use video and software while working on an interesting project. Likewise, a history student might be required to develop a historical website as an assignment, in the process, learning technology skills such as Web design and software programming. The student also will have to learn how to find reliable research resource, as well as a thing or two about copyright use.[23]

Employers and hiring

In the twentieth century, the United States established an education system that produced educated citizens and workers, enabled geographic and economic mobility, and largely decreased the inequality of economic outcomes. The new economy in the twenty-first century, on the other hand, requires a new set of educational needs that includes a greater use of science and new technologies by average citizens, more interdisciplinary work, greater understanding of highly complex, interacting systems. This new economy also will entail solving local challenges in the face of globalization and massification, along with a substantial rethinking of retailing, services, and business in general.[24]

As a result, employers often hire graduates with the expectation that they will take on technology-intensive assignments.[25] Companies will be looking for more than a high GPA from a college graduate; they will be looking at the quality of a student's leadership, independence, innovation, and technical literacy. Gary Daugenti, president of Gent and Associates Search Firm, says that, "Businesses today look for a minimum technical proficiency that is at the same level as today's consumers. It is too time consuming and costly to train."[26] Business should not be responsible for providing technology remediation and definitely not for resolving what colleges could have avoided in the first place. A tip for business leaders is to recruit from colleges that offer high-caliber candidates—smart and technically literate students with proven results.

Summary

In a world run almost completely by information technology, it is in everybody's best interest to become technology literate. This is most crucial for today's youth, who should be ingrained with the capabilities not only to use information technology but also to use it critically and wisely. Higher learning institutions should take the initiative to equip their students with these essential technology skills that will not only make their graduates excellent workforce candidates but also provide them with a skill set that they can use in the real world.

CHAPTER SEVEN

Students and Technology

The Internet is an important tool for everyday life and has become a crucial tool for higher education. Students are pervasive users of the Internet for self-learning. Being fast adopters of technology, they have been and will continue to be considered "evergreen." That is, they will usher in new technologies on college campuses, and their use of and response to these technologies will create more opportunities for integration of technology in higher education. While higher education is grappling with how to educate using Web 2.0, the current technology trend, many are now thinking ahead to the next set of college students—Generation V.

Student use of the Internet

A 2008 report from the Pew Internet & American Life Project found that:[1]

- 79% of college Internet users say the Internet has had a positive impact on their college academic experience.
- 73% use the Internet more than the library for research.

- 72% check their email every day.
- 60% think the Internet has improved their relationships with class-mates.
- 56% believe that email has enhanced their relationship with profes-sors.
- 46% say email enables them to express ideas to a professor that they would not have expressed in class.
- 42% of online students say they use the Internet most often to keep in touch with their friends; 38% say they use it most often for academ-ics.
- 72% use email to correspond mostly with friends; 10% mostly with family; 7% mostly with professors.
- College Internet users are twice as likely as other Internet users to download music files compared with all Internet users.
- College Internet users are twice as likely to use instant messaging on any given day compared with the average Internet user.

In a survey conducted by Houghton Mifflin in 2007, it was found that more than 50% of college students use the Internet "to keep up with course work and prepare for exams"; 59% of college students reported using online study aids; 78% said they use online quizzing (the single most popular school-related use of the Internet); 29% use video tutorials; 24% engage in online tutoring; and 16% participate in online study groups.[2]

The Internet as a resource for news and information about science

A 2006 Pew study showed that the convenience of accessing scientific mate-rial on the Web has enabled the Internet to become a resource for news and information about science. Forty million Americans (20%) rely on the Internet as their primary source, second only to TV (41%) and ahead of newspapers (14%) and magazines (14%). This number changes significantly if the user has broadband at home (34% from the Internet and 33% from TV) and increases if the user is under the age of 30 (44% of users ages18–29 get science news and information from the Internet versus 32% who get this information from TV).

Respondents indicated that if they were looking for specific information on a specific topic, they would first turn to the Internet. For example, when asked where they would find information on stem cell research, 67% said they would turn to the Internet whereas 11% said the library. When asked where they get information on climate change, 59% said they use the Internet first, 12% use the library. When it came to information about the origins of life, 42% said they used the Internet, 19% the library, and 11% the Bible or church.[3]

The study also indicated that:

- 70% of the respondents used the Internet to look up the meaning of a scientific concept or term.
- 68% went online to look for an answer to a question about a scientific concept or theory.
- 65% used the Internet to learn more about a science story or discovery they first heard about offline.
- 5% used the Internet to complete a science assignment for school.
- 52% used the Internet to check the accuracy of a scientific fact or statistic.
- 43% downloaded scientific data, graphs, or charts from the Internet.
- 37% used the Internet to compare different or opposing scientific theories.[4]

This research indicates that convenience plays a large role in drawing people to the Internet for scientific information. Seventy-one percent said that the Internet was the most convenient method for gathering information, 13% thought that information via the Internet was more accurate than content gathered elsewhere, and 12% felt that information available online was information they could not find anywhere else. Of those who stated that the Internet would be their first option for finding out more about a topic, 90% stated that they would use a search engine such as Google and Yahoo to find out more about a topic.[5]

College students use the Internet more frequently than the general population

College students are heavy Internet users compared with the general population because the Internet is part of their daily routine. Their usage is also due to having grown up with computers—86% of college students have gone online compared with 59% of the general population. About half (49%) first used the Internet in college and about half (47%) used the Internet at home and prior to attending college.[6] Students say that the Internet has enhanced their education, since they use the Internet to communicate with professors and classmates and to do research and access library materials.[7]

While the Internet activities of some college students differ from those of the general population, most activities are very similar. Most variation occurs within leisure activities: college users are more likely to download music (60% vs. 28%), download music on a given day (14% vs. 4%), and listen to music online (59% vs. 39%).[8]

Technology has become an avenue that students choose to engage with peers and perform their studies. A 2007 study published in the *National Association of Student Personnel Administrators* (NASPA) Journal suggests that students are more involved in the education process when they use technology for academic purposes. When they use technology primarily for social or entertainment, they tend to be less involved in academic life.[9]

The mindset of today's college freshmen class

Beloit College, in Wisconsin, develops a Mindset List every year in an effort to help professors identify the experiences and world views of incoming freshmen each fall. For the class of 2011, most of whom were born in 1989, Beloit found that students' experiences and perceptions of reality were quite different from prior generations, they never rolled down a car window manually; they grew up drinking bottled water, watching high-definition TV, and listening to Rap music; music has always been portable; U2 is a rock group, not a spy plane; women's studies have always been offered on campus; they can write their autobiographies in real time, thanks to MySpace and YouTube; Tiananmen Square is a 2008 Olympics venue, not the scene of a massacre; and what is the Berlin Wall?[10]

Students are rapidly adopting new technologies

Adults between the ages of 18 and 26 are often the first to adopt new technologies and use them in their daily lives, whether at home, in social activities, or at school. In 2007, students and their families spent about $12.8 billion on electronics, up about 22% from 2006—this growth was fueled by sales of laptops, digital cameras, and cell phones such as Apple's iPhone.[11] A recent Pew study noted that 3 out of 4 young adults download and view Internet videos daily.[12] College students are also spending more time on the Internet than they do using any other media: 33%, 16.6%, and 5.5% spend more than 10 hours per week going online, watching television, and listening to music respectively.[13]

Information delivery methods are also changing due to the rapid adoption of new mobile devices such as smart phones. Today, 93% of college students own a cell phone and 58% have an MP3 player.[14] In addition, content distribution venues are actively used. Apple iTunes has more than 1 million downloads a day.[15] It is clear that the digital decade is accelerating. In a 2006 Forrester report, it is predicted that by 2011 the use of consumer technologies, including laptops, HDTV, and camera phones, will double and broadband use and home networks will triple.[16]

This trend is making an impact on college campuses and college life. Students bring with them multiple devices and technologies with an expectation of using them in their campus life. Laptops and cell phones are constants for college students, who are on campus with a record number of devices that enable mobile connectedness. They expect connectedness to extend from the dorm room to the classroom. Modern colleges strive to create sophisticated campuses that meet student needs for mobility and provide pervasive access to the networked world.[17]

Other current college trends include greater mobility; desktop computer usage is down 13% and laptop usage is on the rise. More than 50% of students bring a laptop to campus and spend 3.5 hours a day using campus hotspots for email, instant messaging, and Web surfing. Reviewing podcasts of classes, receiving grades, posting assignments, and instant messaging professors for help are typical tasks. Cell phone usage continues to rise as an additional 1.3 million students using these devices in 2006 communicated through their mobile devices spending on average 20 minutes a day sending and receiving text messages. Music is also a significant part of college-student life, with more than 41% of students owning an MP3 player.[18]

Increased adoption of social networking sites is another trend among college students, where they spend an estimated 6.5 hours per week. "College students look to their friends above any other influences for guidance and approval. The increase in 'friend' access and the evolving definition of 'friend' affords peer networks greater importance than ever."[19]

Generation V—the next wave of college-bound students

While many educators are still trying to assess how to integrate the newest technologies into the lives of Generation Y students (those born between 1981 and 1995), a group of new students is emerging called "Generation V."[20] Generation V, children born in 1996 and on, is growing up on the 3 Vs—Visual, Virtual, and Versatile.

Visual: The students grew up with visual technologies such as Handycams, digital cameras, and YouTube as ways to source information or express themselves.

Virtual: This generation has been exposed to some of the newest gaming consoles such as Wii, Xbox, and PlayStations, as well as virtual reality games such as *Habbo*, *The Sims*, and a variety of multiplayer online games.

Versatile: These students are accustomed to using a variety of devices such as iPods, iPod Touch, and smart phones with ease. Much of their usage is fueled by the constant stream of new products released by various gadget manufacturers. (See figure below)

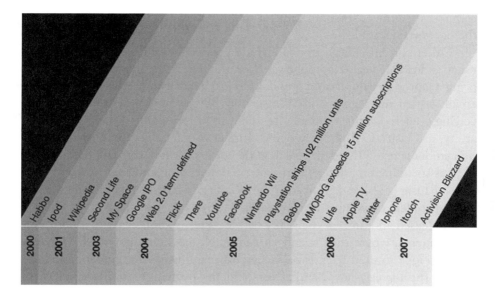

Timeline of innovative new products, services, technologies, and devices launched between 2000–2007. T. Wilen (www.hedtrends.com), 2007.

This new generation of Generation V preteens is quite busy.[21] Parents, due to their own busy schedules, concerns about leaving their children home alone, or the increased availability of academic, social, and athletic options, enroll their children into a variety of activities ranging from sports and martial arts to languages, enrichment classes, and community services. Many parents are now referred to as "helicopter parents" because they hover attentively over their children's educational and extracurricular activities to ensure that their children get into the best possible educational institutions and, if possible, with financial aid. A recent HealthAmerica KidsHealth poll found that 41% of children ages 9 to 13 surveyed said that they feel stressed either most of the time or always because they have too much to do. More than three-quarters of those surveyed said that they wished they had more free time.[22]

Overscheduling is a growing problem for American families. "A cultural phenomenon is taking place where parents are being told that the right way to raise their kids is to involve them in every enrichment opportunity possible, even if it means leaving the entire family feeling anxious and stressed," says Dr. Alvin Rosenfeld, author of *The Over-scheduled Child: Avoiding the Hyper-Parenting Trap* (A. Rosenfeld, 2001).

Dr. David Elkind, a professor of child development at Tufts University, adds, "The notion that education is a race has become quite prevalent and part of the conventional wisdom. And this race begins at infancy. Videos and software designed to give kids as young as 6 months old a leg up on the competition are being sold at toy stores around the country."[23]

A 2001 study by Marc Prensky[25] suggests that the brain development of children growing up today may be different than previous generations because of the influx of multiple experiences many children have through technology.[24] Kids ages 2 to 14 in the United States are using and interacting with consumer electronic devices in larger numbers and more frequently than ever before, and they are more adept at dealing with digital content than other age groups.[26] It is clear that this generation is used to having overscheduled days coupled with an enormous wealth of information resources, making them efficient multitaskers and communicators. Yet many educators in higher education refuse to acknowledge that each generation will evolve and become accustomed to a variety of learning resources—more so than previous generations.

The tertiary system has been slow to change due to tenure, faculty retirement policies and/or lack of focus on technology culture. Generation V college entrants will want access to education resources in the same manner that they access them today, using the 3Vs (visual multimedia, virtual reality and gaming, versatile). Educators must realize that neither these students nor their parents will pick a college that does not prepare them well upon graduating, especially with the rising costs of college education.

Summary

The Internet has become a key tool for learning and decision making and offers alternative content distribution and learning mechanisms for educators. College-aged students quickly adopt current consumer trends and do so faster than other segments of the general population, creating delivery and collaboration venues for education. As students rapidly adopt technologies, they raise the bar for college campuses to ensure intellectual vibrancy. These expectations will continue to evolve as new technologies are introduced and continually integrated into student lives.

CHAPTER EIGHT

Faculty
and Technology

As technology continues to rapidly move ahead, it will become increasingly important to have strategies in place to ensure integration and use of technology in the college environment. Unfortunately, in the past few years, faculty in higher education have moved from being creators and innovative users of the Internet to late and resistant adopters.

Faculty and universities were at the forefront of the development of the Internet

Since the development of ARPANET (Advanced Research Projects Agency Network), the world's first operational *packet switching* network that became the basis for the global Internet, college faculty members have played a pioneering role as facilitators of the Internet development in the 1960s and beyond.[1]

ARPANET was developed under the direction of the Advanced Research Projects Agency (ARPA) of the United States Department of Defense from the concept of interconnectedness first published in 1967. By 1969, the idea had become a reality when 4 university computers were networked. ARPA-NET's initial purpose was primarily to communicate with and share computer resources among scientific users at the connected institutions. Data traveled from one computer to another in small packets that went through different paths and were reconstructed at their destination. The advent of TCP/IP protocols in the 1970s made it possible to expand the size of the network, which now had "become a network of networks, in an orderly way."[2]

Not only did college faculty create and develop Internet technologies, they also were some of the first to use email, transfer files, and communicate online. Additionally, universities, in collaboration with the National Science Foundation, formed the Internet's first backbone NSFNet, a high-speed network for academic research projects that required increased computing power. Research universities were also the first to provide wired connections on their campuses in the 1960s, 1970s, and 1980s; other universities have since followed suit, and today all U.S. universities have Internet connections.[3]

Faculty use of the Internet

A 2004 survey conducted by researchers at the University of Chicago among college faculty found that 90% of faculty members interviewed have been using computers for at least 11 years and that 34% have used them for more than 20 years. Faculty who had been teaching for 10 to 15 years learned to use the Internet in school, whereas faculty teaching for more than 15 years learned to use the Internet when they first became faculty members. They use the Internet at least 4 hours a week; 40% of the educators interviewed are online at least 20 hours a week. Email usage is pervasive, with 82% of faculty reporting that they had been using email for 6 to 15 years—92% of them access email at home and 89% at work.

Nearly all college faculty reported using the Internet to communicate with students, using email, curriculum-based Web sites, or Web boards/forums; 95% use the Internet to make classroom announcements, 71% to provide information on class assignments, 62% to handle attendance matters, 7% to provide feedback on assignments, and 1% to discuss course-related problems.

Faculty surveyed noted that 94% of students emailed them to clarify an assignment, 98% to report an absence, 89% to report that they did not complete an assignment, 89% to find out about a grade, 97% to set up an appointment, 46% to complain about a class, and 52% to complain about an assignment. Email and instant messaging have become standard ways to continue the educational process outside the classroom, according to the educators in this study.

Many were using these tools to encourage student participation in discussions; 67% of faculty reported that the email improved their interaction with students.

While 69% felt that students were generally responsible in their use of email, one concern that faculty expressed was that students were sometimes "too casual" when using email. The professors also noted that email is much preferred by students over face-to-face sessions, and that email communication seems more detached than face-to-face discussions.

College faculty members were divided on the general impact of the Internet in classroom participation: 33% felt that they did not know if the Internet improved the quality of student classroom participation, 26% believed that the quality of student classroom participation was unaffected by Internet use, 22% felt that the Internet improved participation and 19% believed participation had worsened due to the Internet.

Although 13% felt that student writing had improved because of the Internet, 44% felt that plagiarism had increased in student work, and 74% reported using the Internet to check for student plagiarism. Still, 82% felt that the Internet had a positive effect on their teaching.

The study concluded that despite long-term exposure to the Internet, faculty in general were not "techies." For many, the effort required to master new technologies, contend with technology glitches, and accommodate their teaching to fit new technologies hindered rather than helped their teaching.[4]

Barriers precluding widespread acceptance of Internet use in education

Despite continued growth in online education, there are still barriers, including lack of faculty acceptance.[5] "Most academics welcome change in society and hate any change in their immediate environments."[6]

The Internet is constantly changing. Web 2.0 is a current example. While the idea of Web 2.0 is pervasive among young learners, it still is a new concept for faculty. The problem in academia is that students and teachers have been learning and teaching in a typical lecture-based way for decades. Web 2.0, on the other hand, fosters collaboration that challenges decades-old teaching and learning behaviors.[7]

Some institutions are using a variety of methods to help integrate and train faculty on current technologies, including:

- The student Star system at Wake Forest University, in North Carolina, is used to match technology-adept students who act as personal tutors to faculty and administration. This method offers a benefit for the administrator (e.g., private technology tutoring) and the student (e.g., a personal relationship with a key faculty member or dean in addition to a paid campus job).[8]

- Penn State has student tutors for its Angel Course Management System, which offers one-on-one short-term office tutoring.[9]
- The University of Minnesota teaches teaching assistants how to integrate Web technologies into their classes.[10]
- Virginia Tech's Faculty Development Institute (FDI) focuses on teaching faculty how to effectively and efficiently integrate technology into their teaching and research activities.[11]
- The faculty technology center at Westminster College in Utah provides support and technology resources for Westminster instructors seeking to create more efficient, effective, and appealing instruction.[12]
- Bowdoin College in Maine offers online support, a helpdesk, and classes for faculty.[13]
- In New York, St. Lawrence University's Center for Teaching and Learning (CTL) serves a 180-member faculty, providing ongoing faculty development that promotes innovative teaching practices and course design.[14]

Although many institutions are taking individual steps in integrating technology and training faculty, this often is not the case. While many faculty are frustrated by the lack of technical support and the burden sometimes associated when using technology, students are bored by the lack of it. The 20th century has associated learning with schooling, but this model has changed. In the 21st century, devices and digital libraries enable anyone to have access to information, and people are freer today to create their own learning trajectories. Learning theories and instruction are being designed to teach large numbers of students on a standardized curriculum. There continues to be a mismatch of the social organization of schooling and the realities of a global high-tech society—school is increasingly being seen as irrelevant by many students past the primary grades.[15]

Students are now at the forefront of Internet usage

University educators were once the leading "innovators" of technology; however, this title has now shifted to students. Internet developments from innovative companies such as Napster, Facebook, and Google have been developed by students or based on graduate school projects[16] . Students are comfortable with new technologies and expect to use them in the education environment; however, institutions are not always ready or willing to deploy or use them. For students who have grown up with the Internet, the impact is even more profound: they expect their institutions (and others with whom they interact) to use and support these new technologies. According to a report by EDUCAUSE, more than 60% of students agreed that IT used in coursework improved learning, 40% said they were more engaged in courses that incorporated IT, more than one-third believed IT facilitated prompt feedback from their instructors, and more than half felt IT helped them communicate and collaborate more efficiently with their fellow students.[17]

With college students ushering in the use of the Internet in their academic lives, many academic leaders should be and are starting to ask questions, such as:

- How will my college adapt to and use the surge of new technologies to stay relevant?
- How will my institution manage in an environment where students have unlimited access to information?
- How can we facilitate students or researchers who desire to collaborate with others, no matter where they are located, and tap expertise outside the campus walls to enhance and customize their learning?
- How will my campus support self-service learners who challenge the status quo?"[18]

To remain relevant, higher education institutions will face 3 critical challenges within the next 5 years. They will need to learn to:

- Assess newer forms of student work using new mediums (video, podcasts, blogs, and portfolios)
- Take a technology leadership role to enable newer forms of learning and assessment
- Deliver learning to a variety of mobile and personal devices[19]

Summary

Faculty who were once leading in terms of creating and fostering the use of technology in higher education have seemingly been replaced by students who are not only fostering the use of technology in the classroom and higher education learning but are also creating next-generation technologies and companies.

Faculty at many institutions are slow to adopt new technologies and learning models. Although some schools have created programs to help faculty learn how to use technology in teaching and learning, this is not a standard practice. As technology continues to accelerate and provide alternative learning options for students, the question remains: How relevant will technology resistant institutions be in the future?

CHAPTER NINE

Adaptive and Assistive Technology for Use in Higher Education

Patricia D. Wilen, Ph.D.

Career opportunities are increasing for people with disabilities due to advancements in computer technology. Many high-paying jobs, however, require a college education or advanced training in specific skills. A 1999 study by the University of Washington found that U.S. students with disabilities represented only 6% of the postsecondary education undergraduate student body. These disabilities include blindness and visual impairments, deafness and other hearing impairments, mobility or orthopedic impairments, speech and language impairments, health impairments, and learning disabilities. By 2004, this number had almost doubled.[1]

The federal government and many states have mandates that require institutions to provide the disabled reasonable access to educational opportunities. With advancements in technology, students with disabilities are increasingly able to earn a college degree. Two years after high school, 63% of students with disabilities are enrolled in postsecondary education compared to 72% of students without disabilities. Students with disabilities are more likely to enroll in 2-year courses, with 42% enrolled in 4-year courses compared to 62% of students without disabilities; 16% of students with disabilities earned a B.A. degree compared to 27% of those without disabilities, while 25% of students with and without disabilities earned associate degrees or vocational certificates.[2]

Disabled students report that faculty attitudes are a key factor in having a successful college experience.[3] While most instructors were willing to accommodate their disabled students, some faculty were less willing to provide alternate assignments, copies of lecture notes, tape-recorded assignments, and proofreaders.[4] Most schools, however, were found to offer support services to disabled students upon request. These services include alternate exam formats or additional exam time (88%), tutors (77%), scribes (69%), priority registration (62%), adaptive equipment or technology (58%), textbooks on tape (55%), sign language interpreters (45%), and course substitutions or waivers (42%).[5]

Due to widespread use of technology in the United States, many universities require incoming freshmen to own a laptop computer and, more recently, mobile technology. Technology is now used in higher education to do research, participate in synchronous classes, download assignments, and even take entire courses at a distance. This has put many students with disabilities—particularly those with visual, auditory, and motor impairments—at a disadvantage. Distance learning has been both a boon and a problem for persons with disabilities. People with severe motor disabilities can work from the comfort of their home and at their own pace. On the other hand, they may miss the social interaction provided by an on-campus experience, as well as on-campus services such as computer labs and tutorial centers.

However, newer technologies and increased software and hardware resources are now available that can assist the disabled when working with computers or printed materials. Virtual classrooms, interactive audio and video, instant messaging, blogs, wikis, and other tools are helping eliminate the barriers to education faced by disabled persons, as well as increase their level of socialization. These new resources (assistive technology) also help persons with various disabilities increase their participation in the coursework and toward earning a college degree. Assistive technology includes screen readers, talking Web browsers, printed text readers, Braille translators (text-to-Braille and Braille-to-text), screen magnifiers, special computer keyboards, and "motion control" technology that allows one to operate a computer through head or eye movements, for example.

Proloquo AssistiveWare is one example of motion control technology software. Developed for the Mac OS X, Proloquo is a multipurpose, multilingual speech and communications solution that helps enable those with vision, hearing, motor disabilities, and learning disabilities use the Macintosh more easily. Proloquo includes a comprehensive Augmentative and Alternative Communication system for people who cannot speak, a speech feedback feature that responds to keystrokes and can be used in any application for people and children with learning disabilities, and technology that converts text to audio files and iPod-ready iTunes tracks, providing a quick voice-access menu for changing voices in various languages.[6]

Mac OS X has a free built-in feature called Universal Access that enables those with vision disabilities to perform voice-overs, zoom in or out, and make changes to the screen's contrast. People with hearing impairments can make changes to audio and set up flash alerts. And people with motor skill disabilities can use "sticky" keys and "slow" keys to easily use the Macintosh. Systems based on Microsoft Windows have similar accessibility features: Windows Vista, the latest offering from Microsoft, has built-in speech recognition software.

Before buying technology, it is necessary to consider possible challenges a technology might present the person with a particular disability; for what the technology will be used; whether the technology is upgradeable, portable, and compatible; whether training, maintenance, and service plans are available; what the solution will cost, and who will pay for it. Some assistive technology may be free or covered by either government or private insurance plans.[7] The National Organization for Disabilities e-Newsletter and the Accessibility & Disability Information & Resources: Assistive Technology for Computer and Printed Material are valuable resources for researching this information.

The following are some new technologies now available for various disabilities. Some are free, some are not.

Technology for the deaf and hearing impaired

- Most deaf and hearing-impaired students are able to use a computer because hearing is not usually involved. E-mail is an effective way for them to communicate with instructors. Applications that have oral components without text, however, will be a problem. Dr. Sam Slike, a professor at Bloomsburg University of Pennsylvania, uses Wimbas' Live Classroom, an innovative, online course for deaf and hearing-impaired students. Wimba broadcasts a sign-language interpreter through a Webcam and a Sorenson videophone simultaneously, with closed-caption text (via Caption Colorado) to accompany slide presentations and the lecture. Hearing students can listen to the lecture, while deaf or hard-of-hearing students can read the closed-caption text that scrolls across the screen or watch the sign-language interpreter on the video screen. Slike believes that Wimba gives students the feeling of being "right in front of him in real time."[8]

- The Sorenson VP-100, a paperback-sized videophone device, when hooked to a television and a fast Internet connection, provides the deaf and hearing impaired access to Sorenson Media's Video Relay Service (VRS). The VRS is also available through personal computers, Webcams and Sorenson's Envision software that allows the deaf and hearing impaired to see an American Sign Language (ASL) interpreter. The software allows the ASL interpreter to call a hearing-impaired user via a standard telephone line and relay the conversation in real time. The system also allows people with hearing impairments to communicate with one another using sign language transmitted through video at 30 frames per second.[9]

Technology for the blind and visually impaired

- People who have enough vision to read printed materials might seek both screen magnification and voice technology to reduce eyestrain. A scanner and a voice output/speech synthesizer are recommended for users who want the computer to be able to display and speak printed material. Open Book from Freedom Scientific and the Kurzweil 1000 from Kurzweil Educational Systems can be used for speech; both come with voice output capabilities. Zoom Text is suggested for low-vision readers who want screen magnification and speech.[10] For computer users who occasionally require visual verification, both Jobs Access with Speech (JAWS) for Windows and the MAFic magnification software from Freedom Scientific are recommended. JAWS is described as the most widely used screen reader; the Eloquence for JAWS software speech synthesizer can pronounce a variety of languages.[11]
- WebAdapt2Me software from IBM is used at California State University, Long Beach, to access the Internet because it allows low-vision users to change the size of the text and color contrasts for easier viewing. IBM's ViaVoice speech synthesizer can be used with it to read the text out loud.[12]
- Optical Braille Recognition (OBR) software from Sighted Electronics converts Braille to text. The user places a Braille page on a scanner

which converts the Braille to text and then prints the page(s). The program is capable of saving Braille documents to disk as formatted Braille files.[13]

- Wizzard Software's Chameleon Line ViewPlus lets blind people interact with graphical information using a touchpad, eliminating the need for assistants to accommodate Braille labeling. The touchpad also uses computer-generated speech to text out loud.[14]

- Voice Mate from Parrot is a talking phonebook, voice notepad, appointment book, and talking alarm clock, useful to anyone who cannot use a keyboard or write legibly. It is lightweight and can easily be carried in one's pocket.[15]

- PopChart Xpress from Corda Technologies automatically installs JAVA VM 1/3/1 on a Windows platform, allowing users to produce Web-ready, interactive charts and graphs. It is compatible with JAWS for Windows, which allows the blind or people with less vision to see and hear the information presented in the charts.[16]

- Books2Burn is an open-source text-to-speech file for making books on CD using an Apple computer. Books2Burn translates text files into a series of audio files that can then be converted into MP3 or other formats using programs such as LAME or iTunes.[17]

- Lynx is described as one of the most popular text-mode browsers. It is free under the GNU Public License. It works on a variety of platforms including Macintosh (MacLynx), Windows, DOS, UNIX, and VMS. It works well with voice synthesizers and Braille-based technology.[18]

- EmacSpeak, developed by T. V. Raman, a software engineer who has been blind since childhood, works with the text-based UNIX system and can speak the information that is the basis for a visual display. It is free and can be downloaded from the Internet.[19]

- Dolphin's SuperNova Pen for Windows 2000 and XP combines magnification, speech, and Braille for Windows. It is lightweight and can be worn around the neck or carried in one's pocket or purse. It is useful for word-processing tasks, developing PowerPoint presentations, and creating and reading charts.[20]

- Google has an Accessible Web Search engine with an audio component for the visually impaired (http://labs.google.com/accsssible).[21]

- IBM Easy Web Browsing software helps people with limited vision access Web content easily.[22]

- WebbIE, developed by Alasdair King, is a free program that allows Web pages to be read as simple text.[23]

Technology for the deaf and blind

Freedom Scientific developed FSTTY Deaf-Blind Telephone Communication Solution, which allows users with a PAC Mate BX or QX accessible PDA and a refreshable Braille display to place and receive teletypewriter (TTY) calls using any standard analog phone line. Users can read the conversation in either contracted or uncontracted Braille, save conversations as text files, and copy text.[24]

Technology for the physically disabled

Students with physical disabilities are often at a disadvantage when faced with a computer, mainly due to their inability to manipulate the interface. New developments in technology offer alternate keyboard and mouse formats and voice-activated access to the Internet.

- Lomak, short for Light Operated Mouse and Keyboard, is a system that allows people with physical disabilities to use a computer via light sensor technology. A hand or head pointer is used to control a beam of light that enters and/or confirms a specific key or mouse function. The system allows people with muscular dystrophy, cerebral palsy, quadriplegia, arthritis, and other physical disabilities to use a computer. For users who can move their arms, the keyboard is flat and is activated by a hand pointer. For those in a wheelchair, the keyboard is slid into a wrist rest that creates a smooth work surface. For users who do not have arm movement, a light pointer is mounted in a lightweight and fully adjustable headband. The keyboard and the laptop are held in an upright position by an adjustable stand.[25]
- Click-N-Type from Lake Software is free software that works with Windows and DOS applications. It shows a virtual keyboard on the screen for users who cannot type on a physical keyboard.[26]
- Magic Wand Keyboard from In Touch Systems is a miniature keyboard with a built-in mouse that allows someone with limited or no hand/arm movement to fully access any IBM or Apple Macintosh computer. It works with the touch of a handheld stylus or a mouth stick and requires no force. With slight hand or head motion, Magic Wand offers the physically disabled easy access to all computer programs.[27]
- Eyegaze Communication System from LC Technologies, VisionKey

from EyeCan, and Boost Tracer from Boost Technology allow students to use their eyes to operate computers and telephones.[28]

- The Assistive Mouse Adapter from Montrose Secam filters out unin-
tentional hand movements caused by a physical tremor. No additional
software is required. The device is plugged in between the computer
and the mouse and can be adjusted depending on tremor severity.[29]
- SmartNav 4 AT is described as a total hands-free mouse solution with
built-in Dwell Clicking Software and an On-screen Keyboard. This
AT package can be used by people with ALS, spinal cord injuries,
muscular dystrophy, and other special needs. SmartNav comes with
everything needed to control the computer with head motion. www.
naturalpoint.com/smartnav/products.[30]
- The orbiTouch keyless ergonomic keyboard from Blue Orb eliminates
the need to use fingers to type. Its onscreen keyboard is located under
the Accessibility Options in the Windows control panel. It can be used
with a mouse, foot pedal, head pointer, and Eyegaze technology..[31]
- IScan-MP3 from Technical Solutions, also known as SwitchPod, gives
a person with no hand function control of Apple's iPod personal music
player. The iScan-MP3 plugs into the remote control socket and uses a
single switch, which can be mounted onto a wheelchair headrest that
makes available remote control functions.
- LayoutKitchen by Assistiveware is an editor of SwitchXS scan panels,
KeyStrokes keyboards, and Proloquo speech panels. SwitchXS can be
used to create scan panels with just the keys, controls, and functions users need. SwitchXS provides people who can use one or more switches
access to Mac OS X and all standard applications. It also offers full
mouse and keyboard control and numerous scan panels and can be
used by Proloquo users to build communication panels for people who
cannot read or write.
- Swifty from Origin Instruments is an adaptive USB switch interface
that can respond to inputs from a mouse, joystick, or keyboard. It
works with Windows, Macintosh, Linux computers, and many AAC
devices.

Computer games

A common perception among the public is that only specially adapted "accessible" games are available for disabled persons, and that these games are of
interest to kids but not adults. Assistive technology, however, makes it possible

for anyone to play just about any game, including *Unreal Tournament 2004* or *World of Warcraft*. The Assistive Gaming Web site provides assistive gaming technology (*http://www.assistivegaming.com*) for Mac users with disabilities. It also offers information on the latest Mac OS X games, with a special focus on their accessibility. These games were never designed to be played by users with physical disabilities; however, with universal access software, such as onscreen keyboards, these games can be played by the physically impaired. Games played with a keyboard, mouse, joystick, or game pad allow more people with varying physical abilities to play than those that have just keyboard or joystick.[32]

These games of course do have limitations. If information is just visual, then games exclude the visually impaired. Similarly, if information is just verbal, then games exclude the hearing impaired. Once access barriers have been lifted from the world of gaming, online games will provide people with new experiences not available before. "The nice thing about many of the online games is that no one knows you have a disability," says David Niemeijer, publisher of the Assistive Gaming Web site. "In the virtual world there are no disabilities."[33]

Two groups, that provide assistive technologies in gaming are (1) the Heron Sanctuary, which enables disabled persons to function in Second Life by helping them overcome the barriers related to limited keyboarding capability through alternative access technologies; and (2) IGDASIG (International Game Developers Association Special Interest Group), which was formed to help create mainstream games for all regardless of age, disability, or experience.

Some games that employ assistive technologies are:

- AccessibleComputerGamesfromArcess.com (*www.arcess.com*)—easy-to-play single switch games for the physically disabled. These games can be played as single-switch, speech recognition, or expanded keyboard games.
- American Foundation for the Blind free download: Solitaire & Crazy Darts (*www.afb.org/prodsearch.ASP, keyword: games*).
- Space Invaders (*www.thespeciallife.com/space-invaders*).
- UA-Chess—fully functional chess game that is universally accessible and can be played concurrently by persons with visual and hand-motor disabilities (*http://www.ics.forth.gr/hci/ua-games/ua-chess/*).

Cell phones

Cell phones have become a way of life for most people. They have also become very useful tools for the disabled. The phones' small screens and buttons may be problematic for some disabled users, but these products can be linked to other devices that have larger screens, simpler commands, automatic functions, better audio output and cameras, and other help facilities. The hearing impaired can use sign language to communicate over a broad camera link, or the user can call a video device where an operator acts as an intermediary. Video calls can have captions as well as audio outputs so that a hearing person can follow the conversation. Users of relay services can connect incoming calls to an answering machine. During the day, the system automatically redirects calls via the relay service. When users leave their home, they instruct the system to redirect calls to their mobile phones, which will then visually display the text.[34]

Cell phones with cameras allow speech-impaired users to take a picture of an object that they wish to purchase and then show it to the store clerk. Some users are even able to unlock their front doors with cell phones. Cell phones and other mobile devices are becoming increasingly useful on college campuses as discussed elsewhere in this book.

These are but a few of the assistive technologies available to the disabled. Some are in development, while others are already on the market. The Center of Assistive Technology at the University of Buffalo, in New York State, is one of the leading innovators in developing products for the disabled.

The following Web sites offer a wide variety of other adaptive technologies with full descriptions of the products.

- Accessibility & Disability Information & Resources: Assistive Technology for Computer and Printed Material (http://kpope.com/)
- Assistive Technology Literature (http://www.abledata.com)
- Assistive Technology Journal (www.Atnet.org)
- Braille Monitor (*www.nfb.org*)
- Chronicle of Higher Education: Information Technology (www.chronicle.com)
- Free Assistive Technologies AT: gives a list of Web sites and descriptions of 175 assistive technologies now available
- International Braille Research Center (IBRC) (www.braille.org)
- National Organizationon Disability e-Newsletter (http://www.nod.org)
- Niemeijer Consult (*http://www.niemconsult.com/*)

Learning Environments

CHAPTER TEN

Learning Environments

Learning environments: Addressing the current challenges in higher education

In some of the prior chapters in this book, we took a look at just a few of the current trends in technology and higher education; numerous more trends continue to evolve daily. In the following section, we discuss how institutions can cope with the influx of technologies and how to satisfy students' desire to use technology as a part of their education.

Learning environment defined

Learning environments are essentially the result of the blurring of lines between traditional higher education—where learning and resources are available in classrooms and on campus—and popular resources such as blogs, social networking sites, wikis, and video gaming; and the increasing innovations in technology such as Web 2.0, virtual museums, and virtual worlds like Second Life.

In a learning environment, students have a choice in how they learn, which resources they use, and where they obtain the knowledge they need to be successful academically. In a learning environment, a student has unrestricted access to all information resources both in the physical world and in the virtual world; in effect, physical barriers to learning and research no longer exist. Through a flexible learning environment, students can customize their learning experience to their unique needs and preferences.

This section takes an in-depth look at the learning environment concept, an example of how individuals develop their own unique learning environments, and how to apply this concept to the higher education environment.

People use the Internet for daily life decisions

People today have become increasingly dependent on the Internet to give them the information they need for decision making. In a report by the Pew Internet and American Life Project, researchers note that in 2005,[1] the following percentage of adults used the Internet:

- 54%, to help someone cope with an illness
- 50%, in career training
- 45%, for making financial decisions
- 43%, to look for a home
- 42%, to decide on a school or college for themselves or for their children
- 24%, to do research prior to buying a car
- 14%, to switch jobs.

When people use the Internet to gather information or learn about something that they otherwise would have to acquire by more traditional means such as the classroom or a book, they have effectively created their own learning environments.

To better understand a learning environment, try to recollect a recent major life event such as getting married, selecting a college, buying a house or car, or addressing a health issue. That is, identify an event where credible information needed to be collected in a compressed period of time. Then think through how you went about gathering information and learning about the subject.

Here is my example. My mother-in-law was diagnosed with breast cancer in 2007. It was unexpected and took her and the family by surprise. She had limited knowledge and access to the Internet and electronic materials and lived too far from her local library. Her learning environment was limited to a medical manual that was outdated, her doctor, local family, and whoever she could reach via phone. She reached out to family for answers. We in turn felt obligated to quickly educate ourselves on the topic of breast cancer so that we could support her and talk to her and her physicians.

My personal learning environment entailed investigating her physicians' credentials and those of her radiologist, surgeon, and family practitioner. I did this by searching online medical databases, university databases, and official hospital Web sites that are freely available on the Web. I also went to top university medical Web sites to learn more about the cancer and its growth stages and find statistics on its survival rates as well as information about treatment options. I also visited Web sites where cancer survivors submitted their experiences, advice, and recommendations. I read recent alerts and updates on various medical blogs to keep current on topical issues.

My husband took a different path. He was not as well versed on what resources were available on the topic, so he typed the query "What is breast cancer?" into the Google search engine. A variety of search results appeared on the screen—varying from Wikipedia and Webopedia—offering definitions on medical sites such as WebMD.com and Medline.com as well as various physician sites. He reviewed the various sites and eventually found himself overwhelmed with the number of resources, not knowing quite which ones to trust and which ones were accurate.

He decided that he would pursue "Ask the expert" sites such as *www.justanswer.com* and *www.kasamba.com*, where one can review experts' bios and pay by the minute for online, real-time advice that one chooses to use. Payment is based on customer satisfaction and experts are ranked by users. My husband found quite a few medical experts who helped guide him quickly through the questioning process and to educational resources that might help him understand the cancer, what his mother might be dealing with, and what type of questions to ask her physician.

Within 24 hours, the two of us—although pursuing very different learning paths—had accumulated most of the knowledge we needed. In addition, we both tapped into a variety of online and offline resources to accomplish our goals. Furthermore, each of us took a unique approach to the learning process. Within 48 hours, we shipped to his mother a package of reading materials and set up phone conference calls between her, us, and her physicians to help her understand the disease and what would happen over the next few weeks. She felt relieved.

This is an example of a personal learning environment. We will now take a look at a student and how she might approach learning in today's environment.

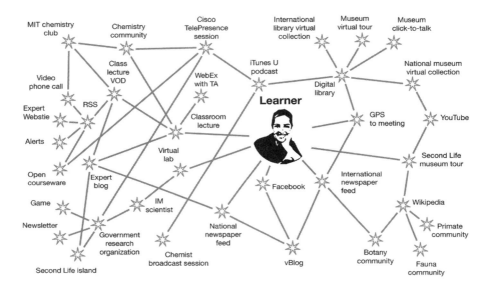

Figure 1—Allison, the freshman college student

Figure 1 traces the learning environment of Allison, a college freshman. This figure depicts how she makes use of a number of resources both physical and virtual through a number of formats and devices depending on her unique learning needs.

Allison is a freshman at a residential college, intending to major in biochemistry. She is taking 2 classes for her major: biology 1 and general chemistry 1. While biology comes easy to her, she finds that she needs to spend more time with chemistry.

Fortunately, both classes are recorded on video and posted to the university's Web site almost immediately after each class. Allison can view the lectures from any of her computing devices: iPod, mobile phone, laptop computer, or desktop PC. As a result, she does not have to take as many notes during class and can pay more attention to the professors to improve her comprehension.

Allison is a collaborative learner: she regularly visits the class Web sites for both classes. The sites are hosted on university servers and updated by the professors or their TAs (teaching assistants). Both classes have a community forum feature on each Web site so that students such as Allison can share their notes, ask questions, and receive immediate feedback not only from the professors/TAs but also from other students. In the biology class forum, Allison is a much more active participant: she asks some questions but she is mostly able to answer questions from her classmates. Allison is also active in the chemistry class forum, mostly asking for clarification on topics that still confuse her.

Allison also has regular sessions with her TAs, who maintain both physical and virtual office hours using collaboration technologies such as WebEx. Allison receives alerts on her personal digital assistant (PDA) to remind her of the weekly meetings and also on her global positioning system (GPS) to receive information about where the meetings will be held. The TAs also hold weekly group sessions in person and online to discuss the course materials and lectures. These sessions are recorded and made available to students as podcasts.

Allison visits other college Web sites and uses open courseware materials to help with her studies, and subscribes to Really Simple Syndication (RSS) feeds that notify her when new biology and chemistry information is available. She visits the college library on campus and has access to knowledgeable librarians through the campus call center; instant messaging; Second Life online, 3-D virtual world; and the library click-to-talk Web site any time she needs them.

Noticing Allison's biology expertise, the TA for her biology class suggests that Allison work as a volunteer contributor to Wikipedia, submitting her research as she develops it. The TA also introduces Allison in a video phone call to a key biology researcher in another country who is seeking students to help with research.

For her end-of-term biology project, Allison decides to visit 4 key biology museums and report on her findings. She selects museums in Egypt for their marine biology expertise, England for fauna biology, Scotland for primate biology, and Papua New Guinea for butterfly biology.

Because she cannot physically go to these museums, Allison visits their virtual sites, which are different from typical Web sites. At each "museum," Allison accesses the virtual collection and holds click-to-talk sessions with the museum's researchers. Impressed with her questions, the researchers invite Allison to attend their special multimedia seminars through a dial-in session using the IP phone on her laptop computer.

Allison decides to present her findings using an electronic portfolio format that includes videos and audio clips. The portfolio is like a mashup with digital storytelling that includes key photos from Flickr.com and a critical analysis of the ways in which biology is applied in real life. Her project is lauded by her professor, her TA, and her classmates for its thorough research and sharp presentation.

In the chemistry class online forum, one student mentions that there is a chemistry-related game for the Xbox that professors at Purdue developed to build students' interest in chemistry.[2] Allison tries out the game, in which the main character travels through a series of rooms and uses tools that emit acid, heat, or cold air to fight aliens. Every room has its own set of chemistry-based challenges students must solve to advance to the next room. As an avid video game player, Allison finds the game a fun way to learn basic chemistry concepts.

Allison's chemistry assignment is a bit more difficult for her. For inspiration and guidance, she decides to join the college chemistry club on Facebook. Through the social network, she connects with several other women who are working on similar assignments. The women are from different universities but share a common interest in chemistry. They invite Allison to several interesting events that she would not have known about on her own.

One of the events is a special videoconferencing session with Dr. Roger Kornburg, 2006 Nobel Laureate in chemistry. To attend the session, Allison schedules a time to use the campus virtual presence facility. Allison is so impressed with Dr. Kornburg that she subscribes to his video blog, also called a "vlog." Fortunately for Allison, the National Science Foundation (NSF) also videotaped one of Kornburg's recent conference panels. Allison signs up as an NSF student member to receive alerts about events, newsletters, podcasts, lectures, and symposiums on specific topics of interest.

Later in the week, Allison meets her college chemistry club in Second Life to visit the campus' new virtual chemistry lab. The class also visits Second Life's Drexel Island to witness molecular docking and talk to researchers about their experiments. The class then tours Nature Island, which is full of chemistry blogs, wikis, and other information. The island also includes a molecule simulator with which visitors can interact.

Allison is so excited she cashes in some Linden dollars (money people use in Second Life to conduct commerce) to have her avatar (Allison's character in Second Life) outfitted for the event—because you never know whom you might meet at the chemistry social afterward.

She finally decides to create a 5-minute video on applied uses of chemistry in real-life situations for her chemistry project. She wants to do a great job so she can post it to YouTube and see how many hits she gets. Needless to say,

Allison receives top grades for this chemistry project as well, and her professor played Allison's YouTube video during one of the class lectures.

The purpose of the example of Allison is to demonstrate how an academic institution enabled a student to create a personalized learning environment so she could take full advantage of all resources available to her—online and of-fline, physical and virtual, and 24 hours a day, 7 days a week.

In this environment, the student had the opportunity to excel in her subjects as well as seek assistance with more difficult concepts. She used a variety of tools (gaming, video, online communities, virtual reality, social networks) to support her unique learning style, which resulted in a deeper understanding and interest in both subjects she researched.

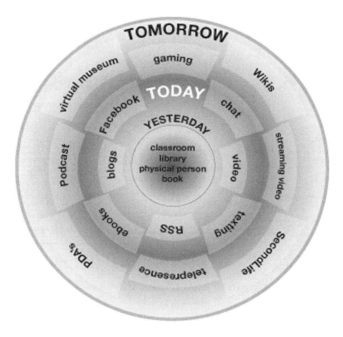

Figure 2—Expanded Learning Resources

Figure 2 shows the expansion of learning resources over time. In the center of the circle is where many people have had their college learning experience in the past. Traditionally, the resources were limited to a classroom space with books and paper materials, and professors on a physical college campus. For many those resources were all that was available; learning was limited to what the professor could bring into the classroom or what the library had on its shelves.

The circles that span out from the center show the progression of resources that have become available over recent years. These resources (blogs, wikis, electronic books, etc.) complement what already exists and help learners expand "their pie" of available resources. Unlike the early years of education, not all of the resources readily available today are physical. As we follow the circles out, we see additional resources that are becoming available for learners today, and we see how learners given access to these resources could have an abundance of tools from which to choose or with which to customize their learning. A key point in the learning environment model is that learners can pick resources according to their own personal learning styles and preferences (paper, in-person, video, virtual). Today there is enough flexibility and choice available to make this possible.

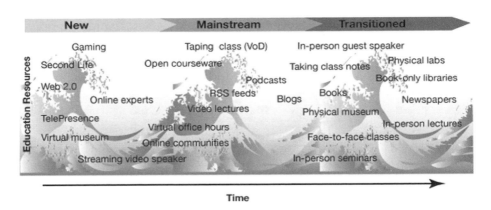

Figure 3—Rapid transition of higher education resources

Figure 3 depicts the transition of learning resources as ocean waves from left (newest) to right (oldest). On the right side are traditional learning resources such as in-person class speakers, notepads, notebooks, textbooks, newspapers, paper journals, face-to-face classes, physical museums, physical historical sites, and so on. These learning resources still exist and many are used today.

The center section presents resources that have entered the environment in recent years and are in use in higher education institutions today. In some cases, the resources in the center have substituted for the resources on the right: a blog for a newspaper, wikis instead of class notes, or virtual museums in place of physical museums. In other cases, the new resources enhance existing resources by providing professors and students more options for teaching and learning, such as taping the class for replay and later group study sessions; podcasting lectures; distributing lectures on iTunes U; hosting a guest lecture via video or RSS feeds; accessing digital library collections; and participating in online communities.

On the far left are some of the newer resources that we are seeing today in higher education. Some resources are being explored, and some are being adopted and used with other resources. These include virtual reality, gaming, and some of the newer Web 2.0 technologies.

Many of these newer resources will enjoy quick adoption in higher education because their use for noneducational purposes is already prevalent. YouTube hosts over 6 million videos; this figure is growing at about 20% every month.[3] Facebook is used by 85% of college students and has 67 million active users[4]; 84 blogs are created every minute and 17 posts published every second.[5] Other resources such as gaming will take longer to reach the mainstream because specific hardware and software are typically required. At the same time, some traditional resources such as books might be replaced or augmented by newer options such as blogs and electronic journals. What is important to note is that technology is in constant evolution and will continue to provide learners more choices. Educators can now offer our students many more options than in the past so that they may customize and enhance their own personal learning environment.

Summary

This chapter summarized the concept of a learning environment. In a learning environment, students have a choice about how they learn, which resources they use, and where they obtain the knowledge they need to be successful. Since a learning environment provides a student with unrestricted access to all knowledge resources in both physical and virtual worlds, barriers to learning and research no longer exist. As educators, it is important that you help facilitate learning environments on our college campuses by providing students access to the resources, many of which are available and free. Through a flexible learning environment, students can customize their learning experience to their unique needs and preferences, enhancing their overall education.

CHAPTER ELEVEN

Transparent Learning Environments

Distance Learning

Higher education institutions already are seeing the impact of modern technologies as they continue to converge, simplify learning, and blur the lines between on-campus and off-campus. We also are seeing the growth of distance learning and the use of newer technologies in both on- and off-campus courses. The impact of next-generation technologies on distance learning will be particularly profound. Tools previously associated with distance learning, such as single-interface and passive text, now are significantly enhanced and replaced with many of the newer technologies used in physical classrooms, further blurring the lines, creating a single learning environment. Students now can freely select from a variety of course options that might include a hybrid campus (with both on- and off-campus interactivity), allowing virtual participation through gaming, avatars, and mobile learning. Distance learning and classroom learning, as we know it, no longer exist separately but rather have merged into a transparent learning environment.

Distance learning defined

Traditionally, a "distance learner" is defined as a student who is not connected to a campus classroom and is not physically present. This usually requires no face-to-face meetings between students and instructors either in the classroom or via a video course. This person has full access to campus materials even though he or she may not be on campus at all.

To reach distance learners, higher education institutions have used alternative methods such as correspondence, online delivery, and TV. Hybrid learning also has become popular among many institutions, where students spend part of the time on campus and part of the time using distance education tools. The instructor combines elements of online distance learning courses with traditional courses to replace some classroom sessions with virtual sessions.[1]

Growth of distance learning

An estimated 1.5 billion people will have Internet access in 2011, with the biggest growth in the online population occurring in Brazil, Russia, India, and China.[2] Extrapolated projections from the United Nations and IDP Education Australia, a global education agent and development organization, indicate that the total demand for higher education in 2025 will be from 263 million students, 170 million of whom will come from China, India, and other Asian countries.[3] For every foreign student who studies in the United States, there are 3 to 5 students who would "consume" U.S. education online if given access.[4]

In 2006, the online student population exceeded 1.5 million, representing 8.6% of all students at degree-granting institutions.[5] A Sloan Consortium study found that online enrollments increased 9.7% in 2006 and have been growing substantially faster than the overall higher education enrollment growth rate of 1.5%. This trend is expected to continue. The study noted that almost 3.5 million students (nearly 20% of the total) were taking at least one online course during the fall 2006 term in the United States, a nearly 10% increase over the number reported the previous year. The study also noted that 2-year associate's institutions have had the highest growth rates and account for more than one-half of all online enrollments in the past 5 years.[6]

In addition, there are notable, successful global distance learning programs and institutions that offer a full range of programs and degrees, such as the Open University in the United Kingdom, Athabasca University in Canada, Phoenix University in the United States, Tech De Monterrey in Mexico, and the Open University in Hong Kong.[7]

With the popularity and success of these programs, distance learning has become an ever-growing avenue toward higher education.

The benefits of advanced degrees

According to the U.S. census bureau, American workers with an undergraduate degree earn on average $23,291 per year more than those with a high school diploma, and holders of an advanced degree earn an average of $51,206 more than those with undergraduate degrees.[8] Multiple degrees also are motivating students to return to school or attend classes while working. A master of business administration (MBA) graduate earned $92,360 during his or her first year on the job in 2006, which was up 4.2% from the year before.[9] The likelihood that an MBA candidate would be offered a job before graduation is increasing steadily, from 36% in 2003, to 42% in 2004, and 50% in 2005.[10] More and more new jobs in nanotechnology, health, and sciences now are requiring a more complex set of skills and knowledge from applicants.[11]

Universities that offer graduate-level distance learning courses toward an advanced degree include Stanford University, which offers online master's degrees in engineering. These courses provide a service to an ever-growing population of workers who require advanced degrees to remain relevant or to excel in their careers.[12] The Tseng College at CSU Northridge offers advanced degree programs ranging from communication disorders and sciences to engineering management. The Duke Fuqua School of Business has a very notable distance learning executive MBA program. These programs can be completed entirely through distance learning programs.[13]

Distance learning benefits for colleges

Broadband penetration and adoption have opened up new avenues for college education. Pew's 2007 report on home broadband adoption noted that 47% of all adult Americans had a home broadband connection.[14] An IDC study reports that 133 million U.S. adults, which is roughly two-thirds of the adult population, have access to the Internet, which creates an opportunity for colleges to reach an untapped educational market.[15]

A number of higher education institutions have started to create online programs in order to stay relevant with these students: 87% of 4-year colleges offered distance learning in 2004, and this number has been steadily growing;

65% of online courses will have discussion forums in 2005, thus indicating that bandwidth performance has improved to support online collaborations and the creation of better learning environments for distance learners.[16] College objectives for online learning include improving student access, increasing the rate of degree completion, and addressing the increasing appeal to traditional students. Cost reduction and containing costs are among the least cited in terms of objectives for institutions.[17]

The line separating distance learning and on-campus learning blurs

Credible content and expertise increasingly are available online (see chapter five) through digitized library initiatives, open courseware programs, content digitization programs (such as Google Book Search), and virtual museums (such as the Louvre and the National Air and Space Museum). Learners are no longer limited to a single source for acquiring and sharing knowledge. The barriers to education that may have previously existed are being eliminated, and classroom learning and distance learning are starting to utilize many of the same learning resources. "Virtual classrooms, two-way interactive audio, video, synchronous and asynchronous computer-based interactions are being added on distance education. In the twenty-first century, more hybrid distance learning environments can be combined in one virtual classroom,"[18] according to the authors of *Distance Learning: The Essential Guide*. Today, there isn't just one single concept of learning: one can use a multitude of instruments, such as computer-assisted learning, Web learning, virtual learning, online training, and digital training.

The new technological paradigm is an indispensable concept for all educational organizations when it comes to utilizing technology for distance learning. The evolution to social and Web 2.0 technologies has morphed distance learning into a highly networked society where students' roles have changed from being passive to being extremely interactive. Traditional software applications have transitioned to Internet services, as the traditional passive form of eLearning transforms into a more collaborative learning environment that includes discussion forums, blended learning, virtual classrooms, podcasts, mobile learning, games, blogs, and wikis. Students as a result have newer resources and use convenient communication modes, including email and instant messaging. Web 2.0 has created a significant paradigm shift in distance learning.[19]

In a 2004 paper by researchers at the Institute of Educational Technology in the UK, the effects of incorporating 4 technologies (blogging, audioconferencing, instant messaging, and Harvard's rotisserie system) in a distance learning Master's course were examined. The course, "Learning in the Connected Economy," was held in October 2003 at the Open University in the United Kingdom. It was noted that student feedback on the use of tools was positive. The study anticipated that as students become more accustomed to the new technologies, there would be a shift toward implementing a range of technologies in distance courses.[20]

A 2002 University of Memphis study comparing learning through online courses to classroom-based learning found that students perceived that their learning experience was the same or significantly better online than in classroom-based courses. Students said that they learned more from online courses than in the classroom, possibly because more time was spent with online learning materials than in classroom-based courses, and that students appreciated the wealth of information that the Internet provided.[21]

Open courseware initiatives

Open content initiatives, such as the OpenCourseWare (OCW) Consortium, with more than 100 universities from more than 20 countries offering courses and content freely to both on- and off-campus students, has made online learning widely available.[22] Many universities have started their own open content Web sites on top of participating in the OCW Consortium, including MIT, Tufts University, and Johns Hopkins University. University of California, Berkeley's open content initiative is offering more than 82 courses, 3600 hours, and 79 events. UC Berkeley has "provided students with a powerful supplemental study tool to review lecture material, but it has also gained notoriety from a diverse and rapidly growing public constituency of life-long learners. Every semester, an increasing number of students request podcasts of their courses, and our statistics, which show more than 10 million downloads this past year, indicate to us that our audience expects more portability, more quality, and more quantity from our program."[23]

In addition, YouTube's education channel, along with iTunes U, has more than 500 universities participating, and there are newer venues releasing content daily, such as the website BigThink, which features leaders and experts in their respective fields, on a variety of topics with special appeal to the academic community.[24] These sites provide open content 24x7, accessible to learners anywhere.

Virtual reality and mobile devices as instructional tools

Gaming and virtual reality are viable instructional tools for online learning. For example, North Carolina State University (NCSU) has created a graduate distance education course entitled WolfDen. Rather than listen to lectures or repeat equations, learners participate in immersed worlds. Researchers noted that 3-dimensional worlds can provide a number of education possibilities, including extending the classroom as a medium for distance education. The course combined content and pedagogy with a multiplayer educational gaming application (MEGA). It has 2 major goals: to find a viable source for synchronous, online course delivery in a MEGA and to pilot a project for learners to design and create role-playing video games in a 3-dimensional virtual environment as a supplement to current instruction.[25] Some benefits discussed included how avatars in virtual learning environments (VLEs) can contribute to the learning experience by giving students a sense of social presence and investment in the learning community that may otherwise be difficult to access.[26]

Mobile learning also has been used with success in distance learning programs. In a program called PocketED (2005), Coastline Community College, in collaboration with the U.S. Coast Guard Institute (USCGI), is offering college courses to U.S. military service members through PDAs and Pocket PCs. The courses come complete with instructional audio and video, so they are accessible by learners even when out of touch with onshore distance learning facilities. The courses all have the same components of a feature-rich, online Internet course including audio and video. For example, Coastline Management and Supervision 100 PocketED course contains more than 90 screens of content, 65 full-motion video interviews and instructional video clips, 23 audio reviews of textbook readings, support screens, navigation tutorial videos, and interactive exercises.[27]

The University of Wisconsin College of Engineering is piloting a distance education master of engineering course on pocket PCs. It was found that the key to delivering courses on handhelds is providing recorded lectures and course notes on the handheld. This allows students to have all the course materials with them at all times so, when they have some free time, they can view the content.[28]

Cheating

Cheating at school has been going on for centuries, but today's professors express concern about increased opportunities for cheating and plagiarism with the growth of online courses and the wealth of material available on the Web. Cheating is not a problem unique to distance learning; it also happens in a traditional classroom setting.

Some notable numbers on cheating:

- In 2002, 47 students at Simon Fraser University turned in nearly the same economics paper.[29]
- In a 1999 study at Duke University of 2,100 students surveyed on 21 campuses across the country, more than two-thirds of the students admitted to one or more instances of serious cheating, such as copying from another student on a test, plagiarizing, or submitting work done by another student.[30]
- A study at Rutgers University found that 54% of students admitted to plagiarizing from the Internet; 74% of students admitted that at least once during the past school year they had engaged in "serious" cheating; and 47% of students believe their teachers sometimes choose to ignore students who are cheating.[31]
- A 2002 study by Rochester Institute of Technology polled 698 undergraduate students at 9 institutions of higher learning. It found that 16.5% of the respondents reported plagiarizing "sometimes," while 50.4% claimed that their peers "often" or "very frequently" committed plagiarism. Slightly more respondents said they plagiarized conventional text more than online documents, and almost 100% agreed that their peers plagiarized conventional text.[32]

These statistics indicate that plagiarism is prevalent in both the traditional and online classrooms. However, although these statistics show that cheating remains a serious academic problem, it is unclear as to whether the Internet has really increased the percentage of students who cheat. If online classes and papers are more susceptible to cheating than paper-based assignments, there are a number of options for online instructors to detect plagiarism by running student-submitted assignments through plagiarism-detecting Web sites or software programs.[33]

Some solutions

According to some educators, many college students seem to have no idea what cheating is about. Some of this may be due to the accessibility of free information on the Internet and the lack of understanding of how to address copyright issues. Many have decided to address cheating with students at the beginning of class.[34] Instructors need to establish firm rules that deter online cheating, such as advising their students that writing samples will be collected, term papers will be filtered through plagiarism-detecting software, pop quizzes will be given throughout the semester, and that weekly participation in the discussion boards is a class requirement.[35]

Papers and plagiarism

Today, students have several resources from which to plagiarize both in classroom and online. Plagiarism of papers is one key area. There are a number of Web sites that offer term papers for a cost, such as Schoolsucks.com and Cheater.com. A 2003 study at Coastal Carolina University had identified 250 active term paper and essay Web sites.[36] In addition, there is a proliferation of freely available books, journals, speeches, and conferences that can be found online and copied.

To identify plagiarism, many educators use Web site search tools, such as Google, where a sentence or phrase can be entered into the search box and lists of possible matches are returned indicating the source. Although easy to use and effective, this means of crosschecking places the onus on the professor. A number of instructors also use a Web site service, such as the popular Turnitin, which claims, "every paper submitted is returned in the form of a customized Originality Report. Results are based on exhaustive searches of billions of pages from both current and archived instances of the Internet, millions of student papers previously submitted to www.turnitin.com, and commercial databases of journal articles and periodicals."[37] Proactively, some online institutions require students to use Turnitin as a regular practice before submitting papers.[38] This helps the student understand what plagiarism is and to advance their writing skills before even submitting a paper. It also relieves the professor of the burden. There also are some commercial software options, such as the Glatt Plagiarism Screening Program, which eliminates every fifth word of the suspected paper and replaces the words with a blank space.[39]

Testing and exams

Another area of concern in distance learning is the examination process, where a student might be more inclined to send someone else to take an exam, solicit personal assistance during exams, access resources during the exam to look up questions, or have access to previous exam questions and answers from a previous examinee.

One solution that instructors use is to place a time restriction on exams. This has been most successful when used in short, multiple-choice quizzes. For example, if an exam consists of 10 multiple choice questions, and a student has 9 minutes to complete the exam, the chances of the student looking up each answer is slim because of the time restriction.[40] Other test strategies include randomizing test questions so that no two students have the same questions in the same order at the same time. Some institutions use proctoring centers where students report to a center for course registration and also for testing. The proctor might require the student to provide an essay, give a handwriting sample, or be photographed for later matching. In some proctored centers, video cameras may be set up for surveillance of the test environment, and students are encouraged to use a hotline to phone in observed cheating.[41]

Biometric solutions now are being used in deterring cheating in distance learning. These include verification methods, such as fingerprints, face recognition, handwriting, voice recognition, and iris scans to ensure identity. Troy University is placing Web cameras (Securexam Remote Proctor) in student homes to monitor exams. The device sits next to a student's computer while he or she takes an online exam. It reads the student's fingerprints, has a microphone that picks up sound, and a camera that captures a 360-degree view. The device helps instructors determine if students are getting any kind of assistance while taking their tests. It also locks down the computer to keep students from using search engines, such as Google, to find the answers.

Online institutions, such as the University of Phoenix, use methods other than testing to assess students, such as writing assignments and message board interaction. Bellevue Online University relies on written assignments, rather than exams, in their programs. Penn Foster College allows open books during testing for courses that require thoughtful integration of the concepts, rather than regurgitation of text.[42]

Another option is online threaded discussions that allow instructors to post discussion-type questions to which all students can respond. These discussions are not asynchronous, which allows students to respond at their leisure within a given time period. Threaded discussions encourage students to communicate, discuss, and debate topics with each other. They also provide instructors with countless examples of a student's writing style, which can be very useful in determining if a student has plagiarized a paper.[43]

Distance learning has created a number of options for students. It also opens up challenges that need to be addressed as with any new situation. With the advent of some of the newer venues for learning, such as Web 2.0 technologies, gaming, and virtual reality, perhaps newer forms of pedagogy and assessment will emerge that will resolve some of the current issues in online cheating.

Summary

Distance learning is on the rise globally as a venue to provide higher education to students. Studies have indicated that students enjoy courses in an online format, and many feel that they learn more in this format than in a classroom. The advent of Web 2.0 has created a shift in distance learning from a passive state to an active and collaborative learning environment, thus enhancing the overall learning experience. In addition, newer content distribution providers, such as YouTube and iTunes U, have provided other avenues for students to access information. Virtual environments, such as Second Life and other virtual museums, have created alternative places for students to visit and learn without leaving the personal computer. Many of these new technologies are used in both the classroom environment and in distance learning. As technologies continue to advance, simplify, and expand, there will be little or no differentiation between on- and off-campus learning.

CHAPTER TWELVE

Centers of Excellence, On-campus Strategy to Learning Environments

This section outlines a possible path by outlining a visualization exercise that higher education institutions could take to get started with creating learning environments.

Connected Centers of Excellence

The Internet already has enabled the transformation of higher education by streamlining campus administrative processes, enhancing facilities such as dorms and classrooms, enabling digital libraries, expanding access to distance learning, and creating more engaging learning environments through video and simulations. Given the proliferation of new technologies and devices on campus, and more expected in the future, institutions are trying to understand how to get started with creating next-generation learning environments, continuous technology evaluation, training, and adoption. These technologies include Web 2.0, multimedia, virtual presence, gaming, and next-generation mobile devices. This is particularly challenging because a college campus may have a multitude of stakeholders (administration, faculty, and students) with varying needs and levels of expertise, as well as varying campus technology implementations, budgets, and goals. The task may seem daunting and unachievable.

This chapter discusses how educators can take advantage of known trends in higher education, such as the increase of building construction and renovation of existing buildings, the evolution of space to collaborative commons, the continual evolution of technology and the desire for more interdisciplinary integration (e.g., integration of Web 2.0 and other social technologies) to start a next-generation learning environment. As buildings are constructed, many colleges already are evaluating how to update these facilities to support current and next-generation technology needs. At the same time, institutions are developing collaborative commons in central buildings where a number of campus constituents already meet, research, study, and socialize. In addition, institutions are evaluating new technologies and services on campus. A Building commas could become the neutral area where stakeholders pilot, test, evaluate, and train new and emerging technologies and services before rolling them out across the entire campus. This chapter proposes a visualization exercise to evolve current campus commons into next generation Centers of Excellence.

Significant spending on overall construction and renovation

Building construction and renovation at higher education institutions have been underway for some time. A total of $14.523 billion was spent on college construction in 2005. About two-thirds of the amount was for construction of entirely new buildings. The remaining one-third was split between adding new space to existing buildings ($2.068 billion), and upgrading existing buildings ($2.663 billion). Many esteemed institutions, such as Harvard, Cambridge, and Princeton, state that their buildings are being designed to last 100 years or more.[1]

Campus Commons are under development

Changes in physical aspects of traditional learning spaces, such as classrooms, schools, and dorms, have been well documented. As technologies, applications, and smart services increase, additional areas, such as libraries, language labs, and computer labs, will transform into hubs of technologies. In addition to new and renovated buildings, many higher education institutions, have created

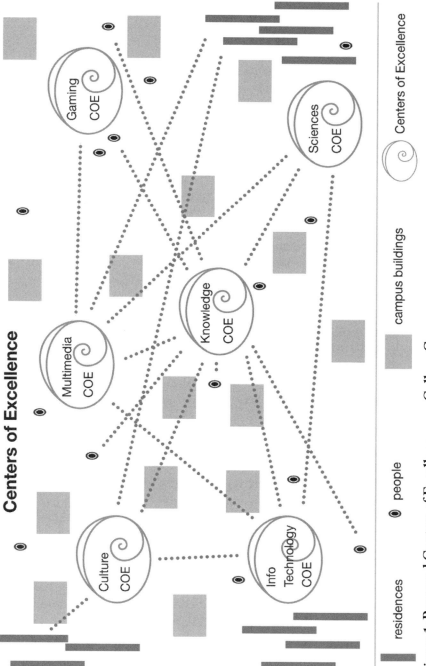

Figure 1: Proposed Centers of Excellence on a College Campus

campus commons that redefine how traditional buildings, rooms, and spaces, such as libraries and computer labs, language labs, are designed, built, and used. Libraries have been at the forefront of this conversion as books are increasingly digitized and space reevaluated. Many universities have used the extra space to transform their libraries into campus commons by building food courts, creating social gathering areas, and adding collaborative seating arrangements.[2] Other universities are reevaluating their computer labs as laptop computers and mobile devices replace desktop computers, creating more free space. The same thing also is happening with language labs as more content, such as language audio and video tutorials, is made available online.

Technology deployment creates smart buildings

In addition to campus commons, new technologies, including wireless, video, virtual technologies, gaming, and Web 2.0, are being integrated into building spaces, such as student residences and classrooms, to create smart buildings. Some notable examples are listed below.

- Wake Forest has a number of uses for PDAs on campus, ranging from academic purposes to party management.[3]
- Bryant University uses digital signage in the student union to have real-time updates on activities, as well as places for students to post their club activities, events, and news (*http://svconline.com/education/ features/digital_signage_bryant_university/*).
- Bentley College is one of only 6 academic institutions in the nation with its own financial "Trading Room" that simulates a stock exchange floor environment (*http://www.gradprofiles.com/bentley.html*).
- UCLA's Chemistry department has Computing and Visualization Centers that house supercomputers networked with other parallel supercomputers all over the country; the computers are being used for calculation-intensive research (http://www.chem.ucla.edu/brochure/ fac-1.html).
- Eastern Michigan University has a gaming center in the student commons (*http://www.emich.edu/studentcenter/*).
- Carnegie Mellon has a virtual concierge service named "Valerie" in Newell-Simon Hall, home of the School of Computer Science (*http:// www.cmu.edu/cmnews/extra/040219_valerie.html*).

Outside of the United States, academic institutions are starting to use these technologies to facilitate learning. At the Singapore Management University, students use tablet PCs to interact with smart video classroom screens to join and share in class discussions.[4] The University of Lancashire uses oversized 3D screens in classrooms (http://www.uclan.ac.uk/computing).

Challenges and opportunities from existing approaches

Although the creations of campus commons and smart buildings are positive moves, several challenges to these approaches exist. First, many smart buildings and classrooms are designed to meet the needs of only a single discipline so they do not facilitate interdisciplinary integration or encourage student and faculty traffic. For example, a smart science lab is intended only for the biology or chemistry departments or a new computer lab for the computer science department. Second, these spaces often do not take into account the need to continually test, evaluate, and deploy new technologies, so the labs quickly become outdated. Third, the services of these commons often are similar to services already offered by other constituents on campus and not shared, so building these common areas may be financially inefficient and services underutilized.

To address these challenges and highlight new opportunities, higher education institutions should ask the following questions.

- How do we keep our facilities current with the rapid influx of new technologies?
- How do we ensure our buildings remain useful and are broadly used for their planned lifespan?
- How do we continually test new technologies and services without relying on a broad campus deployment?
- How can we test new technologies and services with a broad population sample that includes administration, faculty, and students?
- How can we provide services, including mobile access, to stakeholders on and off campus?
- Is there a way to create a methodology to assess campus space for integrated and expanded use as it becomes available for renovation?
- Can we keep this space "evergreen," or always renewable? This is important so that new buildings incorporate existing accepted trends, such as flexible spaces, video integration, smart boards, and Internet Protocol (IP) enablement, as well as consistently measure and evaluate newer technologies and services including smart devices, Web 2.0 technologies, virtual reality, video, and presence technologies.

- Can we involve a broad base of users to evaluate new technologies and services and not limit the participation to a group of users on campus.

Centers of Excellence—framework for success

A solution to some of these challenges is to create a framework of "Connected Centers of Excellence." This framework addresses how to create a central area on campus—"the hub"—where knowledge is created, shared, and resourced, where institutions connect to the hub from other centers on and off campus, as well as on virtual locations or "spokes." The hub and the spokes would not only share common services, technologies, and resources but also have unique core competencies. In this framework, the centers will have a core mission (knowledge, culture, gaming, etc.), provide a variety of services, and become test beds for new developing applications, technologies, and services while still offering key specialized expertise. Centers of Excellence will share services to support the increasingly complex interdisciplinary learning environments. Centers of Excellence will be linked and kept "evergreen" so they do not become dated as technologies advance. In addition, these facilities have multipurpose common teaching and learning spaces and could become financially self-sustaining through the inclusion of retail establishments, services, and even digital advertising to help defer costs, as already seen with many multipurpose retail spaces.

Library Center of Excellence—the hub

A simple way to get started is to pilot the concept in a building that is slated for renovation and is enjoying high foot traffic from students and faculty. Libraries are a good place to begin exploring the concept of Centers of Excellence because they are desirable areas for reinvention, given that libraries often are at a central location on campus, are typically used or visited not only by the student body and faculty but also by administrative staff, and will greatly benefit from a reduction of physical book volume. Many libraries on campus already have evolved from purely book storage centers to knowledge hubs where information is exchanged and ideas can be explored using materials and resources such as reference books, research papers, published journals, and comprehensive collections that are part of the library's core offerings. Libraries, as the central campus physical hub, have become very viable centers for socializing and collaborative learning.

- The largest users of libraries are young adults aged 18–30.[5]
- Internet users are twice more likely to patronize libraries than non-Internet users.[6]
- More than two-thirds of library users use computers in the library.[7]
- 65% of library users look up information on the Internet at the library, and 62% use the library computers to check library resources.[8]
- Academic libraries holdings are estimated at $211 billion.[9]
- Of the total 16 billion books held globally, 3.5 billion are estimated to be in academic institutions.[10]
- Of the 1,947,600,000 items circulated each year in the United States, 122,000,000 are circulated by academic libraries.[11]

With the advent of new networking technologies, the library has been evolving for the past few years and will continue to evolve in a number of ways. Many library systems today utilize increased digitized collections, preserved digital archives, and improved methods of data storage, retrieval, curation, and service. Librarian skills will continually evolve to respond to the changing needs and expectations of populations. Students and faculty will increasingly demand access to library resources and services and expect digital presence with academic systems and social computing. Information technology will shape the practice of scholarly inquiry, requiring more technology-related services and technology-rich user environments. Higher education is increasingly viewed as a business, with a degree of accountability in addressing the needs of the "customers," which, in the case of universities, are the students, faculty, and staff. Online learning will continue to expand and libraries will need to gear resources toward delivering to a distributed academic community. Demand for free public access to data and research is expected to go up as well. Library facilities will progressively be integrated with research, teaching, learning programs, technology, and student services. The role of the library has shifted from managing collections to knowledge creation. It is clear that libraries are positioned for change.

Visioning Session

Visioning sessions help bring together stakeholders into a neutral format to brainstorm and provide ideas about the future as well as identify practical needs and goals. Sessions such as these are fairly common when embarking on new projects of concern to the community. The session often entails a review of a variety of research findings, best practices, and benchmarks. It may include far-reaching ideas on where the project could go if there were no limitations from organization or budget. Part of the process may include storyboarding activities that help us understand what can be enhanced or simplified. For the purpose of this chapter, we will explore how a library can evolve into a Knowledge Center of Excellence (and move beyond that) by incorporating ideas from a variety of experts and stakeholders.

Determine a central mission and academic purpose

The first step is to determine a central mission and purpose for the new Center. For example one individual suggested "The Campus Library Commons will be a Knowledge Center of Excellence and become an important part of our institution's learning environment and knowledge creation through the integration of information, technologies, collaborative learning, and research."

Propose supporting ideas

The next step is to brainstorm on supporting ideas that support the central purpose. Here are a few examples that individuals proposed:

- The Center's leadership will be the Chief Knowledge Officer (CKO) who will have an understanding and vision for the aggregate campus needs for learning, information reference, and knowledge creation.
- The Center's staff are individuals who are not only experienced and expert in knowledge creation and reference (library science) but also are facilitators of activities that will draw people to the Center by initiating collaboration, interaction, and the social construction of knowledge.
- The CKO will partner with the Chief Information Officer (CIO). Together these 2 officials have a comprehensive understanding of cross campus teaching, learning, and technology needs and will work in unison to integrate knowledge and technology.
- The Knowledge Center of Excellence is the central point for core library services such as reference, research, information repository, search, training, and study and a test bed for new technologies. Here, new pedagogy and assessment tools are evaluated and adopted, tech-

nologies and learning tools are tested, ideas exchanged, collaboration fostered, and results measured. It is a neutral place to experiment with new and unfamiliar technologies.

- The Knowledge Center of Excellence provides a neutral area for training faculty how to integrate technology into learning (technical literacy) as well as a place for students to learn how to discern quality information in a technology environment (information literacy).
- This Knowledge Center of Excellence will be fully integrated into the student and faculty lifestyles and will be inclusive of retail services, the newest technologies, and flexible, collaborative, and social environments. It will be open 24/7 for both on- and off-campus needs and inquiries.
- The Knowledge Center of Excellence will link and share technologies and services to provide a consistent offering to all departments and schools on campus.
- The Knowledge Center of Excellence will link to other Centers on campus by sharing commonly used services.
- The Knowledge Center will be the key social gathering place for students, faculty and administration. The place to be seen.

Dr. Joseph Cevetello, who obtained his doctorate in teaching, curriculum, and learning environments from Harvard University, has spent the past several years investigating the changing role of the library. He believes that:

The library will become a learning collaborative space and less of an information marketplace as it has been in the past; individuals will spend time in these spaces because of their need for collaboration, social interaction, and access to technology tools and resources to facilitate knowledge creation. One of the most primary challenges in this regard is not in the construction or imagining of these spaces, it is in giving these spaces a name that befits their function. Current thinking about academic libraries is stuck in the mindset akin to how people thought about the first automobiles. For a significant period of time, automobiles were termed "horseless carriages"; yet, the automobile was a wholly different and unique mode of transportation. In a similar fashion, twenty years from now, we will have a wholly different designation for what we currently term "library." The Knowledge Commons is one suggestion, but whatever moniker, the purpose of the library has been radically changed by its interaction with 21st-century technologies and the students and faculty who are adept in their use.

Storyboard the process flow and activities

Storyboarding is a common exercise used in art, media, and TV; however, it has applications in other areas and can be applied to the design of Centers of Excellence as well. In this exercise, a storyboard flowchart is used to document the activities and the process flow of what needs to take place in a library from the user's perspective. This exercise is valuable because it tracks the actual paths of students, researchers, and faculty. It seeks to find areas for efficiency. For example, our group after storyboarding noted that the library had multiple stop points (circulation, reference, technical questions) that could be consolidated into one location with a concierge that could save the visitor time and enhance the visitor experience. A storyboard process might start with the current state and then document the future state. Storyboards are helpful because they create a reference point that all can use when they envision the surrounding space, and they can be rough representations of what the finished product should be able to provide. These storyboards either can be drawn, diagramed as flow charts, or as text.

Envision the Space

The next step in a visioning session is to envision what the space might look like or what stakeholders might want to explore; this is done based on research of what the best practices and benchmarking are in other institutions and industries. This can be an enjoyable experience for those involved as it helps put a picture to the concept as well as letting people imagine the possibilities without constraints. For the purposes of this exercise, a variety of spaces are benchmarked globally and notes were taken on best practices or ideas.[12] In one previous occasion, when this exercise was implemented, an architectural design student (estimated age 22), without any knowledge of some of the concepts discussed, was invited to explore and design what he thought this space might look like, including his own preferences and design background to help push the idea even further. In addition, modern IT development and technologies were added to help envision what services could be tested throughout the Center of Excellence. This section outlines the vision that was collectively built and then drafted into a visual format.

Exterior

The building will be round and surrounded with glass, with 3 floors. It will have multiple walkways to enter the building from each side of campus. There is natural light and greenery built into the building plans. The building is round to encourage collaboration rather than isolated corners or cubicles. It is mostly glass so as to allow and use natural light where possible (with shades for privacy).

The reason for 3 floors is to ensure that it is not a book storage facility but rather a place where people will utilize the full space and available resources. Books will be creatively housed in the sides of the glass walls (like art, rather than stored paper) and automatically retrieved through automated research kiosks throughout the facility. The books within the walls are visible, accessible, and become an integral part of the building. The rooftop is utilized for indoor/outdoor events, meetings, and social activities.

Interior

Space is open and flexible and can be fully utilized; the furniture is flexible, mobile ergonomic, and comfortable. Flexible and open design (furniture, walls, flooring) is key so that the rooms and flooring can be rearranged as technologies and needs change.

The atrium has natural light and greenery throughout, with circular stairways that connect floors. Elevators that run up and down the outside of the building allow visitors to see various aspects of the campus. Dispersed throughout, on walls and carts, are current newspapers, related periodicals, top-selling books, and magazines. Hot-docking desks are interspersed around the concierge for quick work and collaboration stops. Multiple building entrances enable more foot traffic from various parts of campus and encourage passerby familiarity and discussions. A variety of current retail outlets, restaurants, coffee shops, trendy food stands, and lounges offer social gathering areas for and create revenue streams (or cost recovery) for the Knowledge Center of Excellence. Food orders, reservations, and retail purchases are enabled from any device.

Technology

The entire building is Internet protocol (IP)-enabled and hosts a variety of smart technologies: wireless sensors monitor a variety of building services such as security, heat, air conditioning, lights, and security. RFID tagging, identity recognition, high-definition (HD) videoconferencing (TelePresence), and digital signage are some other technologies that can be employed. Ample broadband will be necessary for high-bandwidth needs. Smart/multipurpose rooms and labs can be reserved through an automated calendaring system as a way to integrate the classes with the reference sections (flexible walls can reduce or increase the size of the spaces). A variety of mobile devices are available, such as mobile laptop carts and PDAs, all for onsite use, with power stations and strips for cell phones. It is a predominantly paperless and fully wireless environment; many books are digitized and easily accessible through a multitude of devices and may be downloaded and stored. Physical books are available through automated book systems, such as a kiosk and RFID, with each book tagged for easy inventory, checkout, and security needs.

Research assistance and helpdesk inquires can be supported 24/7 in person, by call centers, or Question Point (www.questionpoint.org), a virtual reference service maintained by the Online Computer Library Center (OCLC), and other similar services. Meeting requests for expert sessions can be reserved using calendaring applications and facilitated through a call center, conferencing sessions, videoconferencing, or Second Life.

Shared services

The library is not limited to the physical walls of the facility but links and shares services with other Campus Commons, such as computer rooms (Computer Commons), language labs (Language Commons), or gaming lounges (Gaming Commons). In this manner, knowledge and services are integrated throughout the campus regardless of location. A 24/7 call center ensures that service levels are high. Collaboration software tools including Click to Talk, which makes VoIP calls at the click of an object, ensure that distance is not an issue. The library is replicated in Second Life to ensure virtual access.

The following section outlines a vision of how this center could be organized based on the activities that occur in the center. The first floor is the main social area where most people would do collaborative work. The second floor is the quiet zone. The third floor is the lifestyle area.

Floor 1—social and collaborative area

Central Concierge—this easy-to-access area is staffed with experts in reference, technology, and services. This service would replace more traditional roles of the reference desk, the circulation desk, and the helpdesk to create a one-stop destination for all service needs that is easy to access in a variety of methods. Concierge personnel are not confined to this area; wireless headsets, easily connect to experts within the facility, as well as in other Centers of Excellence. Some might be virtual through high-definition videoconferencing, Second Life, instant messaging, and Click to Talk applications.

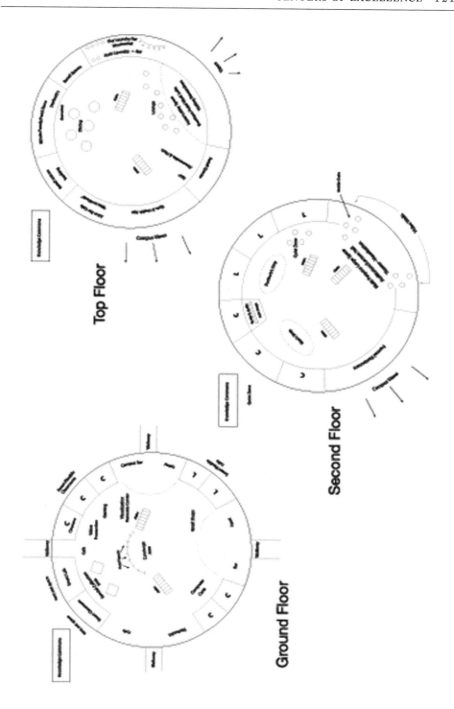

Kiosks are available to locate people and track GPS coordinates in the facility, which also can be done on personal devices. Helpdesk IP video phones are pervasive so, from any location, you can dial 1 for reference, 2 for IT support, 3 for general inquiries, so on and so forth and talk to someone. Hot docking desks are interspersed around the concierge for quick work and collaboration stops.

First floor services offer gaming areas where multiperson assignments can be played in groups or new games created. There is a video production center with resources needed to create multimedia assignments and a visualization research and development center (visual computing of experimental data) for research assistance. The library's rotating collections can be viewed as an interactive display that includes digital signage tutorials, hands-on experience, and video tutorials. Retail spaces are dispersed throughout the floor for convenience and revenue streams and to encourage social collaboration. Collaboration areas (large and small) are available for group study, classes, and guest sessions. Food courts, bars, and coffee shops are pervasive and encourage late night group sessions.

Most academic libraries have special collections or archives, which tend to be holdings that are unique to that institution. The Knowledge Center of Excellence can be the place to make these collections come alive through virtualization technologies. Special collections, centers, and archives have never had the opportunity to be so pertinent, interactive, and alive.

For example, as an illustration a collection "LA Voting During the Great Depression" at the Center for the Study of Los Angeles at Loyola Marymount University could be made accessible to the greater LA community in ways not possible previously through the use of virtual reality, video and immersive technology. An interactive map of 1932 Los Angeles is projected on a video wall in front of the viewer upon entering the space. This aerial map could be overlaid with digital graphics representing voting districts and actual voter turnout percentages. Visitors could scroll through virtual maps, by election, through the map interface. If the viewer chooses the street view, they can experience a virtual 3D walk through downtown streets, created by scanning photographs into a (Virtual Reality) simulator. In essence, they would be transported to Depression Era LA and could walk up to a polling station and enter it to experience the space. They could examine a virtual polling machine and, in front of them, in a display case, might be an actual polling receipt, as well as a 1930s polling machine. The visitor could step back, click on the user interface, and view a satellite map of 2008 Los Angeles presented with polling and voter turnout percentages by districts. (Dr. Joe Cevetello, Director of Information Technology and Director of Academic Technology, Loyola Marymount University, Santa Monica)

Floor 2—the quiet zone

Most libraries, even when undergoing change to include more social activity, do keep sections of the library for quiet reading, work, or reflection. For the purposes of this exercise, a floor is designated as a quiet zone. Quiet zones, with comfortable seating areas, ensure that no cell phones interrupt individual study and reading. Eclectic and trendy fast food food options, such as a chocolate lounge, sushi bar, tapas tables, and tearooms, are dispersed throughout the floor. Some of these could be automated, have single seats, or offer takeaway food options. Multipurpose soundproof classrooms and labs are available for on-campus lectures, research sessions, or off-campus rental. Each is equipped with smart technologies, such as high-definition videoconferencing, whiteboards, and wireless devices. Multipurpose rooms can be partitioned into smaller spaces for small group study. A multipurpose auditorium is available for performances, lectures, theater, and large group activities. This space can be partitioned; it is acoustically designed and soundproof. It has a ceiling-to-floor screen for visualization research projections. A soundproof formal restaurant is on this floor accepting online reservations. The food and spaces thematically change every 6 months and are perhaps affiliated with or provided by the local culinary institute. Within the restaurant, there is a media bar, a place where learners can sync their handheld devices, watch taped lecture videos, and download podcasts and music in a lounge bar environment. Within the restaurant is a video wall lounge that can be used for a variety of digital displays— guest speakers, video clips, entertainment, and the like.

Floor 3—practical lifestyle and research floor

Many institutions have talked about the library becoming a 24/7 facility and a place where students, faculty, and researchers could safely come and go and stay for as long as they wish. However, many of these libraries have not thought through how an individual might actually have the ability to stay longer if only minimal services are available. The practical lifestyle floor offers a solution to this problem by adding a number of lifestyle services: gym, childcare, security, and even a hotel so that individuals can use the facility 24/7.

In addition, many research universities have been exploring ways to tap into research data as they happen in real life, in real time. One interviewee noted. "A lifestyle floor could enable connected research, for example, on health and nutrition, where real-time data would be gathered, evaluated, and showcased (digital signage) with all available resources within reach (periodicals, research kiosks, journals, data files, etc.), thus creating a convenient real-time

24/7 research area."

For example, the data from the workout facility are tied to the food services throughout the building, the grocery store and the health club machines. An individual's diet and exercise plan can be evaluated and assessed by researchers who might be working in the lab, offsite or staying in the hotel. Statistical data easily can be displayed using digital signage in addition to online access.

The floor would include other lifestyle services such as a spa (with online reservation system), an automated, IP-enabled laundry bar (also with online reservation system), an automated dry cleaning service, and a grocery store (automated bar code checkout). A child care center is within the gym, with video monitoring from any device. There also is a health food café with IP-enabled takeout. Digital signage helps diners determine nutrition-balanced meals for in or out service. Boutique hotel loft work/sleep spaces are for rent for visiting researchers.

Rooftop

The rooftop is included in this design as a flexible space that could have a variety of uses. The outdoor roof is open for social gatherings and entertainment. A covered rooftop provides space for indoor activities. The rooftop can be utilized for research, most appropriately perhaps for astronomy, botany, or green studies.

Conclusion

Creating a higher education, technology-rich learning environment is possible today. Many institutions are trying to envision how to enable and share all of the educational resources on their campus using technology. Connected Centers of Excellence are an achievable goal and can be established practically on campuses today. The Library Commons, or some other central building under renovation, can be an ideal location to start and pilot the campus vision. Some of the key points for getting started include understanding the needs of the campus and the stakeholders, defining the core mission for a selected space, storyboarding the use process, and determining key services and resources that need to be supported, as well as planning for support and continuity and even letting your imagination run wild.

Reflections on Technology and Its Growing Influence in Higher Educations

CHAPTER THIRTEEN

Forward through a Rearview Mirror

What the History of Technology in Higher Education Tells Us about Its Future

Joseph Cevetello, Ed.D.

> When faced with a totally new situation, we tend always to attach ourselves to the objects, to the flavor of the most recent past. We look at the present through a rear-view mirror. We march backwards into the future.
>
> —Marshall McLuhan (*The Medium Is the Massage*, 1967)

For well over a century, the application of technology in the service of formalized higher education has been a recurrent and popular theme, with a great variety of technologies that pundits have suggested will influence education for the better. In the 1920s, applying technology meant learning by film and correspondence; in the 1930s and 1940s, it signified learning through radio; in the 1950s and 1960s, it denoted learning through television; in the 1970s, it implied learning through video; in the 1980s, it indicated learning through computers; and in the 1990s, to computer-mediated learning over the Internet.[1] Until the present, each of these "educational" technologies has had a life cycle; each was supposed to radically transform, if not end, education as it was known at the time; each invariably fell short of expectations.

Successive waves of technology proponents employed rhetoric thick with claims about the revolutionizing effect these technologies would have; yet, very few spoke about the history of earlier educational technologies and how they influenced education. Such an historical examination of the impact of these technologies upon the improvement of instruction or upon the practice of teaching and learning reveals a marginal effect at best, and at worst, a bleak picture of technologies that are "oversold and underused."[2]

Historian Larry Cuban's seminal work on technology use in education reveals that there is a cycle to the introduction of new technologies in education:[3] advocates make hyperbolic claims about the efficacy of the new technologies promising improved instruction and radical reform of education; enthusiasts encourage the spending of substantial amounts of funds for the large-scale introduction of new technologies into schools; advocates make little attempt to understand the culture or history of the technology; research usually demonstrates that the "new technology" is no more effective than learning with traditional technologies, and that promises invariably fall short; disappointment and disillusionment ensue while teachers, administrators, and school organizations are blamed for the failings of the technology.

Despite the variety of technology involved, two constants remain: the recurrence of this cycle whenever a *new* technology is introduced, and the historical perspectives of successive technology supporters. Cuban is critical of the technology pundits and their disregard of the history of technology. He criticizes them for seeing "History [as] a source of problems more than of insight."[4] Ultimately, Cuban suggests that a mature historical perspective might do a great deal toward changing this cycle and, possibly, achieving better results in the application of technology in educational contexts.

Historian David Noble's[5] work on the history of correspondence education and distance learning also sheds insight into the questionable effects of technology use in higher education, as does Postman's work.[6] Most recently Selwyn has stated that "the formal use of computer technologies in many areas of higher education could best be described as sporadic, uneven, and often 'low level.'"[7]

Thus, we observe that for more than 100 years, the desire to deliver education with technology has remained a consistent aspiration of educators, pundits, and learners alike. Yet, the impact of the vast majority of these technologies has been marginal at best—not a history of abundant success. Instead, the use and application of technology in education have been a history of robust and great promise with little real impact. Technologists, information technology professionals, educational proponents, or those companies who help create and produce technology rarely reference this history. Consequently, this lack of historical context handicaps meaningful discourse about educational technology use and prevents us from coming to a meaningful understanding of how to use technology correctly and effectively in educational contexts.

We can no longer ignore this history. If we do, we will be doomed to repeat it. Yet, how can we dare believe that current technologies and claims about how they will improve the learning environment in higher education will be different? How do we avoid the pitfalls and disappointment of previous proponents and the technology they supported? How do we, to turn a phrase, not doom ourselves to repeat the past? Why *is* it different today?

Why today is different

Given the strength of the above historical indictment, we would be foolish to propose increased and significant integration of technology into the curriculum unless there was something truly significant and different about today's educational environment. Yet, there is cause for optimism as there are several significant trends and developments that truly delineate the current state and its potential from previous eras.

To begin, there is the sheer ubiquity of digital technology available to us today. Currently, 83% of all U.S. households have broadband Internet access, and this will increase to 94% by 2011.[8] Worldwide there are 270 million people who can access the Internet wirelessly; by 2012 there will be more than 310 million.[9] The sheer numbers of higher education institutions that offer wireless Internet access have increased dramatically over the past 5 years, and trends indicate that within 3 to 5 years nearly all campuses will provide wireless Internet access anywhere on campus. Not just campuses, but whole cities will be wireless, and wireless convergence between cellular, satellite, and Wife systems will mean that ubiquitous wireless communication will become the expected standard of service.

Wireless ubiquity has been concomitant with a rise in mobile computer usage. The rate of mobile computer ownership continues to grow while desktop ownership remains stagnant. Current global ownership of mobile computers is at 34%.[10] By 2010, in the United States, 53% of all households will own a laptop.[11] Soon, more mobile computers than desktops will be produced by the personal computer industry. Already, 98% of all first-year students at universities and colleges come with their own computers, and almost three-quarters (74%) of these are mobile computers.[12] Students also use other wireless devices, such as smart phones, that are more a "palmtop" computer than phone, and which allow for powerful communication and computing capabilities. Concurrent with these powerful and ubiquitous computing and networking tools come expectations from students—today they expect to be able to be on the Internet, connected and engaged through computer-mediated technology 24 hours a day, 7 days a week.

Before wireless Internet access and mobile computing, institutions and faculty had more powerful technologies than what was commonly available to students. Today, students come to campus with technologies as powerful as, if not more powerful than, what is available to faculty, and students are pushing faculty and the institutions to adopt greater amounts of technology. One recent example is social networking sites, such as MySpace and Facebook, which are phenomenally popular with students who spend hundreds if not thousands of hours interacting through them. Innovative institutions are seeking to harness what is happening in these spaces and, consequently, faculty are following their students and attempting to adopt this kind of open, collaborative, informal medium. This indeed makes a profound difference to the introduction of previous technology in higher education. The traditional balance of institutions being in control of technology has been overturned and the personal computing advantage is with the students. This far-reaching and rapid dissemination of digital technology, which began in the later part of the twentieth century, has been termed "digital singularity"—a shift so fundamental that there is absolutely no turning back.[13]

Global platform

A second profound change is that the global platform of the Internet provides today's student with access to a seemingly limitless flow of information. In contrast to previous generations, the average student today has at his/her fingertips more expert information than any one single faculty member could provide. Faculty can no longer expect that they are the experts in class, or outside it. At any given moment, in any class, students can call up a wealth of thoughts and knowledge that will challenge their instructor's primacy. Some faculty have reacted to this by banning mobile computers and Internet searches in their classrooms. Yet, ultimately, this is sheer folly, as faculty cannot ban their students from accessing this information when not in their classroom. Previously, faculty and universities relied on the fact that their greatest resources were their knowledge and their intellectual property; these were scarce and could be controlled and disseminated from the brick and mortar of their campuses to the public as they saw fit. The Internet and the World Wide Web have inexorably altered that reality and, in turn, created a third profound difference with the past—the abundance of content.

Content abundance

MIT was a harbinger of this trend when it launched its OpenCourseWare (OCW) initiative in 2001. OCW's goal was to encourage all faculty members to publish their syllabi, lecture notes, research, and other knowledge on the Web, to be accessible by anyone, anywhere with an Internet browser, at no cost. Today, more than 1 million visitors per month access the OCW site.

Within the past year, both Yale and Harvard have announced open access initiatives to disseminate knowledge created by their faculty to the world at no cost.[14] Other institutions have similar initiatives, but when three of the most respected and influential universities in the United States are providing the intellectual property of their faculty to the world at no cost, a major shift in how higher education views knowledge dissemination is underway.

Content abundance also is evidenced in the book and library digitization projects currently underway within higher education and outside of it. The Google Book Search Project plans to scan and digitize 32 million books within 10 years.[15] Other initiatives from Amazon and the Open Library Project also will bring an unprecedented amount of text to the digital world within the next decade. These projects have challenged the core principles of the library and its role in twenty-first century education. This content abundance will have a profound effect on how we educate in the ensuing decades. We are experiencing, in the words of social critic Neil Postman, an "information glut" awash in an unprecedented sea of facts and figures; it is not that we suffer from too little information; it is that we suffer from too much.[16] Higher education, and our society in general, will have to grapple with this issue for many years to come.

Digital natives

The fourth profound difference is that the average undergraduate student today is more adept, more skilled, and more knowledgeable about how to use digital technologies than the average faculty member. It is not uncommon that today's undergraduates learned how to use a computer keyboard before they learned how to handwrite and have never known a time without some type of computer being available to them. They are accustomed to being connected and engaged with some type of computer throughout the majority of their day, especially on the Internet, using social networking sites, searching, accessing, publishing, instant messaging, listening to music, watching video—81% of the respondents in the ECAR student study report using a social networking site on a regular basis.[17] Three in four young adult Internet users watch or download video online.[18] These students are able to process and engage in multiple activities simultaneously through "attentional deployment" or "continuous partial attention" defined as a continuous flow of interactions in which students are able to partially concentrate on any one activity at the same time as focusing on all.[19]

This is the realm of the "digital native," those individuals who are native speakers of the language of computers, video games, and the Internet.[20] To the "native," technology is part of their environment—interwoven, ubiquitous, and permeating their school, work, and social lives like the wireless waves that provide them with Internet access. The difference in how these "digital natives" view, think, and interact with technology is perhaps the most profound change that today's higher education institution must take into account. If nothing else, the use of technology in higher education will follow a different path than previous epochs because our students will demand it. In short, "today's students are no longer the people our educational system was designed to teach."[21]

Crisis of significance

Cultural anthropologist Michael Wesch suggests that this creates a "crisis of significance" for higher education. He suggests that the most significant problem in higher education today is the problem of significance itself. To Wesch, significance reflects culture and there is a wide gap between the culture of our digitally adept students and our "digitally immigrant" faculty.[22] Our students engage, collaborate, and communicate in a decentralized digital world where information is plentiful; yet, their classrooms mostly are centralized, passive, analog environments that control information and make little use of digital tools. In surveying his students, Wesch discovered that more than half stated that they did not like school, but that not a single student said they did not like learning. In short, school is not significant to their lives, but learning is. Prensky and Wesch suggest that today's student exhibits a great appreciation for learning in digital environments, but the typical higher education classroom is sparse in its integration of digital tools. Marshall McLuhan stated almost the same more than 40 years ago in reference to the effects of television on classroom learning, "Today's child is . . . bewildered when he enters the nineteenth-century environment that still characterizes the educational establishment where information is scarce but ordered and structured by fragmented, classified patterns, subjects, and schedules."[23]

Learning spaces have been mostly unchanged since the middle of the last century; yet, the ubiquity of technology in the age of "digital singularity" suggests that there is a significant and profound shift in how our students interact with technology, and a corresponding impetus for technology integration and infusion in higher education environments that might well follow a different path than previously.

To summarize, there are profound and significant differences in today's environment for the integration of technology as compared to the recent past. I have focused on four of the most significant:

- Digital technology is ubiquitous.
- The Internet provides a global platform with seemingly limitless access to information.
- Content is abundant; information and knowledge are not scarce and are easy to access at little to no cost.
- Students are extremely comfortable and facile in the digital world. They are "native" to it and expect it to permeate all aspects of their lives.

What is the same?

Lest we feel that the current state is totally dissimilar to the past, let us examine the constants in our education environments vis-à-vis the application of technology, for we have as much to learn from these similarities to the past as we do from the differences.

Evolution vs. revolution

To begin, we must acknowledge that most technology trends begin as an attempt at radical reform of education practice. Invariably, a particular technology's pundits will claim that "X" technology must be adopted to "revolutionize" how we educate. This is essential, they claim, to either boost achievement, to create citizens who have the skills necessary to succeed, or just to keep up with other schools, countries, or peoples. Many proponents will claim all three and point to an impending crisis in education. Yet, as inevitable as these claims are, the reality is that the promised revolution does not come. Things are never that easy in educational culture, "limited implementation of technology is inevitable."[24]

One significant reason is that higher education is a very established, old, and deep culture.[25] The traditional "grammar of schooling" is tenacious and must be reckoned with. Our conceptions of learning and teaching are deeply enculturated and not easily altered, and this "grammar" extends far beyond the physical boundaries of the classroom. It is present in asynchronous and virtual learning environments as well.[26] History informs us that the most successful educational reforms and innovations have been those that have been (1) structural add-ons to existing schooling; (2) noncontroversial; (3) supported by influential constituencies; or (4) required by law.[27]

All too often, educational reformers place too much emphasis on the logical and instrumental, believing that the proper application of technology will lead to profound change. They either ignore the culture, norms, and mores of education or believe that the reform they are proposing will mitigate them. Inevitably, the revolution begins to slow, promises invariably fall short, and the reform stalls.

There are a great many reasons for this as seen through a number of studies examining school reform and change.[28] Suffice it to say that those technologies that can be deployed as an addition to current educational practice have been those that have had the most success. Consider the blackboard, which was first introduced to wide application in the mid-nineteenth century. Its success ensured that for the better part of the twentieth century, it was practically impossible to imagine a classroom without some kind of large mounted writing tablet for instructor use. In an evolutionary sense, the blackboard was an improvement upon the small, individual tablets that students and teachers had been using. Consider also Blackboard, the course management system (CMS). Again, the CMS was not a revolutionary technology, as it was only a technological improvement to allow for electronic distribution of materials and content to students. Today, there is hardly an institution in the United States that does not have some form of CMS, and more than 80% of all students report using a CMS during their time in higher education.[29] Further, in the above illustrations, the blackboard and the CMS were not technologies that sought a radical reformation of the organization of education; they were evolutionary additions to current practice. Eventually, over time, the blackboard did have as major an impact on modern schooling as any technology, but it was an evolutionary adaptation of the individual slate—it did not attempt to wipe the slate clean. In short, most successful technology implementations share a common trait of being evolutionary and not revolutionary in nature.[30]

Universities are in the knowledge creation business

As mentioned previously, our society is suffering under a glut of information, but we must take care to remember that information is only the first step toward knowledge. In fact, part of the way that we can deal with our current information overload is to focus on the process that turns information into knowledge and, in so doing, recognize that universities provide important epistemological frameworks in which to comprehend and make sense of information.

Postman's work examines the distinctions between information and knowledge. To Postman, information is defined as some form of statement about fact, which may or may not be correct. Postman emphasizes that the Internet, until now, has been the ultimate information medium, presenting us with as much potentially valuable information as poor information. Knowledge, on the other hand, is information embedded in some context and the ability to process it toward an end. Universities have been one of the primary institutions that have provided individuals the environment and context in which to learn how to interpret information and construct knowledge. In fact, modern universities and schools were created in reaction to the printed text (information) brought about by Gutenberg and movable type. Yet the information available to anyone with an Internet browser is exponentially greater than what was available just 100 years ago. Thus, the purpose of the university has become even more important in our information-rich environment.[31]

Furthermore, universities can help with the ultimate goal of knowledge creation—"the capacity to know what body of knowledge is relevant to the solution of significant problems," which Postman defines as wisdom.[32] Here again, the primary vehicle for individuals to learn how to develop this practice of inquiry is the institution of higher education, and technologies that assist this inquiry can provide strong support to this endeavor.

Universities serve an important social function

An often overlooked, but equally important, dimension of our universities is that they are communal and societal training grounds and, as such, are places and destinations for socialization. In this function, they provide an environment in which to learn social skills, independence, and valuable lessons in the progression toward adulthood. Yet, despite the fact that this is one of its more important functions, this social aspect is mostly ignored by those individuals advocating for technology incorporation and reform. In the mid-1990s, there was a great deal of hype in the popular and academic literature that the Internet and computing technology would eliminate the need for brick-and-mortar campuses. It was suggested that when the average person with an Internet connection could stay at home, access a wealth of information, and engage in "eLearning," there would be no need for colleges or universities to have physical campuses. A good many of these pundits viewed such possibilities solely through a technology lens, ignoring the social, cultural, and organizational aspects of any traditional university. They claimed that most universities would close their physical campuses within a decade. Yet, today, more than 15 years later, such radical change has not happened. eLearning is more popular than ever, but the vibrancy of physical campuses remains. In 2005, there were 3.1 million students enrolled in online learning courses, and this number is expected to triple to 9.8 million in 2012.[33] At the same time, physical campuses and enrollments continue to expand. Currently, there are 4276 institutions of higher education in the United States, 200 more than in 1998.[34] In 1998, there were 14.5 million students enrolled in higher education and in 2008, 16.1 million; this number is estimated to grow to 18 million by 2012.[35] Contrary to the calls of pundits that eLearning would revolutionize the educational establishment, the reality has been more of an evolutionary impact upon brick-and-mortar campuses to provide virtual and computer-mediated learning environments in addition to the physical.

Further, online environments have not been able to replace the type of interaction and knowledge that is exchanged through the sharing of physical space. Perhaps no better statement about the importance of social proximity, interaction, and university culture has ever been made than the one made in reference to one of the highest profile technology initiatives of the past decade—the OCW initiative. In announcing the initiative, MIT president Charles Vest was very clear that OCW was not an MIT education and reaffirmed the unique value of a face-to-face interaction on a residential campus. "Our central value is people and the human experience of faculty working with students in classrooms and laboratories, and students learning from each other in the kind of intensive environment we create in our residential university."[36]

Three aspects of curriculum transformation— content, method, and medium

In the majority of technology introductions in higher education, there has been a pernicious and fatal misconception in the application of technology. That misconception has been to focus on technology and to ascribe to it a power and a potential to transform, while ignoring the contextual and organizational aspects of the environment. Past technology proponents have tended to forget that technology is a tool, a means to an end, and not the end in itself. For any technology implementation to be successful, whether it is in business, government, or education, the organizational and cultural aspects of the environment in which the technology is introduced must be considered at least on an even par with the technology.[37]

There is, however, an additional manner in which the focus on the technical adversely affects the success of technology use in education, and this concerns curriculum design and development. Its importance is unquestionable, for it is through the curriculum that environments are constructed that allow for knowledge creation and transfer. All too often, however, technology proponents have focused on technology at the detriment of sound curricular design. To illustrate this, let us consider three important components of a curriculum utilizing technology—content, method, and medium.

To begin, there needs to be some compelling content, that is, some type of valuable knowledge or information that an instructor wishes to impart to a student—without this there would be no reason for the learning activity. Typically, this knowledge is divided into standard discipline designations, such as mathematics, biology, or management science. Whatever the content, the key question an instructor must ask is: What is it that I want my students to know?

Next, the instructor requires a framework or pedagogy to deliver the information/knowledge. Thus, the method or instructional strategy frames the manner in which the student and instructor interact while working with the content. Behaviorism, problem-based learning, constructivism, distributed learning, cognitive apprenticeship, direct instruction, inquiry-based learning, and the like are all examples of instructional methods or strategies. A lecture-based, instructor-controlled classroom session is one example of an instructional strategy; a constructivist "learning by doing" session would be another. There is a wide array of philosophies, methods, and strategies that can be employed in any given learning situation. Regardless of the method, the questions one must ask to guide the choice of method and instructional strategy are: What do I want to achieve? What type of knowledge do I want my students to have? How will I know when I have achieved it? What activities need to occur to construct the type of knowledge I wish to create?

The third aspect of curricular design is the technology itself. This technology or medium, in the words of McLuhan, also consists of a wide array of choices.[38] We already have referenced radio, film, television, and a course management system such as BlackBoard, but there seemingly is an endless variety of technologies that can be used in educational contexts: virtual environments, simulations, gaming, and videoconferencing technologies are just a few examples. So far as technology is concerned, the questions an instructor should ask are: In what environment can an activity be presented? What technologies can assist my instructional method and acquisition of content?

Good curriculum design requires that the difference between medium and method be recognized and appreciated. For too long, researchers and educators in the field of technology-mediated learning either ignored this distinction or conflated learning medium with method. Bold statements about how asynchronous learning is essentially collaborative—more so than face-to-face learning—hold little value and illuminate the real nature of technology-enhanced learning even less. As noted previously, attributing more efficacy and power to technology is one of the primary reasons that most technology reforms in higher education fail; yet, this is as rampant today as it has been in the recent past.

Claims that online learning is active learning or that eLearning is more collaborative than learning without technology are nonsensical.[39] A lecture-based, drill-and-response course can be created in a CMS as easily as a constructivist, project-based course. Few educators would think about making a blanket pronouncement about face-to-face learning being inherently passive; yet, such statements are made routinely about the use of technology in educational contexts. In the words of Cuban:

> Smart people have said for decades that personal computers, laptops, and hand-held devices are only vehicles for transporting instructional methods; machines are not what teachers do in classrooms. Teachers ask questions, give examples, lecture, guide discussion, drill, use small groups, individualize instruction, organize project-based learning, and craft blends of these teaching practices.[40]

A well-designed curriculum that uses educational technology, therefore, needs to have a clear content or subject matter identified, a complementary method or instructional strategy that allows for this content to be transferred from instructor to student, and a corresponding medium that allows for content and knowledge to be exchanged. Further, the sequence of curricular design should follow content, method, and medium. Far too often, however, those seeking to introduce technology into their teaching focus first on the technology and then—only secondarily, if at all—on the instructional strategy. Even those skilled in thinking about how to construct learning environments fall prey to this type of thinking. My own experience with faculty in a variety of higher education institutions has demonstrated that the vast majority will focus on the technology: "I need to create a course that is online, show me how to do this in our CMS," as opposed to, "I want to create an environment where my students will engage in a simulated commodities market to address issues of corruption, manipulation, and fraud. What online technologies can help me achieve this?" Said in another way, technology should not be our focus. Instead, it should be transparent and in the service of the organization, communication, and construction of our most valuable asset—knowledge. If we ignore this insight, we do so at our and our students' peril.

To summarize, there are several important similarities or constants in higher education that have affected technology adoption and use. I have identified four of the most important:

- Evolution vs. revolution—the most successful technology innovations have been evolutionary in nature.
- Universities are in the knowledge creation business—knowledge, understanding what it is, and how to create it, is the ultimate goal of the university. Technology should be focused on assisting in this activity.
- Universities serve an important social function—universities have been and will continue to be destinations and important social environments for youth.
- Content, method, and medium—Good curriculum design incorporating technology, must recognize the 3 important aspects of a sound curricular strategy and must not ascribe too much influence to technology.

Challenges to the work of the academy

Thus far, we have examined key differences and similarities between the current and the past environments in higher education with respect to educational technology use. In a sense, we have been looking in the rearview mirror to gather insight and to reflect on successful and unsuccessful implementations of technology in educational contexts. We undertook this examination to learn from the past, so as not to repeat the same mistakes and failings of technology in the service of education.

The above lessons are significant and the wisdom gained from examining the past can be applied to a wide array of current issues in higher education. Let us now attempt to do this as we examine two key areas of the core mission of the university—knowledge creation and dissemination.

From scarcity to abundance

The networked world of the Internet and the digitization of text, audio, and video have caused nothing less than a major paradigm shift in how universities approach the creation of knowledge, its codification, and its distribution. This same networked world has served students who are savvy consumers of information and knowledge, who are facile and comfortable with digital technology, and who approach learning, communication, and interaction with others in a manner wholly different than that of students before the explosion of the Internet. There is no doubt that Tim Berners Lee's brilliant idea—the World Wide Web—has unleashed an interconnected world that has known no parallel in history. It is inexorable and inevitable, and we in education must coexist with it.

The networked world allows any university to have an almost limitless global reach. It is the ultimate distribution mechanism of information, allowing for mass distribution at little cost. In contrast, for a good deal of the twentieth century, access to distribution mechanisms was limited or costly. Print publishing, film, radio, and television production required specialized equipment, personnel, and substantial funds, and the average university sought to outsource the production of print materials and texts to specialized publishers. The majority of universities, in short, created knowledge but abdicated their interests in the channels of distribution and, in some cases, the control of their intellectual capital, because of the high cost of production and distribution. Today, however, publishing truly has become "desktop," unbound from dedicated machinery and technology. Any faculty member with a laptop can publish their work on the Web at practically no cost as a PDF, Web stream, or podcast. Knowledge dissemination has gone from a model of scarcity to a model of abundance. Table 1 illustrates some of the key distinctions between the twentieth and the twenty-first centuries in terms of how universities distributed knowledge.

Having access to a global distribution mechanism, and the ability to control this medium, is nothing less than a tremendous and paradigmatic change for higher education. Hahn suggests that this shift will require new models of scholarly knowledge dissemination and communication, which will challenge our traditional idea of publication:

> In the past, it was useful to equate scholarly communication with the publication of monographs and journals, a process that could be clearly distinguished from other communication practices employed by scholars. The substantial expense, organized effort, and prolonged production and distribution process all readily distinguished communication involving tangible publications. These historic distinctions are now substantially blurred. As most forms of communication become untethered from the production of physical artifacts, some of the terminology of scholarly communication has been stretched to adapt. At the same time, publishing itself has become a term of much fuzziness.[41]

Pre-Internet	Post-Internet
Scarcity	Abundance
Finite or limited distribution	Limitless distribution
Slow process	Immediate process
High cost	Low cost
Needs dedicated means of production	Uses technology widely available in personal computing devices
Cedes control	Retains control
Text primary	Text, audio, and video

Table 1: Knowledge Distribution Prior to the Internet and Post-Internet

A world of abundant information and knowledge accessible by anyone, anywhere, at any time calls for a faculty that embraces the digital means of content distribution. Our students are proficient with digital distribution systems such as YouTube, Wikipedia, and iTunes U, and, in fact, they would prefer that such distribution systems be widely adopted in higher education. A recent study demonstrates a distinct difference in preference for electronic texts versus printed texts between faculty and students, with students preferring e-Texts at 2 to 3 times the rate of faculty members.[42] Podcasting and the iTunes U distribution system, made available to higher education institutions at no cost by Apple Inc., have seen dramatic growth in their ability to distribute all forms of digital information in a standard format. By the beginning of 2008, iTunes U had become the largest distribution medium of scholarly content available on the Web.[43] Today, early adopter faculty members are choosing to directly publish their cutting-edge research via podcast through iTunes U at no cost. Any student or member of the general public can learn about cutting-edge research from University of California Los Angeles, University of California Berkeley, and Stanford by downloading the research directly through the iTunes U.

These new models of scholarly knowledge distribution empower universities and faculty to distribute knowledge and reach an audience in an unprecedented manner. For a good deal of their history, modern universities were the distributers and publishers of their content. Consequently, university presses were created to publish the knowledge and research of their faculty. In the middle to latter part of the twentieth century, however, the role of the university press changed as the cost of production caused many universities to outsource this activity. Those university presses that remained tended to become boutique publishers for the general public rather than distributers of content from their faculty to their students.

iTunes U, Web publishing, and eTexts now enable universities to again control and distribute their work and allow for the rebirth of the university press. In iTunes U, for example, faculty can create a digital text and distribute it to students and the general public using only a mobile computer. Information can be published "just-in-time," literally hours before students need the content, and it can be edited and redistributed at any time. In addition, any digital content, including video, audio, animation, or text, can be published and, most importantly, faculty members can do it themselves, without special equipment or additional personnel.

In such a world, the means of distribution have changed. As a result, questions at the core of what it means to be "faculty" must be examined, for example: What do peer review, authorship, and tenure mean in such an environment? Who is the referee or arbiter of whether what is being published is valid?

At the moment, the means of distribution have matured, but the debate about how this is impacting the process of review has only just begun, "right now we're still living with the habits of information scarcity because that's what we have had for hundreds of years. Scholarly communication before the Internet required the intermediation of publishers. The costliness of publishing became an invisible constraint that drove nearly all of our decisions."[44] Old models are being questioned and decisions about the meaning of scholarship are yet to be made, but a lively discourse about scholarship and authorship is underway. "Perhaps rightly, on the digital frontier, peer review has been an area of extremely limited innovation. Even disciplines that practice widespread pre-publication distribution of manuscripts largely adopted those practices prior to the development of the Internet. Disciplines generally have transferred their existing peer review process directly onto new publishing models."[45]

Wisdom of the crowd or of the expert

In a world where anyone can publish, the question of who is the arbiter of what is valid and right takes on a renewed significance. Perhaps, we may garner some insight into how to answer this by examining a current debate outside of academe. Let us look at the current discourse concerning issues of review, validity, and value as it concerns *Encyclopedia Britannica* and Wikipedia.

Wikipedia is a Web-based encyclopedia that quickly has become an authoritative source of information on the Web. The Wikipedia model represents an open social network of individuals who voluntarily create, vet, and publish knowledge. These individuals may or may not have credentials or extensive background in the topics they write about, and the editing and vetting of these articles can be performed by anyone who is able to access the site. In contrast, the content in *Encyclopedia Britannica* is controlled by a closed group of established and credentialed individuals who, oftentimes, are considered to be the experts in their field. A core set of editors responsible for accuracy tightly controls the vetting of information. These entities represent an "amateur" model in the case of Wikipedia, and a "professional" model with respect to *Encyclopedia Britannica*.

In 2005, a study was conducted that sought to answer the question of which of the above is more accurate and reliable. The journal *Nature* compared the accuracy of entries in Wikipedia and *Britannica* and found a small difference in accuracy of information: Wikipedia contained 4 inaccuracies per entry, and *Britannica* 3.[46] In one sense, *Britannica* was slightly more accurate; however, a more important distinction concerns how long the inaccuracies remain. Wikipedia's inaccuracies can be remedied as quickly as any user discovers them, whereas *Britannica*'s remain far longer. In a sense, therefore, Wikipedia is more accurate because inaccuracies can be corrected almost immediately.

The distinctions between the disparate models of Wikipedia and *Encyclopedia Britannica* will be interesting to observe. The new publishing model of direct digital publishing is causing established models of what is valid, reliable, and authoritative to be radically rethought. With regards to higher education, we should not expect that such questions would have any less of an impact on authorship, review, and even the system of promotion and tenure. We would be wise, however, to reflect upon the historical lessons we discussed above, lest we believe that peer review, tenure, or traditional publishing will cease to exist in the near term. Higher education is a resilient culture that has responded well to change that is evolutionary in nature, as previously discussed. Yet there can be no doubt that the global platform of the Internet, the ubiquity of digital distribution technology, and information abundance will deeply challenge the practice of knowledge creation and distribution in the academy.

Challenges in the learning space

A second key venue where knowledge is created and distributed is the "learning space." Since the arrival of formalized schooling, this has meant the classroom—a physical space where faculty and students gather to interact, exchange, and learn. With the advent of email discussion groups in the 1980s, and the creation of the Web-based CMS in the 1990s, classroom also has come to denote as much a meeting place that exists in the bits of the computer-generated world, as a space in the atoms of the physical. This extension of the learning space is as important a challenge to the academy as any other and one that continues to be a major topic of discussion. With respect to learning environments, spaces, and classrooms, we will consider 2 important questions:

- What is a classroom in an environment where students can interact without being physically present in the same space?
- What is a learning space in a world where access to information is ubiquitous?

A dichotomy of views has evolved around whether we should embrace technology-infused learning environments or shut technology out of the classroom. In recent years, substantial opinions have been expressed on both sides. There have been those who argue that mobile technology in the classroom adversely affects learning and encourages students to be inattentive or unengaged in the classroom, as they use their laptops and wireless connectivity to communicate with friends, email, surf the Web, or game. To confront this, some instructors have taken the step of banning laptop use in the classroom or of asking that wireless access be restricted during class time. In contrast, there are a great many university classrooms that require mobile technology. For well over a decade now, schools such as Dartmouth, Drexel, Harvard Business School, and Clemson University, have asked their students to purchase a laptop as a requirement of their program of study. Such initiatives are termed "required buys" or 1-to-1 programs (one mobile computer per student). Currently there are more than 200 universities in the United States that have some form of mobile requirement, and the clear trend is that such programs are on the rise. The impetus for such programs is reinforced by the fact that almost 75% of all first-year students have a mobile computer.[47] These institutions reason, if 3 in 4 students come with a mobile computer, why not standardize and require students to purchase them?

Given these trends and the fluency of today's student with digital technology, it would seem to be sheer folly to close our learning spaces to the most powerful tools that students possess. Such thought would simply be replicating one of the cardinal errors of infusion of technology into education—focusing on the technology rather than the method or instructional strategy of how the technology is used. In fact, introducing a mobile computing requirement without considering how students should create knowledge is a recipe for failure, since it ignores the precepts of sound curriculum design outlined previously. Faculty who continue to use the same lectures and activities that they used in a nonwired classroom in an environment where mobile technology is ubiquitous will no doubt find the technology to be a distraction. There can be little doubt that faculty must rethink how they wish to deliver knowledge to have a successful learning experience. "The process of composing texts in a world full of new media technologies requires us to reconfigure teaching and learning in remarkably innovative and, perhaps, ungrammatical ways."[48]

Let us imagine, however, that we have created a "right-minded" curriculum that uses mobile technology in its service. There still remains the important question of layout and design of the physical environment that supports such learning. This question is very much a part of the academic discourse at the moment; the Cox Center at Emory University and the Wallenberg Center at Stanford are two places where proper learning space design is under consideration. In addition, there is a growing body of literature concerning learning space design that examines how learning space intersects technology and learning theory. This work suggests several key components to be considered in designing learning spaces to account for technology ubiquity. They are: flexibility, comfort, sensory stimulation, "decenteredness," and technology support.[49] These aspects allow for collaboration between and among students who are physically present and those who are in virtual environments. They allow for a variety of instructional strategies and methods to be employed; they seek to integrate the preferences of the digitally fluent student; and they allow for collaboration with and through technology in the construction of knowledge. To be successful, and to allow for environments that reflect the precepts of good curricular design, we need to construct learning environments that have robust wireless networking, convenient access to electrical power, and mobile furniture for an ergonomic and comfortable space in which to learn, as well as multiple nodes of group and individual learning in a contiguous space.

An additional consideration is that physical space must allow for easy access to virtual space and vice versa. In an educational environment where more than 80% of all students have used an online course management system, and increasing percentages are using Second Life and other virtual environments to interact, the connection between the virtual space and the physical space should be seamless. Our students are in many ways as adept and comfortable with online learning environments as they are with the traditional, physical learning space, and the distinction and preference that the digital immigrant might express for the physical space is not as strongly felt by the digital native; 81% of all undergraduate students have used a social networking site, and (going by conservative estimates) spend on average two hours per day—that is, upward of 700 hours per year—maintaining relationships in a virtual world. Technology provides an environment in which "natives" can learn and are facile moving between the virtual and the physical learning space. Accordingly, universities need to craft environments that are integrated hybrids of the face-to-face and the computer-mediated worlds and to pay as much attention to the creation of virtual environments as they do to their physical structures.

> First, campuses can expect the boundaries between virtual and brick-and-mortar learning environments to continue to blur. Students and instructors will need access to their virtual learning environments while seated in their brick-and-mortar classrooms. Second, as campuses accept the notion that virtual spaces are actually classrooms, they can begin to apply the same care and consideration to decisions about course management systems and campus portals as they do to decisions about new construction and renovation. Of utmost importance is the usability of these virtual spaces.[50]

Ultimately, as technology use in the learning space evolves, we will not speak of face-to-face, or online, or virtual learning: we will simply speak of learning.[51] We would expect that successful technology use in the curriculum would arrive at a convergence of the learning space with the other curriculum elements of method and medium. If we use the past as our guide, we can expect the boundaries to continue to blur, and that learning space will connote a synthetic blend of the virtual and the physical. "We need to construct shared, distributed, reflective practicums in which experiences are collected, vetted, clustered, commented on, and tried out in new contexts."[52] This will require our faculty to be as adept in the computer-mediated world as they are in the flesh. We should not expect a zero-sum game between the physical and the virtual learning space but an ecosystem that could provide a better environment than its individual parts.

Conclusion

> Now, more than a decade into the Internet Age, there have been great advances and compelling opportunities for creating new systems of communication that fully serve research and scholarship. However, it has proven to be the case that technological advances are not sufficient for cultural change; many improvements are dearly bought by effort and conflict. We are at an interesting point in the current paradigm shift, one where we have made significant progress on the journey but clearly still have a long way to go.[53]

For well over a century, the application of technology in the service of education has been a study of great promise but of disappointing practice. This chapter has been a brief examination of some of the reasons why. In our analysis, we examined key similarities and differences between the past and the present in terms of technology and the higher education environment. The important differences in our society are the ubiquity of digital technology; the global platform of the Internet; content abundance; and the facility and ease of the "digital native" student with technology. The key similarities to past technology introductions are that the most successful technology innovations in education have been evolutionary; that technology should assist in the creation, evaluation, and distribution of knowledge; that universities serve an important social function and will continue to be destinations and important social environments for youth; that curriculum design incorporating technology must recognize the important aspects of a sound curricular strategy—content, method, medium—and must not ascribe too much influence to technology.

In examining these similarities and differences, I have suggested that today's "digital singularity" is of such significance that the current state of technology use in education might well escape the traditional cycle of technology hyperbole and failure that Cuban's work so brilliantly outlines. Yet this will be the case only if sufficient heed is paid to the fundamentals of sound curriculum design that seeks to employ technology in its service as a means to an end and not as an end in itself. Without a sufficient and correct understanding of the precepts of curricular design, the application of technology will not be successful, no matter how great and substantially superior the current technology environment is as compared to the past.

As an illustration, consider the following from a recent Web posting in *The Wired Campus* section of the *Chronicle of Higher Education*:

A Future without Courses?

With all the information on the Internet, and with all the ways that students can connect with experts via Web 2.0 tools, who needs traditional courses? George Siemens, an education-technology consultant, argues that the day may soon come when the course outlives its usefulness.

"When content and conversations are distributed, we no longer need to have courses in their current iteration," he says in a 15-minute PowerPoint presentation on his Web site. "We can instead create a global classroom with distributed learners from virtually every corner of the world participating in learning experiences, providing learning resources, creating learning resources, and playing a peer-mentoring role to others through the process."

It's a provocative point, but he offers no clear path to that future. And he concedes that some form of accreditation would be needed to give a seal of approval to all that distributed, self-guided learning. That's a caveat as big as Harvard's main library.

The argument seems a bit like the pronouncements that come, from time to time, predicting the death of the book. It is a fun thought exercise, even if the book never does die.[54]

Are the claims outlined above just the latest installment in the hyperbolic cycle of technology introduction or a possibly different future? This chapter would suggest that we consider the above through a historical lens before we decide to dismiss or embrace this vision. Only then can we determine if the above vision is an oasis off in the distance or just a mirage. The question of whether the "future without courses" will come to pass will be left to the reader and to the test of time.

It has been my contention that in understanding these historical differences and similarities we might be better able to chart a more successful course in the future. In this spirit, we examined two key aspects of higher education practice: (1) knowledge creation and dissemination and (2) learning space. There are no other venues in higher education where the potential of transformation through the correct integration and application of technology holds greater promise. I suggest that this examination will help inform the debate and enrich the discourse, so that we may avoid the problems of the past and help to begin to create a history of successful and transformational change in education with technology.

CHAPTER FOURTEEN

Learning 2.0: Revisiting the 7 Principles

Lev S. Gonick, Ph.D.

Blink: Learning 2.0 is a framework for understanding how to leverage a new generation of collaboration technologies, commonly referred to as Web 2.0, to help realize the full potential of the university learning environment. This chapter is a self-reflective and critical narrative that explores how technologies, such as blogs, wikis, tag clouds, mashups, mobile platforms, Second Life, 3D virtual worlds, digital storytelling, and others, can advance more than 25 years of understanding of what constitutes good practices in the process of discovery and the journey learning. Specifically, the chapter focuses on the new paradigm of participatory learning as a reflection of a broader participatory culture to (1) encourage active learning, (2) advance peer-to-peer cooperation among students, (3) emphasize time on task and project and time management, (4) provide prompt and authentic feedback through mentoring and communicating high expectations.

Click frame 1: [Context]

I have chosen to tell the story in the first person.

Students entering colleges lecture halls today have almost no recollection of a time before the World Wide Web. Most will never own a landline phone, knowing only a mobile and wireless world. They are less interested in television than any generation before and will not watch television on a fixed program schedule for much longer.[1] Most of our students will never read a newspaper. More than half of them have created media content, of whom roughly a third (circa 2005) have shared the content they had created. Email is something their parents did.[2] They are a text-messaging generation that wants to be heard through their and their friends' authored content. Expert views carry no more implicit trust or editorial authority than unknown peers. Community connectedness and a deeply structured experiential and participatory culture are at the heart of their Internet experience.

Click frame 2: Pre-History

It was a rather different time before Facebook, blogging, and other social networking tools became part of the collective consciousness of today's youth. Samantha debated with her peers at the Model United Nations. Today, she is a professor of international relations. Toni participated in fieldwork as an international volunteer in an AIDS clinic in Zimbabwe. Her resulting thesis turned her to the world of publishing, where she remains professionally engaged. Marc learned about international commodity flows using hyperstack to present his term work. Today, he is a trade specialist for a national government authority. Steven wrote scripts on the third world for community radio before he ever left his hometown. After college, he spent years traveling the world. Later, he became a human rights advocate in the Sudan dispute, long before it received international attention. Ingrid wrote scripts for a documentary on prostitution and later pursued a career in journalism. Jim produced, edited, and distributed a video news digest on an international conference on the Laws of the Sea. Later, he worked as a media producer. Rebecca spent a semester working with women in a township in Africa. After completing her Ph.D. research in Malawi, she began directing an international development program at a major university.

(Inter)active, collaborative, and student-centered learning strategies are nothing new. They remain a powerful force in education.

Click frame 3: Dilemma

One must learn by doing the thing, for though you think you know it—you have no certainty until you try. (Sophocles, 5th c. B.C.E.)

For more than 25 years, we have known that "[a]ll genuine learning is active, not passive. It is a process of discovery in which the student is the main agent, not the teacher."[3] Twenty-five years ago, the notion of students participating in, and taking ownership of, learning was a significant part of the answer to a series of national blue ribbon panels on the crisis of undergraduate education. This panel was supported by the American Association of Higher Education and the Education Commission of the States, with backing from the Johnson Foundation and others. As one of the panelists noted, "Students learn what they care about and remember what they understand."[4]

Perhaps the most enduring of those major reports was Arthur W. Chickering and Zelda F. Gamson's *Seven Principles for Good Practice in Undergraduate Education.* As I began prepping my very first university course, while still finishing my Ph.D., in the spring of 1987, their article in the *American Association for Higher Education Bulletin* (March 1987) had a profound impact on my syllabus design and, upon reflection, on my entire career as educator, teacher, technologist, futurist, university administrator, and parent. "Learning," they wrote, "is not a spectator sport. Students do not learn much just by sitting in class listening to teachers, memorizing pre-packaged assignments, and spitting out answers. They must talk about what they are learning, write about it, relate it to past experiences, and apply it to their daily lives. They must make what they learn part of themselves."[5] Good practice in undergraduate education, according to these two esteemed educators, includes the following:

- encourages contact between students and faculty
- develops reciprocity and cooperation among students
- encourages active learning
- gives prompt feedback
- emphasizes time on task
- communicates high expectations
- respects diverse talents and ways of learning

Over the next two decades, research from learning specialists became the subject of the emerging work of brain researchers and cognitive scientists. When brain researchers started using functional magnetic resonance imaging, scientists began a detailed signal mapping project charting the very different parts of the human brain—the right and left brain hemispheres (a discovery that was subsequently significantly refined).[6] Most people and most types of learning draw upon right brain thinking. Designing curriculum that addresses right brain attributes like random, intuitive, holistic, subjective and attempts to synthesize experience is a difficult process. Those designing most curricula are among those least able to call on their own approach to learning. Subject experts, also known as university faculty—most of whom learned their subject and their passion for research through their exposure to the lecture mode (typically left hemisphere dominant learners)—are at a significant disadvantage. Left brain learners are logical, sequential, rational, analytical, and are well suited to absorb the pieces and parts of a problem needing to be solved. The system of structured learning developed by faculty over the past several generations has been biased in favor of their own way of learning. The limits of left brain dominant approach are not only based on important insights on learning theory and brain research, the left brain approach also faces challenges as we scale the information and knowledge creation and recall requirements in the Information Age. Nobel Laureate Herbert Simon summed up the new reality and the new challenge for learners and their teachers. "Knowing has shifted from being able to remember and repeat information to being able to find and use it" (Simon, 1996). The explosion of information and the emergence of information technologies served as a major catalyst in the transformation of the learning enterprise.

Click frame 4: Learning 1.0 and the emergence of information technology for learning

In the 1970s, computing was anything but a massive collaborative platform for innovation, experience, and participation; computing was about programming, coding, keypunch cards, number crunching, and some statistical analysis. Mostly, it was about late nights at the university computing center, waiting for your box of Hollerith cards to run at 2 A.M. only to find a job control language error reflecting some kind of data entry mistake deep in the box of cards, requiring another day of work. That is, if you could get to a keypunch terminal. Public opinion polling, survey research, simulations, and crude text editors, such as vi and Emacs, were all beginning to find their way into the temples of the college mainframes. To be sure, there was some early flirting with questions related to human-computer interfacing and its potential relevance to learning by organizations. In addition to pioneering engineering work by the likes of Doug Engelbart and, later, Alan Kay, institutional exploration came in the form of projects such as the National Science Foundation (NSF) as it looked to seed new frontiers. In 1978, NSF awarded EDUCOM, the predecessor (along with CAUSE) to EDUCAUSE, a grant for $360,000 for the study of computer-based sharing in teaching and research. Almost none of the crystal ball gazers of the mainframe world on the university campuses saw growing interest in active learning strategies. Fewer than 400 persons attended the EDUCOM meetings in the early 1980s, and the organization, later the largest trade organization of higher education and technology, had cash and cash equivalent balances of $7,733 as late as June 1984.[7] No wonder, in retrospect, that few thought the emergence of the Osborne 1 microcomputer on campuses in the spring of 1981 as having much consequence for the future of learning. In the same year, even more obscure in terms of potential for collaboration and learning at the time was the arrival and release of the Pac-Man arcade game in college bars. The 2 solitudes of active learning, portfolios and the rise of microcomputing and graphical interfaces would have to wait almost another decade before the very first popular demonstrations of information technology for learning would become evident in the mainstream of the academy.

From the second half of the 1980s to the early 1990s—in the days of Elm (email client) email, Archie, Veronica, Gopher, Apple Hyperstack multimedia tools, reel-to-reel tape recorders, and incredibly complicated and expensive Broadcast Video U-matic (BVU) format for video recording (and even more arcane editing tools)—an emerging generation of students found interest in relatively esoteric subject matters linked to their experience in uncovering insight and meaning through case methods, role playing, technology-enabled simulation, and simple and crude telecommunication tools. While the link between active learning and the use of connectivity through technology may appear to be obvious today, as late as the birth of commercial Internet in 1993, there was simply little, if any, connection but for the earliest of adopters.

Following 2 years of association with the Kennedy School at Harvard's Pew program in Case Teaching for International Studies, I took a sabbatical in the fall of 1993. Arizona State University (ASU) was interested in my work in using case method as an active learning strategy. As the first versions of something known as the Mosaic Web browser were released in the late fall of 1993, there was only passing interest at ASU in the VIPER Seminar (Virtual International Political Economy Research Seminar project, which I was offering from my garage in Scottsdale. The only thing I asked for was an email alias as *cyperprof@asu.edu*.

It was in the fall of 1993 when the technology was first used in learning. Using simple navigating and collaboration tools developed by Tim Berners

Lee and his colleagues at CERN, along with first-generation digital repository and fetching tools, dozens of students and faculty colleagues in New Zealand, Japan, Colombia, South Africa, the United Kingdom, and across the United States and Canada met asynchronously using 300 baud modems for an entire semester of engaged and active learning. International research and learning teams used emerging asynchronous communications to develop shared curriculum and engage in common research activities. In early 1994, just as the first releases of HTML became available to a few thousand users around the world, leading educators in dozens of programs, from dance to nursing, began looking for a framework for making sense of the new instructional tool set, whose potential was every bit as exciting as it was disruptive and threatening. Gary Wolfe in his article "The (Second Phase of the) Revolution Has Begun" (*Wired Magazine*, October 1994, Issue 2.1) not only portended the demise of Prodigy, AOL, and Compuserv, but also affirmed the audacious suggestion by mavericks such as Marc Andreesen of Netscape that the graphical interface of the browser was going to emerge as the world's standard interface. Enter Learning 1.0 and the 7 principles.

Click frame 5: The day before the revolution

In 1995, with the temperature hovering above 115 degrees, 250 educational technologists got together in Scottsdale, Arizona. The meeting was called under the auspices of the Teaching, Learning, and Technology Group and its founder, Steve Gilbert. Beyond sharing early best practices and anecdotes, a heated conversation unfolded as the group debated the findings of a survey conducted by Kenneth (Casey) Green, founding director of the Campus Computing Project. In late 1994, Green published data, from approximately 800 universities across the United States, from computing directors and other campus technology leaders on the emerging use of technology on the college campus. His findings, presented in his analysis of the then fifth year of his national survey in 1994, caused a stir among the gathered academic technologists. Green noted that while more than 90% of respondents to his national survey agreed that CD-ROMs would be an important source of content and instructional resource of the next several years, there was an emerging surge of activity in leveraging the nascent campus network and its access to the experimental World Wide Web as a platform for academic technology and instruction. In his data, Green uncovered that from 1993 to 1994, there was a jump of nearly 10% in interest in the positioning of the Internet as an instructional platform. Interest in the nascent World Wide Web as a learning platform rose from 5.3

in 1993 to 5.7 (on a 1–7 scale). More provocative was Green's finding that as many as 1 in 12 courses was using email as an instructional tool, where only the year before it had been zero courses. While he hedged his bet by concluding that, "movement of IT into the classroom and college over the past decade has been slow," those gathered in the Arizona sun looked at these findings as empirical evidence of the coming revolution. Indeed, this was the day before the revolution on the college campus. Within 12 months, nearly 100% of all 4-year public and private universities had their first Web sites, more than 1 in 5 courses were using email, and more than 25% of college courses would be using a tool called PowerPoint™ available in the then new Microsoft Office 95 (version 7), based on Windows 95.

In November 1994, Steve Gilbert and his colleague Stephen Ehrmann, at the time associated with Annenberg/CPB, had formed the TLT Group as an activity of the American Association for Higher Education. That fall, they formed the very first Teaching, Learning, and Technology Roundtable (TLTR) in Washington, D.C. with fewer than 100 registrants. They asked what difference these emerging technologies were likely to have on assessment and learning. Gilbert travelled the country running workshops at hundreds of universities, probing and agitating for consideration of new organizational models on the campus to support the growing excitement over the use of these technologies. Gilbert also was concerned and prescient in his insight that the technological imperative unleashed by the Internet might well connect campuses, but unless we were deliberate in the designing of the learning experience we were at risk of disconnecting learners from each other and from their faculty mentors.

Early and uncurbed enthusiasm in the transformational potential of these emergent technologies on the campus led to lively and sometimes heated debate. Language borrowed from the early nineteenth century found its way back into the lexicon of college technologists and their critics. Neo-Luddites such as Postman (Neil Postman, *Amusing Ourselves to Death: Public Discourse in the Age of Show Business*, 2006, Penguin Books), Roszak (Theodore Roszak, http://www.commondreams.org/views04/0128–05.htm), Noble (David Noble, http://communication.ucsd.edu/dl/ddm4.html), and other critics of technology and its impact on the learning ecosystem gave rise to a collective resurgence of re-reading Byron's 1812 defense of Luddites. Neo-Luddites invoked the language of Utopianism to describe the work of French philosopher Jacques Ellul (*The Technological Society*, 1964, Vintage Books) and his historical lineage all the way to Ray Kurzweil's (*The Singularity Is Near: When Humans Transcend Biology*, 2006, Viking Penguin Group), vision of fusing of human and artificial intelligence, while celebrating their own dystopian views of technology.

In the shadows of these important philosophical debates, coupled with growing trepidation on the impact of the outcomes of those debates on the central issues of control over the workplace and identity politics, Ehrmann and Chickering published an important article in the fall of 1996 called "Implementing the Seven Principles: Technology as a Lever."[8] They attempted to shift the debate by asking how one might leverage these new and at best immature technologies to advance student success and the associated value of the research gathered in developing the inventory of the 7 principles for good practice in undergraduate experience.

Click frame 6: Motivating students

What motivated you as a student while you were a university student?

While it is true that many students come to university to have their world changed, that preconditioned state of mind is a necessary but insufficient condition. The journey of learning and developing critical thinking and other skills and competencies is most highly correlated to both structured and informal interactions between students and their faculty mentors. It is, whether we acknowledge it or not, the heart of the learning enterprise. Helping realize a young person's full potential is the art of the mentor and it is the first of the 7 principles. Quality contact between instructors and their students is the single most important predictor associated with motivating and engaging students. When asked retrospectively what accounts for their sense of academic accomplishment as a student during their college years, the literature cited presents the relationship between learner and professor as the single most reported variable (Chickering and Gamson, 1987). Attending university is as much about learning about yourself, what you imagine is possible for yourself and those around you, as the subject matter of the courses and assignments you undertake. As students transition to and through this developmental stage, the experience and reflective wisdom of the faculty person can help students get through the inevitable tough times and keep them motivated and aspiring to new heights. Moreover, beyond the readings, assignments, and exams, students report that their university experience is greatly enriched through the opportunities enabling to them to get to know a few faculty members. Retrospectively, most students report that their intellectual curiosity and civic sensibilities can be traced to their interaction with faculty mentors who encouraged them to think about their values and to reach up to make future plans of their own. How, then, could this new electronic communication technology known as email and the nascent World Wide Web help accelerate and deepen the value of faculty-student relations?

For those who went to university before the advent of email, opportunities for interaction with faculty was limited to scheduled office hours and the ritual of the professor posting a question or an essay topic, a response being submitted in the form of an essay, and then awaiting the marginal red-penned notes, end-comments, and a grade from the professor. The "conversation," if one can call it that, was fairly impoverished and usually did not extend beyond that sequence. Indeed, by the time that ritual was completed, more often than not, the class and the professor were well on their way to other topics and conversations. Beyond the obvious ease of iterative communication between students and their faculty colleagues, Ehrmann and Chickering observed that, "the result [of using email] seems more intimate, protected, and convenient than the more intimidating demands of face-to-face communication with faculty."[9] In one of my early offerings of the virtual political economy seminar on globalization and culture,[10] aboriginal students in Ralph Pettman's course in New Zealand, Native American students in Arizona, and First Nation's students from the University of Guelph, in Ontario, Canada, all found their voices in a clarion set of text-based exchanges with their faculty and peers, sharing poetry, stories, and community views of the steamrolling effect of globalization on themselves and their communities. The intimacy and power of those exchanges had a profound impact on all involved in the seminar. Upon reflection, the relative anonymity of asynchronous communication helped to accentuate the value of the relative immediacy of asynchronous electronic communication that nevertheless privileged the reflective practice of writing. Different from students interacting in face-to-face classes, or waiting at the end of the class for a word with the professor, the practice of exchanging letters brought with it an opportunity to ask deeper questions and call on more authentic exchanges from both the students involved and the faculty, who were early adopters of the experimental platform.

As Ehrmann and Chickering (1996) surveyed the landscape of the emergent technology, while they continued to privilege the hierarchical nature and value of direct faculty-student relations, they were correct in highlighting the powerful impact of asynchronous learning made possible by electronic communication, in particular the growing ubiquity of email as a service on the university campus. They also were quick to point to the emerging treasure of electronic repositories of learning materials that faculty could make available to each other and to their students through the Web. Among the many challenges to this exciting new reality was the question of managing the scaling of the practice of electronic exchange. The ease of communication quickly generated an expectation that faculty would be available 24X7 and that virtual office time grew to infinity through the artifact of the email inbox. More subtle at the time, the hierarchy and associated deference that faculty enjoyed for hundreds of years as educational oracles were about to be challenged. Finally, if faculty-student communication could be enhanced through direct email communication, the relationships also could be abused and the relationship and role of professor and student could be ignored, with students using the same mode of communication to circumvent the received power and authority of the student-faculty relationship. Learning 1.0 on the Internet was exciting but full of discontinuities.

For nearly a decade, the reliability, robustness, and capacity of the technological infrastructure served as a significant rate-limiting factor. While there was no shortage of great expectations, the ability of the faculty and the support community to advance and help deepen the quality of mentoring relationships, augmented or enabled through electronic communications, was shortchanged because of the maturity of the technology itself. Innovators among the faculty and staff became conditioned to the 'best effort' and 'work around' in helping to manage their faculty-student relationships: managing, but not' really advancing the mentoring role that many hoped would emerge as a result of the new, exciting, but largely immature technology. Early showcasing events would routinely start with a caveat and sometimes an apology—something to the effect, "we ended up defaulting to a sub-optimal educational goal or learning approach because, in the end, the technology software, hardware, or network environment would not support the goal or approach."

Second-generation, advanced (switched) networking technologies, and more robust and enterprise-focused software solutions entered the enterprise around the turn of the century. More than any other technological factor, these new university networks made possible not only a more reliable infrastructure but also one that could sustain the explosion of creative and innovative practices and applications that quickly followed. Voice and video joined data as modalities of communication enabled over the network. In addition, the enabling speed and reliability (to support quality of service for voice and video) enabled and supported the acceleration of electronic commerce and transaction technology that moved beyond "just managing" relationships between client and service provider. The twin developments of using technology to advance the value of customer intimacy (knowing how to begin to customize online experiences at scale through Web sites such as Amazon.com, Progressive Insurance, and Real Networks,) and of advancing the value of self-service (and ultimately "pro-sumer" paradigms) together set the stage for the era of Web 2.0. The challenge became to design new ways of leveraging the sage wisdom of the mentoring faculty and the augmentation of student learning.

In this new era, whose impact we are just beginning to fully experience and understand, advancing faculty-student relationships mediated through technology has begun to shift from managing students to managing the transactions between students and faculty. The insight offered by Chickering and Gamson in the mid-1980s was less about the ability to have more faculty-student contact (a necessary but insufficient condition) and more to do with the quality of the relationship and the nature of the mentoring role. Email in the Learning 1.0 era could be more intimate than some forms of traditional twentieth-century faculty-student interaction. Some students and faculty found reflecting and expressing themselves in the asynchronous modality easier than in the more typical interaction that occurs during the more standard office hour or after-class scrum. Oftentimes, however, the nature of those communications was largely unidirectional, replicating the asymmetric relationship between student and professor in the traditional classroom. The current generation of students still may be socialized to defer to their more senior faculty colleagues but they are the products of a participatory culture. While some may despair the "wisdom of the crowds" sensibilities that can contribute to the erosion of the traditional role and identity of the expert, new and powerful learning relationships can and are being integrated into the student experience. Faculty can resist the participatory culture or use it as a starting point in building impactful relationships with their students. From my vantage point, the most exciting part about Web 2.0 tools is the faculties' ability to leverage these participatory-enabling technologies and combine them with creative pedagogies to open an almost endless number of paths for deeper learning, discovery, and exploration. The emergence of electronic portfolios has allowed students to archive and share their technology-enabled learning outcomes in environments that approach authentic assessment and learning. Because the culture is participatory, and students come with experience and some expertise, knowledge sharing and cocreation are very much part of the underlying zeitgeist of this generation of learners. This is an important precondition for supporting and encouraging engaged learning. If we make a concerted effort to embrace and extend our mentoring roles as faculty leveraging these tools, we may not only produce students motivated to research, motivated to take responsibility for their learning, motivated to understand and experience the value of team building and teamwork but perhaps some longer-term impact as well.

Public support for the role of higher education institutions in our society is on a 25-year (or more) secular decline. From my own vantage point, an important part of the credibility gap is the growing sense that we in higher education, need to make clearer our relevance to, and engagement with, our students. Public support for higher education is at the heart of democracy and, as such, the risk of continuing diminution of public support is not trivial. The inherent resistance to change is not surprising but the stakes are higher than ever before. Web 2.0 makes possible a more relevant learning experience for students to connect their academic experiences in the formal learning environment to the participatory culture that surrounds them and now competes for attention cycles with class time. The emergence of the participatory culture is itself the product of more than 40 years of broad societal movement associated with postindustrial society and the emergence of the information age economy. For students, the challenge is to find connections between their information-rich, multisensory, multitasking, discovery-based informal learning environment and the rather static, hierarchical, single-threaded stand-up traditional learning environment that still dominates most universities. For many students, there is a growing disconnect between their formal education associated with classes and seat time and all the other time spent learning through informal, peer and discovery-based learning. We should be careful to ask which they find more valuable. The opportunity to leverage is the profound engagement that students have in the overall learning environment across most of the day. Engaging students by extending their motivation and commitment to their social networking worlds stands at the core of the opportunity to deepen the quality and value of the relationship between faculty mentor and student learner in the twenty-first century.

Faculty mentorship in the Learning 2.0 era combines 2 arcs of activity: (1) choreographing a wide range of learning opportunities and (2) providing formative assessment, feedback, validation, guidance, and the transference of the value of inquiry, reflection, and positive skepticism. Michael Wesch's project-based world simulation program engages as many as 400 undergraduate anthropology students in the use of video and rich-media technology.[11] Students are immersed in the discovery of ethnographic methods through the development of group-based project work that enables students to see the world in their own image through the assembly of video artifacts. With millions of downloads, the final capstone video products are a combination of collective portraiture, performance art, ethnographic studies, and critical thinking. His extraordinarily popular class projects, such as "A Vision of Students Today,"[12] have served to inspire, provoke, and lead to ongoing dialog among students and the academic community attempting to better understand the intersection of the ivory tower in the era of social networks. As students and their faculty colleagues engage in mentoring relationships, their reflective practices are an integrated part of the learning experience, enabled through a workgroup blog that invites comments and critical reflection.

Ed Lamoureaux (aka Professor Beliveau, as his avatar is known in the virtual world platform Second Life) conducts 2 of his communications courses on field research "inworld," that is to say, in the virtual world. He has turned the emergent space of the Second Life virtual world (with approximately 13 million residents and an economy of nearly $1 million a day) into the subject of research and learning among his students. Theirs is a community of practice committed to a better understanding of virtual worlds through the lens of participant observation.[13] Lamoureaux is mentoring his students in communications and new media as well as his own peers (at Bradley and throughout the academy), in a new form of faculty development and support in learning from, and participating in, the creation of best practices of mentoring in the virtual world.

Because social networking technologies can bridge the formal and informal education worlds, many members of the faculty have used pervasive Web 2.0 tools, such as Facebook, to engage directly with students in order to encourage and prod them into considering extending their experiences to various causes, groups, and educational experiments in the emergent social learning space. Another means of faculty mentoring is the extending of writing across curricula to the blogosphere. Many students are well versed in the participatory culture of blogging and related forms of self-expression and authorship. Offering students the opportunity to practice the integration of research skills, critical thinking, and reflection through blogging affords the faculty opportunities for formative feedback and interactive exchanges with an individual student and/or a small team of students. Early critiques of Learning 1.0 included accentuating the differences between face-to-face learning and learning using asynchronous environments. Today, faculty use skype, and a growing menu of videoconferencing and conference tools to both extend and deepen their roles as mentors outside the formal learning environment. Faculty also use a hybrid approach to take advantage of face-to-face or voice-to-voice communications as they relate to learning objectives and faculty sensibilities of the value of such environments. Other faculty have used tags and wiki projects to support engaged and participatory student experiences. At the same time, while these tools support co-creation methodologies for learning, they also enable faculty to offer incisive interventions to support specific learning objectives. In addition, the availability of these new tools enables other forms of learning, such as peer-to-peer learning.

While email, IM, and Twitter can be an important part of the mentoring role of faculty throughout and beyond the student experience on campus, new opportunities in the Learning 2.0 portfolio are available. The Learning 2.0 environment can more readily support scaling to keep the faculty mentoring role front and center in shaping the learning and life experiences of young people who come to universities and colleges to have their world changed.

Click frame 7: Reciprocity

There was a time when student peer-to-peer activity did not mean illegal downloading of copyright materials across the college high-speed network but rather a framework for student team collaboration. In Chickering and Gamson's framework, learning in structured teamwork was modeled not only for life after university but also augmented the journey. In their words, "Good learning, like good work, is collaborative and social, not competitive and isolated."[14] While the tradition of the solitary scholar sitting between stacks of books in a dust-filled library may conjure up a classic image of the goal of being a student, the cumulative research challenged the notion that the only way to learn was to move into the library carrel at the beginning of the semester and throw away the key. Team efforts, discussion groups, study forums, and other structured interaction strategies help to sharpen one's own ideas by sharing and reacting to feedback from peers. Having to articulate, communicate, defend, and reflect on one's ideas and insights as a university student, whether in class or in the spillover to the cafeteria, is an important part of learning how to develop active listening skills while unlearning the habit of not working with others.

Ehrmann and Chickering expressed some surprise that computer-based tools, specifically email, served as an important enabler of peer-to-peer collaboration for students. Structuring learning to leverage the asynchronous nature of email made possible, for perhaps the first time ever, a meaningful and efficient near-time option for both the busy working adult student, as well as the student who works part time—a growing reality that well over half, and closer to 3 out of 5 students, were balancing their university experience with the need to work, at least part-time.[15] Enabling students to use simple electronic repositories for checking in and checking out peer-reviewed drafts of essays is both powerful and efficient. Allowing students, across geographic space, to collaborate together was both innovative and potentially transformational. As faculty experimented, it became clear that a wide range of cooperative learning activities, from research and writing to copyediting and presentation development, were all now readily possible through rather simple and effective technology-mediated learning environments. Students found that working together in teams allowed them to individually contribute their personal strengths to the team while learning from their peers. It also became clear that having to prepare and help your peers understand some theory, case, or research project was a valuable way to actually assess the materials oneself. Perhaps most profound was the growing realization that the network itself was to have a deep transformational impact. Students in places that were generally cut off from the rest of the world could, if they were motivated and guided by their faculty mentors, work with peers in Europe, Latin America, or North America on the full breadth of the learning enterprise. The global village of learners was being enabled by fiber optical networks, visionary faculty, and other university thought leaders. As the global village becomes real, surely the global political economy would evolve to fully leverage the network to support financial transactions, product design, and, ultimately, a more fully integrated world economy. Forward-thinking universities saw the opportunities both to support emerging national education markets, such as Vietnam and China, as well as to leverage the network to offer well educated nationals opportunities to participate as tutors, mentors, and/or peers with others plugged in across the world. In the mid-1990s, bold new ventures and consortia began to sprout up offering new business models to attract a new generation of learners. They, in turn, could connect to one another and be part of the end of the traditional development paradigm of first world versus third world, us versus them. The new communication paradigm created its own divide but it was, and remains, a provocative platform for accelerating learning opportunities. The first fruits back in the Learning 1.0 era were suggestive and pregnant with possibilities. Students collaborated in teams across vast geographies to deliver work. But, as often is the case, what we came to know in that first wave of peer-to-peer learning also served to limit the imagination of the possible. Taking education to the edge of the possible ran into early calcification of the technology-mediated learning world.

In the burst of activity in the Learning 1.0 era, form very quickly followed function, and there we got stuck. Networks allowed efficient transfer and exchange of text and, later, low-quality images. Our educational technology solutions were likewise fixed on extending the long tradition of the written word into cyberspace. In December 1995, Silicon Graphics Inc. (SGI) announced a product whose code name was Cosmo.[16] At the annual meeting of the National Association of Broadcasters in the spring of 1996, Cosmo was advertised as "enabling the second Web" and purported to support the very first rich and streaming media over IP network solution. With the assistance of chief engineer, Michael Corgan, I wrote a position paper which outlined the value of enabling a peer-to-peer student network based on student-created, rich-media content. My short-term goal was to justify the acquisition of an SGI mediabase server solution. Together, the team of instructional designers, engineers, educational technologists, and pioneering faculty colleagues, such as James Manley and Liliane Fucaloro, created MediaVision at Cal Poly in 1997. MediaVision was one of the first large-scale, university-based IP streaming media projects. For 2 years, we traveled the land (and the world), with streaming media server and network ports and client browsers in tow, encouraging and cajoling those who would listen to support rich-media content creation by and for students. Although international textbook publishers, software executives, high-ranking politicians, and the cognoscenti among the higher education and technology leadership all supported Internet text-based student collaboration, almost no one fully grasped the potential of peer-to-peer rich media. Saul Landau, award-winning documentary filmmaker, writer, poet, social activist, and policy analyst, moved from Washington, D.C. to Southern California to take the first Hugh O. LaBounty Chair of Applied Interdisciplinary Knowledge at Cal Poly Pomona. Landau, working along with his students, spent 3 years on studying film, art, lighting, literature, and the politics of the lives of the young people in and around Pomona, California, The result was a series of award-winning telenovelas with titles such as "Doing It Pomona Style," "Life Is Good," and "You Can't Cross the Same River Twice"—all written, scored, and produced by students.[17] Students involved in the project not only received recognition for their work, a number of them also continued to engage in the creative media arts world and/or community activism after graduation. The power of peer-to-peer, rich-media collaboration among students would wait another nearly 10 years before it would harness the technology to engage students in collaborative digital storytelling as an integral part of the university curriculum.

Landau's innovative work as a faculty mentor and champion of peer-to-peer learning, combining student cocreation with MediaVision as a platform technology, included early experiments in what would emerge nearly 15 years later as the core of the Learning 2.0 era. YouTube and iTunes U are the most prominent examples of a platform that allows student teams (along with faculty-mentored efforts) to publish a wide range of rich-media content as expressions of their interest in both exploratory culture, as well as in authentic learning outcomes.

Learning 2.0 began, in some ways, not so much as a logical follow-on response to the Learning 1.0 world, but rather as a response to an important deficit that the university world would need to confront in the late 1990s. From the student-centered view of the world, as Web 2.0 emerged, early editing tools that enabled sampling, editing, and ripping of music to share with friends generated a tidal wave of peer-to-peer activity. Of course, not all of the activity was ethical although it certainly enabled plenty of opportunity to discuss the ethics of intellectual property, cultural expression, and its relationship to human creativity and the entertainment economy. Educational projects and methodologies, such as digital storytelling provided a creative and ethical framework for encouraging students to work together to create original or near original content.[18] Digital storytelling, encourages students to tell personal stories about themselves and their families. As variously practiced, the technique encourages practice in research, oral interviewing, outlining, writing, peer critique, and the production of short video stories.[19] The results can help students understand the power of peer learning as well as gain insights into the paradoxes of peer-to-peer network activities. One of the central features of the Web 2.0/Learning 2.0 era is the shift from local, campus-based hosting of content and tools to services hosted on the Web, such as YouTube and iTunes U. As student produced content (as well as content created by faculty and staff) reaches a global audience through these externalized, service-based solutions, the campus technology community is grappling with how to confront and perhaps leverage these service platforms. The consumerization of these powerful peer-to-peer learning ecosystems challenges the once advanced and privileged role that campus technology once offered. Email, once a sacred piece of campus-owned technology, has been superseded by 'cloud' services from Yahoo, Google, and Microsoft. Many on campus sought to recapture eyeballs on campus through the introduction of portal technologies. With the exception of some transactional services that are still locked behind the campus fire walls, portals are melting away. More flexible, consumer based frameworks for gathering, assembling, and reassembling content and experiences are the essence of social networks. While campus IT administrators often are preoccupied with how to lock down content, these new platforms are almost entirely outside the authority of the campus technology community. Students are voting with their feet and the clicks of their mice as their expectation of being able to extend their interest in creating and sharing content across the blurred lines dividing formal and informal education while at university is well served by these external platform technologies.

About the same time, around 2005, universities were learning from their community and business partners that the world had changed. Universities now were being asked to help prepare students to work in teams and have skills such as project management, cross-functional organization, and disciplinary exposure, along with a demonstrated ability to communicate well with one another. Students began using Web 2.0 tools to respond to these requirements. While there are notable headline-grabbing exceptions, students began teaching their faculty colleagues the opportunities afforded by these new tools to advance the learning experience. Early peer-learning communities emerged leveraging integrated platforms such as iCohere[20] or Eluminate.[21] As Web 2.0 emerged, faculty and instructional designers began to realize another important characteristic of the technology with implications for the academy. Students wanted more flexibility in designing their peer-based learning environments. Large, complex, and integrated environments began to give way to frameworks that offered not only integrated tools but also relatively easy ways of adding personalized services from other social networking environments. Students could use MySpace, Zoho, Yahoo, Microsoft Live, Google Apps for Education, Ning,[22] Pageflakes,[23] or any number of Ajax-enabled portal-like frameworks as starting points for their peer-to-peer activities, and then snap in relevant community learning tools and other widgets. Using a range of tools, from GoogleDocs for file sharing to mashup projects (combing geographical information systems such as GoogleMaps and their APIs to hook into other data sources), students have helped each other and have contributed to the fashioning and designing of the Learning 2.0 era. Inherent in much of the participatory peer-learning experiences was the growing realization that passive, book only learning needed to be blended or mashed up with a range of other active learning strategies.

Click frame 8: Active

There was a time, not so long ago, when experiential and hands-on learning were radical concepts within the university curriculum. When Chickering and Gamson pointed out that learning was not a spectator sport, they were contrarians in a mainstream academic environment in which the faculty-centered view of the learning ecosystem was largely unchallenged. Here is the essence of their analysis. "Students do not learn much just sitting in class listening to teachers, memorizing prepackaged assignments, and spitting out answers. They must talk about what they are learning, write reflectively about it, relate it to past experiences, and apply it to their daily lives. They must make what they learn part of themselves." (Chickering and Gamson, 1987). (*http://honolulu. hawaii.edu/intranet/committees/FacDevCom/guidebk/teachtip/7princip.htm*)

Borrowing from traditional technologies and their associated apprentice approach to learning by doing, champions of the learning with technology 1.0 era turned to the manner in which new technology could enrich and augment these tried and true approaches. Use of technology to support real-time problem solving for statistics courses, rather than the tradition of proofs and drills at the chalkboard, was one example. Experiments that were too dangerous, costly, and/or difficult to carry out in the real world could be simulated using new computer-modeling technology. Finally, in surveying the way in which new technology had been leveraged to implement this third principle in the framework, Ehrmann and Chickering pointed out the value of running computer-based 'if-then' scenarios in various sciences (and by extension, in other disciplines). Simulations would allow students to experiment with, for example, Darwin's finches to better understand experimental outcomes and would give them in simulation exercises the ability to manipulate the various variables that led to species evolution, survival, and decline. Under the leadership of Chuck Schneebeck and Lou Zweier (who had both recently moved from Cal State Long Beach to Sonoma State), the new California State University Center for Distributed Learning began to build simulation engines and collect a growing number of active learning applets and other learning materials in an emerging repository. The project, appropriately known as the Multimedia Educational Resource for Learning and Online Teaching (MERLOT), ran on a platform architected by Jim Spohrer, back then a scientist at Apple Computers (and now director of IBM's Almaden Research Lab), underwritten by NSF funding for Authoring Tools and an Educational Object Economy (EOE). While not all the learning objects in MERLOT were active learning applets, MERLOT was and may very well still be the most ambitious effort to gather and make available peer-reviewed faculty learning tools that can be used. But learning objects were largely conceived of as instructional aids to support the faculty. At the time, too little thought went into the design of repositories that would active become learning objectives and support peer to peer learning opportunities.

How to apply active learning strategies to educational technology to support student success in areas of traditionally difficult subjects, such as physics or other basic sciences, became a hot topic for many disciplinary societies. As the world of science becomes more complex, science education itself becomes more of a challenge, especially if it is taught in the same and largely passive and bookish manner of earlier generations. At world-class institutions such as MIT, the problem was well understood. Award winning and distinguished faculty members such as John Belcher were grappling with the mismatch between traditional teaching methods and how students actually learn. Despite great lecturers, attendance at MIT's freshman physics course dropped to 40% of enrolled students by the end of the term, with a 10% failure rate. Even though MIT freshmen had good math skills, they often had a tough time grasping the concepts of first-year physics. Traditional lectures, although excellent for many purposes, did not convey concepts well because of their passive nature.[24] Belcher and his colleagues launched a multiyear, multimillion dollar investigation and reinvention of the physical, technological, and pedagogical underpinnings of physics instruction under the auspices of MIT's Technology Enabled Active Learning (TEAL) project.[25] There remains much work still to be done to abstract the findings and consider the challenge of replicating, scaling, and identifying the required investment of resources and talents to fully realize and sustain our understanding of technology-enabled active learning across disciplines.

In the Learning 2.0 era, the portfolio of active learning scenarios and opportunities is nearly boundless. Student sensibilities regarding participatory culture makes the pursuit of active learning strategies a compelling undertaking. Blending lessons learned from MIT's TEAL project with the proliferation of social networking and Web 2.0 technologies makes experimentation and prototyping relatively inexpensive and relatively easy to introduce for purposes of feedback and iterative insight. The core insight is to provide students with the opportunity to apply theory to practice and have the opportunity to fail and learn from their errors as well as to celebrate the learning moments when their hypotheses are confirmed or affirmed.

Click frame 9: Feedback

Although they did not use the turn of phrase, Chickering and Gamson laid the early groundwork for what might be termed a "learning genome" project. Instead of approaching learning as hitting the "midpoint" of a cohort of distinctive learners with different learning interests, aptitudes, and degrees of interest, Chickering and Gamson called for an authentic learning and reflective environment based on individualized assessments of existing knowledge and competencies. The journey of university education combined research skills, the development of critical faculties, judgment, and the craft of synthetic reasoning and composition. Timely and salient feedback on effort, coupled with opportunity for self-reflection and evaluation, were the key to a good education.

In addition to email feedback, Learning 1.0 instructional technologies included using word processors for annotated commentary and real-time simulation engines, providing students with opportunities to witness the impact of manipulating variables in an experimental model. In 1987, sociologist Rodney Stark sent me an email on bitnet, introducing me to a new statistical software package that he claimed could be placed on one of the brand new 3.5-inch floppy disks and put on a notebook computer and brought into class to teach interactive statistical analysis. MicroCase statistical software package was among a new breed of software tools that provided opportunities to bring real world scenarios and data into the classroom. Students and faculty could engage in Socratic methods of learning, even in social science statistics. Accessing real and substantial data sets, such as the General Social Survey and cross-national electoral survey data sets, allowed the class to come alive with instant feedback on theories and social science hypotheses. While the pain and phobia around learning social science statistics did not melt into air, student versions of the program available in the newest IBM PCjr lab on campus provided the opportunity to experience computer-aided learning in testing hypotheses and gave an insight into the importance of statistical analysis. By the early 1990s, a wide range of new learning labs were developed, including foreign language labs, and group decision-making labs were developed to advance the idea that computer-aided learning could provide near instant feedback for individual and grouplearning experiences. While personalized study plans, authentic assessment, and learning portfolios would mature over time, Learning 1.0 instructional technology marked a major and valuable improvement over the traditional, paper-based feedback system that had existed for generations.

As we fast forward to the Learning 2.0 era, we notice considerable debate on the value of the new and contested assumption that more and quicker feeds lead to any additional learning outcomes. The ability of Netflix's or Amazon. com's scoring system to offer feedback on student work, professors or courses, or peer activity is not the same as reflective critiques and constructive feedback. The wisdom of the crowds is neither the answer to every question nor the equifinal object of derision and disdain of those who offer critical insights. But, at times, such wisdom comes from people who are themselves unable or unwilling to take the time to offer authentic, timely, or constructive feedback. There is room for using Twitter and IM for some kinds of feedback. At the same time, where appropriate, thoughtful red pen markups on a draft term paper also have a place in the feedback portfolio. The important consideration, which we have learned from speaking to students when they are interviewed on leaving the university, is that although they generally are positive about the knowledge and wisdom of their faculty colleagues, they also are equally consistent that they do not always receive the timely feedback they expected as part of their experiences.

Click frame 10: Time

Time plus effort equals learning. More than just learning the lesson of managing one's time, Chickering and Gamson understood that motivating students to spend more intentional time and energy could lead to a qualitatively different learning experience. Combined with experiential and action-oriented learning, intentional, time on task may not be the most efficient path to teaching and learning to the test. Nevertheless, well-managed use of time on task, combined with the pursuit of deeper learning moments, has the virtue of allowing students to reflect on present knowledge and connect it to previous insights and of building the ability to test the connections between theory and everyday experience. There are, to be sure, a number of critical time efficiency conditions that became immediately apparent as networks connected people and machines to learning resources. Online library resources became available, opening up untold amounts of learning and discovery opportunities. Searching for physical or electronic learning resources also became much more efficient than the tedious practice of learning how to use bound volumes of *Chem Abstracts*, ERIC, and the various disciplinary citation indices, microfiche, or microfilm.

Every year, graduate students from all over the world email, call, or interview me face-to-face to learn about the pathway to becoming a chief information officer. The story I tell is largely based on my experience of using technology in the curriculum as a hook to engage students with subject matter that might otherwise be of little or no interest. When Danny Goodman published version 2 of HyperCard, I could not wait to get it into the hands of my upper-division undergraduate students who were working on commodity flows in the international economy. Apple's Media Lab, co-led by Kristina Woolsey (author of *VizAbility: Visual Language Capability for the Digital Age*, Course Technology) provided visualization software tools that allowed stories to be told in both linear and nonlinear fashion. Students in those courses were intrigued and challenged as they realized that the traditional tyranny of the author in writing narratives was about to undergo a radical change. Systems humanists like Ted Nelson had predicted as early as 1960 that hypertextuality would be a largely disruptive force in fields as disparate as literature and computer science. Hyperlinking allowed authors and those using the tools to explore both sequential narratives (known in the post-modernist literature an tyranny of the author) as well as to follow a more organic, if initially haphazard, path through the hypercard links that predated online hyperlinks known later as universal resource links. Time and again, students found themselves working in the computer lab through the night as they became entirely immersed in the treasure hunt of this new playful world in which new language needed to be invented to describe what kinds of learning was being experienced. Joe Lambert, the pioneer of intergenerational digital learning, helped many of us understand that storytelling appealed to a basic human need to spend time sharing narratives on things that mattered to us. Digital storytelling was an important tool to help students spend time reflecting on their own experiences and their own pathways to learn whether the stories were playful, serious, personal, or the synthesis of the experience of others.

The long-term impact of time on task mediated by networks and computers began to take shape in the early 1990s when Seymour Papert, Sherry Turkle, and a new generation of students including Mitch Resnick and Yasmin Kafai, among others, began to glean insights. Through the lenses of observation, experimentation, and theory, they observed that serious computer play was helping shape and perhaps irrevocably alter the human brain and our socialization within the family, education, and broader group identities. These prophets saw an evolving human condition in which reality would be the blending of the physical and the synthetic worlds. We are ever closer to approaching that condition.

Click frame 11: Expectations

I remember when my friend Max started programming games for a small start-up called Apple, around 1978.

Like a lot of young people in my circles in the late 1970s, Max was creative, very smart, and driven by the "Yiddish mama" syndrome, which is a technical term for high expectations, bookended at home and at school. At the same time, the world around us was in transition. I don't think Max ever became a doctor (although his sister did), a lawyer, or a dentist. However, Max was part of a new pioneering group that was taking early gaming programming[26] and bringing it to the desktop—with new, 2-tone color palettes, exploding treasure chests, and sounds that were, well, different. Max had internalized the expectations around him and there was no stopping him. I always thought Max was different, a kind of boy genius. Ten years later, I realized 2 important things: first, that gaming was going to go online and, second, that, when it did, it would become a very powerful new paradigm for collaboration that would simulate an infinite number of realities from chess to flying airplanes, from medical simulators to revisiting and experiencing the making of history. Gaming would move in parallel from human-machine interfaces to human-human interfacing. The prospects for learning were significant. Gil Brum and a multidisciplinary team at Cal Poly Pomona used gaming platforms to reinvent and recreate a comprehensive, integrated undergraduate science curriculum in the early 1990s. Building on his pioneering work with Smalltalk, Alan Kay along with his colleagues developed Squeak in about the same time frame as a gaming programming language for kids to inspire, provoke, and make possible experiments that could be designed, tested, and evaluated by and for young people. The broader educational consequence of the development of an industry that would supersede the economy of the Hollywood motion picture industry with hundreds of millions participating in these communities of practice was and is the prospect of learners taking responsibility for their own learning in active and experiential fashion.

Expecting students to perform well becomes a self-fulfilling prophecy. This was the essence of Chickering and Gamson's sixth practice. In their 1996 article mentioned above, Ehrmann and Chickering conveyed the insight offered by faculty innovators around the world. Students, as it turns out, were stimulated by the knowledge that their final products would not be just read by their professor and returned for filing in a college folder in the garage. It has been a decade since Google enabled easy search and as a result became the platform enabler of mass collaboration; as a result, students have been taking extra time, effort, and care as they realized that their final college capstone project in their term would be published on the Internet. The same was true in the world of multimedia, digital video production, and digital art and music. The barriers to entry and distribution were still relatively high but communicating that the end product would find new audiences made the process of discovery and the creative process of production an intriguing exercise. Education professor Doreen Nelson, who borrows extensively from the philosopher/educator John Dewey, called that experience the process of designing never-before-seen things. In her applied research work in city-building education, Nelson demonstrates that engaged learning leads to a huge sense of pride, ownership, and a deeper capacity to relate one set of learning experiences to other contexts and situations. Challenging learners to invent never-before-seen objects, projects and experiences for Nelson is at the heart of the education enterprise. More often than not, as Doreen Nelson's philosophy helped to inform, learners step up and routinely surprise the educators with their curiosity, perseverance, and ingenuity.

In the emerging Learning 2.0 era, faculty and other mentors have an opportunity to seize the pulse and impulse of the participatory culture of the current generation of college-age students and harness it through communicating higher expectations. While it is rather common to hear faculty bemoan student readiness for their studies, my own experience has been contrarian. Indeed, the discipline and the rigor associated with learning have always been contextual to a broader set of circumstances. Communicating high expectations, along with many other elements in the teaching portfolio, is causally related to the outcome one can expect to receive. Among the examples of raising expectations and the concomitant goal of having learners take more active responsibility for their learning, one of the most provocative is the emergence of virtual worlds. From Second Life to Wonderland and Croquet, these emergent learning spaces extend the value of communicating high expectations that were once framed in terms of sharing a Webpage or a multimedia presentation with a broader audience. Virtual worlds are big business (over $1 billion of investment in the 12-month period from October 2006 to October 2007, *http://www.virtualworldsmanagement.com/2007/index.html*). They are also a bold frontier for education. According to congressional testimony by Lawrence Johnson, CEO of the nonprofit education group New Media Consortium, "Over the past two years, an estimated 4,000 educational projects have emerged within Second Life alone, and of the 13,400 regions in Second Life that were active at the time of this writing, more than 1,400 of them were being operated by bona fide educational institutions"[27]. The broad experimentation includes dozens of immersive, high-fidelity examples associated with a wide range of academic subjects—health care and wellness, biotechnology, nanotechnology, cross-cultural communications, global warming, human rights education, gaming, cultures and the arts.

The real value, from an educator's perspective, may well be less about time on task, peer learning, and other obvious observations that many others have made. At their best, virtual worlds' education is an invitation to the learner to help conceive, design, build, use, and develop a community of practice. The scripting tools today look like html did in 1993. For digital natives, building gaming environments, although not a pervasive literacy, is not a foreign language either. Incentivizing and raising expectations that students will use these new, powerful, massive, online communities to create their own learning experiences, along with giving opportunities for critical reflection, is a powerful and provocative use of the technology platform for educational outcomes. Those faculty and teachers engaged in this type of never-before-seen, project-based learning are finding that their ability to communicate high expectations are leading to engaged learning by students in ways that are additive in terms of learning outcomes. Research, writing, and presentation are being combined with project management, innovation, creativity, team building, and play representing new forms of literacy for the twenty-first century. As, we turn to the last of Chickering and Gamson's elements in their framework, perhaps the most interesting observation is that the emergent Learning 2.0 suite of learning tools are touching new and different learners.

Click frame 12: Diversity

Not all students are going to find the use of Web 2.0 learning tools of value to their learning style. According to Chickering and Gamson, different students learn differently. Understanding that students need various opportunities to show their different skills and talents is a mark of a good teacher. Helping stretch the student to new and unfamiliar territory becomes doable once we understand where an individual learner starts and how they learn. Early efforts in the Learning 1.0 era to leverage the new World Wide Web revealed core insights. New learners found their voices and new learning communities emerged. Geography became less of a constraint. Sheizaf Rafaeli, then of the Hebrew University in Jerusalem, was among the first communication theorists to outline the multiple-sensory appeal of the Internet.[28] As early as 1996, Rafaeli wrote, "Text, voice, pictures, animation, video, virtual-reality motion codes, even smell, are all already being conveyed on the Net. . . . The Net's capacity for addressing senses far surpasses that of any other medium. In a sense, this indicates that the medium serves less than ever before in a constraining, guiding role." (http://jcmc.indiana.edu/vol1/issue4/rafaeli.html) In 1987, I had a student whose name was Bob. Bob was blind. He once invited me to his dorm room to show me how he was using new technology to play back the notes he was typing in on his Braille computer keyboard. Bob listened back to his notes at nearly twice the speed of normal hearing. He supplemented it with his Braille printer that allowed him a second sensory experience, also with enormous proficiency. He was active in every facet of the class experience. Bob graduated summa cum laude. As a teacher, his experience taught me that new learners could both access and excel in the university environment.

Of course, some learners who excel in traditional learning environments have not found the multisensory appeal to be of much value to their own experience. For important cross-sections of the population for whom learning in general and certainly postsecondary learning in particular were inaccessible, the new Learning 2.0 learning tools make it possible—for some, for the very first time—to access, engage, and become part of the learning community and its broad value for supporting and advancing personal reflection, civic engagement, and appreciation for science, discovery, and aesthetics. My 20-year-old daughter is autistic and lives in a very different world. She has been a parallel learner since she was 2 years old and has a complex of communication challenges consistent with young people on the autism spectrum. I marvel at her skill and aptitude in using Facebook not only for communication with her peers but also for engaging in and appreciating the value of research. Her competency in navigating the world of YouTube for both entertainment and education is remarkable. While she faces some apparent social and communication discomforts in her physical world, she is quick to share photos and provide entirely appropriate tagging and commentaries on Flickr and to socialize with apparent ease in Second Life.

The spectrum from typical learner to learners with differences is immeasurably wide. As we understand better how learners with differences are able to access the treasuries of learning opportunity through technology-mediated tools, we also better understand how typical students learn and discover. Text-to-audio technologies for blind learners turn out to be of enormous value to a wide cross-section of typical auditory learners as well. Visualization tools employed to structure learning for dyslexic learners turn out to be a very valuable tool for visual learners across the population. There is a way to go to realize the full potential of a learning genome project to support personalized education. Understanding and probing how different people learn with the new set of tools in Learning 2.0 is an important contribution to this broader and more ambitious effort.

Transition to Learning 2.0

Every good story has a plot, heroes (and antiheroes), drama, crisis, and resolution. Even if I were a much better story teller with better technique, rhetorical flare, offering more epiphanies and pithy insights, the point of this story is less about revealing a surprise ending or a grand synthesis. Rather, Learning 2.0 is part of a journey that we are on. Our multifaceted worlds (private-public, formal-informal, analog-digital) and all the associated norms, rules, and other principles are at once convergent and emergent in a dialectical manner. Designing learning opportunities to leverage the portfolio of tools now at our disposal will take new forms of educational leadership across the university.

We are less in control of the learning environment than ever before. We can bemoan and critique that reality and/or we can create bold, new opportunities to help the next generation of learners and researchers seize those opportunities to reflect and discover approaches to solve and support the many different challenges facing the human condition and the broader ecosystem in the twenty-first century. If learning is a journey, Learning 2.0 promises to be as disruptive as it is promising over the next 20 years. Embracing the ambiguity of that reality is the last and perhaps only insight I have to offer.

Conclusion and Future Directions

The emergence of the network society and the process of transformation of new information and communication technologies have created a paradigm shift evolving mankind into an information knowledge society.[1] These technologies have changed education by creating new fields of study and new disciplines.[2] The impact has created a new outlook for distance education, creating expanded learning environments for learners both now and in the future.[3]

Key technological trends that will shape the future of knowledge society:

- Broadband Internet access is becoming more widespread, especially in well-advanced economies, driven by peer-to-peer file sharing and always on features
- Weblogs or blogs are becoming a major source of information and communication for internet users
- Podcasting could be a driver for mobile learning
- Short Message Services (SMS) and the Multimedia Messaging Services (MMS) are also becoming important providers of new content and offer ways for people to be mobile and share information
- Open source software and open source content are challenging existing

software and content developers, including educational institutions.[4]

A 2006 Pew study suggests that by 2020 a low-cost, global network will be in place, ensuring global availability of broadband. This network would open up opportunities and competition and continue to "flatten the world."[5] In addition, the Pew study stated that those who are connected will spend more time in compelling virtual worlds. Another study predicted that by the end of 2008, 41 million corporate employees globally will spend at least one day a week teleworking, and 100 million employees will work from home at least one day a month.[6]

So where are we going in the future and what can we expect in higher education?

Learning continues to transition: From passive to collaborative to immersive. Learning will continue to transition from a one-way, lecture-based passive experience to collaborative learning facilitated by Web 2.0 technologies and, eventually, to immersive learning driven by gaming and virtual reality.

Multimedia will continue to converge and be used more widely in education. With the ease of creating and producing multimedia videos on smart mobile devices and cameras, mashups will become easier, more prevalent, and practically cost-free. This will lead to expanded adoption and use in higher education.

Entertainment will impact all areas of education. Movies, music, and sports will be integrated into education, creating new forms of content output such as mashup videos that have snippets of education mixed with TV, music, and movie clips.

New technologies and uses will emerge and impact learning materials. Advanced 3D technologies and effects, such as lighting, animated holograms, e-paper, and realistic views of depth and space, will continue to evolve and be used in research, education, and gaming.

Free content distribution will continue to proliferate and expand. Broadcast TV such as BBC, CBS, ABC, mtvU and video sites, such as BigThink will continue to expand into education. Most of these sites will be free and provide professors with ample teaching and learning materials.

Libraries and other commons will be IT enhanced connected, utilize more

shared services and expand into Centers of Excellence. Common spaces will continue to be renovated and offer places on campus for people to experiment and try new technologies. Many of these Centers will replace classroom and department silos as they will offer more useful services. Library digital collections will become globally connected through organizations such as Online Computer Library Center (www.oclc.org)

Mobile learning in education will advance as devices become cheaper, smarter and easier. Smart phones and devices will continue to expand and proliferate. Each new device will have simpler and enhanced functions, making it easier to read and use content on the device. This will help drive more education uses and applications.

Generation V will drive new use of current technologies and significantly change the education landscape again (current changes are Web 2.0 and social technologies) by 2020. Generation V, having grown up with emerging technologies, will push the next set of applications forward into mainstream education use. These applications include gaming, high-definition video, and virtual reality.

As free education content sites and channels will expand (YouTube.com, MTVu.com, iTunes.com, BigThink.com, etc.) budgets will shift to support content creation and delivery. There will be ample venues for teachers and students to access quality content in a variety of formats. Budgets for teaching and learning materials will be shifted to methods to access and use free materials: broadband, wireless, gaming rooms, video production, visualization centers, high-performance computing, storage, and backup.

Virtual reality will simplify and become more accessible. In the same way Yahoo simplified the World Wide Web and Google simplified search, virtual reality sites, such as Second Life, will deploy breakthrough technologies that will help simplify the site's use and application, thus driving these reality sites into a more mainstream consumer application.

Community resources will be more integrated and accessible to education. Higher Education will not only utilize the vast materials provided through the web but also integrate the digital assets from local resources such as hospitals, libraries and museums for use by local schools and community.

Learners will pursue multiple degrees, certifications, and courses to remain

relevant to job requirements. Most of this will be through distance learning. As new careers are invented and defined, learners will demand more courses, degrees, and certifications to help them maintain relevancy and viability as job candidates. For example, courses and programs on gaming, immersive technology, and advanced video design will be offered.

Interdisciplinary degrees will increase and many will integrate technology and information literacy into the curriculum. Learning how to use technology in education will become integrated into college programs and will not remain as separate courses offered in computer science or by the IT organization. Technology and Information literacy skills will become so critical for learning and working that they will become fully integrated into curriculum programs.

Glossary

by Alva Grace R. Mckee

Active Worlds

A 3D virtual reality platform where users assign themselves a unique name, log into the Active Worlds' virtual world universe, and explore 3D virtual worlds and environments that other users have built (see **Virtual Presence**).

Apple iPod touch

A portable, wireless media player designed and marketed by Apple, featuring a multitouch interface that allows users to find and use information more easily. It is the first generation of the iPod line to include wireless access to Apple's iTunes Store (see **iTunes U**).

Beaming

The communication of data between wireless devices using a beam of infrared light; used in many familiar devices, such as television remote controls and garage door openers. Infrared transmission often is used to transfer information between computing devices, for example, beaming data between a handheld device, such as a personal digital assistant, and a laptop computer.

Bebo

A social networking Web site designed to allow friends to communicate in various ways.

Blended course

Face to face and online course components.

Blog

An online journal or log updated or maintained by a **blogger**. **Blog posts** are published onto the World Wide Web and typically are accessible to anyone with an Internet connection.

Blogger

Author of blog.

Blog post

Entry made on a blog.

Click to Talk

A new form of Web-based communication in which a person clicks an object (a button, image, or text) to request an immediate phone call or voice-over-IP (VoIP) connection to speak with another person in real time.

Creative Commons

A nonprofit organization devoted to expanding the range of creative work legally available for others to build upon and share. The organization has released several copyright licenses known, as **Creative Commons licenses,** which restrict only certain rights, if any, to the work.

Course Management System (CMS) see **Virtual Learning Environment (VLE)**.

del.icio.us

A social bookmarking Web service for storing, sharing, and discovering Internet bookmarks; now part of Yahoo.

Distance education or distance learning

A field of education focusing on the pedagogy/andragogy, technology, and instructional systems design that are incorporated to effectively deliver education to students who are not physically on campus. Teachers and students may communicate at times of their own choosing by exchanging printed or electronic media, or through technology that allows them to communicate in real time. A distance education course that requires a physical, onsite presence for any reason, including the taking of examinations, is considered to be a **hybrid** or **blended course** or program.

eLearning

Computer-enhanced learning using networked and/or multimedia technologies.

Facebook

A social networking Web site launched in 2004. The name of the site refers to the paper facebooks depicting members of the campus community that colleges and preparatory schools give to incoming students, faculty, and staff.

Flickr

A photo-sharing Web site widely used by bloggers as a photo repository. Its popularity has been fueled by its innovative online community tools that allow photos to be tagged and browsed by folksonomic means (see **Folksonomy**).

Folksonomy

The practice and method of collaborative categorization using freely chosen keywords called tags.

Generation V

Comprised of children born in 1995 or later who are growing up on the three V's: Visual, Virtual, and Versatile.

High definition (HD)

Any video system of higher resolution than standard-definition video, most commonly at display resolutions of 1280×720 (720p) or 1920×1080 (1080i or 1080p).

Hybrid

Course that combines distance learning and traditional classroom learning.

iTunes U

A dedicated area within the iTunes Store featuring free content such as course lectures, language lessons, lab demonstrations, sports highlights, and campus tours. It is provided by top U.S. colleges and universities, including Stanford University, University of California, Berkeley, Duke University, and the Massachusetts Institute of Technology.

Learning environment

The blurring of lines between traditional higher education and the ever-increasing, technology-enriched resources that have become popular as learning tools (see **Web 2.0, Blog, Wiki, Distance Education or Learning**).

Learning management system (LMS) see **virtual learning environment (VLE)**.

Live streaming media

Video and audio files that can be viewed by the end user at the same time they are being delivered by the provider. This method speeds the viewing process because the user does not have to wait until the entire file is downloaded before viewing it.

Mashup

A Web application that combines data from more than one source into an integrated experience.

Massively multiplayer online role-playing games (MMORPG)

A genre of online computer role-playing games (CRPGs) in which a large number—often in the thousands—of players interact with one another in a virtual world (see **Role Playing Game**, *World of Warcraft*).

mLearning

The intersection of mobile computing with eLearning; learning enabled by the use of PDAs, mobile phones, and other personal and portable devices (see **eLearning**).

Moodle

A **virtual learning environment (VLE)** with more than 333,000 users (see **VLE**).

Multimedia

Media that use multiple forms of information content and information processing (e.g., text, audio, graphics, animation, video, interactivity) to inform or entertain.

Multimedia messaging service

A technology that is a standard for telephony messaging systems. Allows sending messages that embed multimedia objects, such as images, audio, and video, as opposed to short message service (SMS), which incorporates only text.

MySpace

A popular social networking Web site offering an interactive, user-submitted network of friends, personal profiles, blogs, groups, photos, music, and videos. MySpace currently is the sixth most popular Web site in any language and the third most popular Web site in the United States.

On-demand streaming

Media content transmitted to the client upon request. Examples of this may include taped classes and lectures that are posted on Web sites to download for later review (see **Video on demand VOD**).

Open courseware

Programs or services that provide content from academic courses in the form of lecture video and audio files, documents, and review materials through the Internet. These materials are made available not only to students taking the courses but also to anyone with access to the Web.

Podcasting

The distribution over the Internet of media files using syndication feeds (see **Really simple syndication, RSS**) for playback on portable media players and personal computers. The term "podcast" comes from combining the name of Apple's portable music player, the iPod, with the word "broadcast," although podcast technology is in no way dependent upon the iPod.

Prosumer

A type of consumer who would become involved in the design and manufacture of products, so they could be made to individual specification.

Quality of service

Provides different priorities to various users or data flows or guarantees a certain level of performance to a data flow in accordance with requests from the application program or the Internet service provider policy. Quality of service guarantees are important if the network capacity is limited, for example, in cellular data communication. This especially is true for real-time streaming multimedia applications, such as voice-over IP and IPTV, because these often require a fixed bit rate and are delay sensitive.

Really simple syndication (RSS)

A family of Web feed formats used to publish frequently updated digital content, such as blogs, news feeds, or podcasts. Users of RSS content use programs called feed readers or aggregators. Users simply subscribe to the feeds they want. The reader then checks the feeds to see if any contain new content. If so, the reader retrieves the content and presents it to the user.

Role-playing game (RPG)

A game in which the participants assume the roles of fictional characters and collaboratively create or follow stories (see *World of Warcraft*).

Second Life

A 3D virtual world entirely built and owned by its more than 9 million "residents" from around the globe (see **Virtual presence**).

Short message service (SMS) or text messaging

A technology that allows sending messages purely in text format between two mobile phone devices, as opposed to **Multimedia messaging service (MMS)**, which allows the embedding of multimedia files.

The Sims

A strategic life-simulation computer game (see **Simulation games**)

Simulation games

A game that contains a mixture of skill, chance, and strategy to simulate an aspect of reality (see *The Sims*); describes a diverse category of video games.

Social bookmarking

A bookmarking system or network that enables users to store lists of Internet resources that they find useful. The public can access these lists via a specific network or Web site. Users with similar interests can view the links by topic, category, tags, or randomly (see **del.icio.us**).

Social networking

The practice of expanding the number of one's business and/or social contacts by making connections through individuals (see **Social networking site**).

Social networking site

A Web site that provides a virtual community for people interested in a particular subject or who just want to hang out together. Members create their own online profile with biographical data, pictures, comments about their likes and dislikes, and any other information; members communicate with each other by voice, chat, instant message, videoconference, and blogs. The service typically provides a way for members to contact friends of other members (see **MySpace, Facebook**).

Technical literacy

The ability to use digital technology, communication tools, and networks appropriately to solve information problems includes not only the ability to use technology as a tool to research, organize, evaluate, and communicate information but also the possession of a fundamental understanding of the ethical/legal issues surrounding the access and use of information.

TelePresence

A new technology category offered by Cisco Systems that uses advanced visual, audio, and interactive technologies to deliver a unique "in-person" experience over the network. TelePresence meeting solutions create a "room-within-a-room" environment where life-size, **high-definition** images, along with spatial and discrete audio, enable face-to-face meetings around a single virtual table (see **High definition [HD]**).

Video log or vlog

A Weblog or blog containing video. Regular entries typically are presented in reverse chronological order and often combine embedded video or a video link with supporting text, images, and other metadata (see **Blog**).

Video on demand (VOD)

A system that allows users to select and watch video and clip content over a network as part of an interactive television system (see **On-demand streaming**).

Videoconferencing

A method of conducting a conference between two or more participants, at different sites, by using computer networks to transmit audio and video data.

Virtual presence

Being present via intermediate technologies, usually radio, telephone, television, or the Internet. Virtual presence can denote apparent physical appearance, such as voice, face, and body language (see **Second Life, Active Worlds**).

Virtual learning environment (VLE)

A software system designed to support teaching and learning in an educational setting (see **Moodle**).

Web 2.0

A trend in the use of Web technology and Web design that aims to facilitate creativity, information sharing, and, most notably, collaboration among users, leading to the development and evolution of Web-based communities and hosted services, such as **Social networking site**, **Wikis**, **Blogs**, and **Folksonomy**.

Wiki

A collaborative Web site that can be directly edited by anyone with access to it.

World of Warcraft

An MMORPG where players complete quests and experience the world at their own pace, whether it be a few hours here and there or entire weeks at a time. Additionally, the quest system provides an enormous variety of captivating quests with story elements, dynamic events, and flexible reward systems. **World of Warcraft** features a faster style of play, with less downtime, and an emphasis on combat and tactics against multiple opponents (see **massively multiplayer online role-playing games**).

YouTube

A popular, free Web site that lets users upload, view, and share video clips. Videos can be rated by users. Rating averages, and the number of times a video has been watched, are published, making it easier for users to sort and view the content that they want to watch. Google acquired YouTube in November 2006.

Notes

Chapter 1

1. P. Anderson, "What Is Web 2.0? Ideas, Technologies and Implications for Education," February 2007 (www.jisc.ac.uk/media/documents/techwatch/tsw0701b.pdf).
2. P. Sellers, "MySpace Cowboys," *Fortune,* September 4, 2006 (http://money.cnn.com/magazines/fortune/fortune_archive/2006/09/04/8384727/index.htm).
3. D. Sifry, "State of the Live Web, April 2007," Sifry's Alerts: David Sifry's Daily Musings, April 5, 2007 (www.sifry.com/alerts/archives/000493.html).
4. "Wikipedia: Size Comparisons," March 2008 (http://en.wikipedia.org/wiki/Wikipedia:Size_comparisons).
5. L. Gomes, "Will All of Us Get Our 15 Minutes on a YouTube Video?" *The Wall Street Journal Online*, August 30, 2006 (http://online.wsj.com/public/article_print/SB115689298168048904–5wWyrSwyn6RfVfz9NwLk774VUWc_20070829.html).
6. H. Jenkins, "From YouTube to YouNiversity," *The Chronicle of Higher Education*, February 16, 2007 (http://chronicle.com/weekly/v53/i24/24b00901.htm).
7. N. LaPierre, "Digg User Statistics and the Digg Effect" © 2007 (http://fvvw.com/digg/report.html).
8. "Number of Twitter Users," January 6, 2008 (http://twitterfacts.blogspot.com/2008/01/number-of-twitter-users.html).
9. "College Students Surf Back to Campus on a Wave of Digital Connections," Alloy Mar-

keting, September 2006 (www.alloymarketing.com/investor_relations/news_releases/index.html).

10. "The Horizon Report 2007 Edition," The New Media Consortium and the EDUCAUSE Learning Initiative, 2007 (www.nmc.org/pdf/2007_Horizon_Report.pdf).

11. E. Maloney, "What Web 2.0 Can Teach Us about Learning," *The Chronicle of Higher Education*, January 5, 2007 (http://chronicle.com/weekly/v53/i18/18b02601.htm).

12. B. Alexander, "Web 2.0: A New Wave of Innovation for Teaching and Learning?" *EDUCAUSE Review*, Vol. 41, No. 2, March/April 2006.

13. L. Lessig, *The Future of Ideas* (www.lessig.org/blog/).

14. Dickinson College Blog (http://blog.dickinson.edu/?page_id=885).

15. Henry Jenkins "From YouTube to YouNiversity."

16. C. Safran, D. Helic, and C. Gutl, "E-Learning Practices and Web 2.0," Interactive Computer-Aided Learning Conference, September 2007 (www.iicm.tugraz.at/iicm_papers/ICL2007_csafran_final.pdf).

17. "7 Things You Should Know about RSS," *EDUCAUSE Education Learning Initiative*, April 2007 (www.educause.edu/ir/library/pdf/ELI7024.pdf).

18. Bryan Alexander, "Web 2.0: A New Wave of Innovation for Teaching and Learning?" *Educause Review* (March 2006), pp. 33–44.

19. L.A., Safran et al., "E-Learning Practices."

20. L.A., Safran et al, "E-Learning Practices."

21. T. Bryant, "Social Software in Academia," *EDUCAUSE Quarterly*, 2006, No. 2 (www.educause.edu/ir/library/pdf/EQM0627.pdf.

22. "7 Things You Should Know about Wikipedia," *EDUCAUSE Education Learning Initiative*, June 2007 (www.educause.edu/ir/library/pdf/ELI7026.pdf).

23. M. Arrington, "85% of College Students Use Facebook," *TechCrunch*, September 7, 2005 (www.techcrunch.com/2005/09/07/85-of-college-students-use-facebook/).

24. N. Ellison, C. Steinfield, and C. Lampe, "The Benefits of Facebook 'Friends': Social Capital and College Students' Use of Online Social Network Sites," *Journal of Computer-Mediated Communication*, Vol. 12, No. 4, 2007 <http://jcmc.indiana.edu/vol12/issue4/ellison.html>.

25. "7 Things You Should Know about Facebook II," *EDUCAUSE Education Learning Initiative*, May 2007 (www.educause.edu/ir/library/pdf/ELI7025.pdf).

26. Lee Bryant , "Social Software." *http://www.headshift.com/moments*

27. "7 Things You Should Know about Flickr," *EDUCAUSE Education Learning Initiative*, February 2008 (www.educause.edu/ir/library/pdf/ELI7034.pdf).

28. "7 Things You Should Know about Mapping Mashups," *EDUCAUSE Education Learning Initiative*, July 2006 (www.educause.edu/ir/library/pdf/ELI7016.pdf).

29. T. O'Reilly, "What Is Web 2.0: Design Patterns and Business Model's for the Next Generation Software," OReillyNet.com, September 30, 2005 (www.oreillynet.com/pub/a/oreilly/tim/news/2005/09/30/what-is-Web-2.0.html).

Chapter 2

1. M. Madden, "Online Video," Pew Internet & American Life Project, July 2007. (www.pewinternet.org/pdfs/pip_online_video_2007.pdf)

2. D. Riley, "The Rise of the Prosumer," TechCrunch, June 15, 2007 (www.techcrunch.

com/2007/06/15/the-rise-of-the-prosumer/).

3. A. Sumits, "Global IP Traffic Forecast and Methodology (2005–2011)," Cisco white paper, 2007.

4. Ibid.

5. "mtvU Adds 2.6 Million Subscribers, Launches on Charter, Verizon FiOS, Suddenlink, AT&T and Nearly 70 Other Carriers Nationwide," PRNewswire, January 29, 2008 <http://findarticles.com/p/articles/mi_m4PRN/is_2008_Jan_29/ai_n24238765>.

6. "Acquisition Establishes mtvU as Number Two General Interest Online Destination for College Students," PRNewswire, January 17, 2007 <http://www.prnewswire.com/cgi-bin/stories.pl?ACCT=104&STORY=/www/story/01–17–2007/0004507644&EDATE>.

7. IDC 2005—(http://www.the-infoshop.com/topics/CS25_en.shtml)

8. "Definition—Streaming Video," TechTarget.com <http://searchvoip.techtarget.com/sDefinition/0,,sid66_gci213055,00.html>.

9. http://www.webopedia.comlTERMNNoD.html.

10. "Definition—Videoconference," TechTarget.com <http://searchmobilecomputing.techtarget.com/sDefinition/0,,sid40_gci213291,00.html>.

11. "Definition—Podcasting," TechTarget.com <http://searchunifiedcommunications.techtarget.com/sDefinition/0,,sid186_gci1044707,00.html>.

12. A. Deal, "Podcasting," *Teaching with Technology*, Carnegie Mellon University, June 2007 <http://connect.educause.edu/files/CMU_Podcasting_Jun07.pdf>.

13. "Design Implications of Rich Media (Podcasting) in a Campus Network," © 2007 Cisco Systems.

14. Ibid.

15. Deal, "Podcasting."

16. F. O'Connor, "Podcasting Goes to College," International Data Group (IDG) News Service, July 20, 2006 <http://www.itworld.com/Tech/5042/060720podcastcollege/>.

17. "Design Implications of Rich Media."

18. Deal, "Podcasting."

19. C. Lane, "UW Podcasting: Evaluation of Year One," Report by *Office of Learning Technologies*, University of Washington, 2006 <http://catalyst.washington.edu/research_development/papers/2006/podcasting_year1.pdf>.

20. S. Brittain, P. Glowacki, J. Van Ittersum, and L. Johnson, "Podcasting Lectures," *EDUCAUSE Quarterly*, Vol. 29, No. 3, 2006 <http://www.educause.edu/ir/library/pdf/eqm0634.pdf>.

21. B. L. Kurtz, J. B. Fenwick, and C. C. Ellsworth, "Using Podcasts and Tablet PCs in Computer Science." In *Proceedings of the 45th Annual Southeast Regional Conference*, 2007 <http://portal.acm.org/citation.cfm?id=1233428>.

22. M. Frydenberg, "Principles and Pedagogy: The Two P's of Podcasting in the Information Technology Classroom." In *The Proceedings of ISECON 2006*, Vol. 23, 2006 <http://isedj.org/isecon/2006/3354/>.

23. D. Glaister, "Top of the iTunes Chart: Meet the Professor Who's Making Physics Cool," *The Guardian*, December 2007 <http://www.guardian.co.uk/technology/2007/dec/20/internet?gusrc=rss&feed=technology>.

24. "Podcasting Technology," University College Dublin Media Services Blog, January 2008 <http://ucdblogs.org/mediaservices/?cat=77>.

25. A. Hochman, "OpenCast Community Home," OpenCast Community Web site,

March 2008 <http://confluence.media.berkeley.edu/confluence/display/WCTREQ/OpenCast+Community-+Home;jsessionid=D6830360A829E37541A7F7550F673AC6>.

26. L. Gomes, "Will All of Us Get Our 15 minutes on a YouTube Video?" *Wall Street Journal*, August 30, 2006 <http://online.wsj.com/public/article/SB115689298168048904–5wWyr-Swyn6RfVfz9NwLk774VUWc_20070829.html>.

27. J. R. Young, "Thanks to YouTube, Professors Are Finding New Audiences," *The Chronicle of Higher Education*, January 9, 2008 <http://chronicle.com/free/2008/01/1159n.htm>.

28. "YouTube: Professors Are the Latest Rock-stars with Mashups," Technology + Education Blog <http://technologogy.wordpress.com/2008/01/31/YouTube-professors-are-the-latest-rock-stars-with-mash-ups/>.

29. C. Conway, "YouTube and the Cultural Studies Classroom," *Inside Higher Ed*, Nov. 13, 2006 <www.insidehighered.com/views/2006/11/13/conway>.

30. H. Jenkins, "Learning from YouTube: An Interview with Alex Juhasz," the official Weblog of Henry Jenkins, February 20, 2008 <http://www.henryjenkins.org/2008/02/learning_from_YouTube_an_inter.html>.

31. Y. Anwar, "Campus Launches YouTube Channel," Press Release, UC Berkeley News, October 3, 2008 <http://www.berkeley.edu/news/media/releases/2007/10/03_YouTube.shtml>.

32. "Being Here Is Being There," TelePresence Technology Overview, Cisco Systems Web site <http://www.cisco.com/en/US/products/ps7060/products_category_technologies_overview.html>.

Chapter 3

1.   "Back to College 2007," Consumer Intentions and Actions, BIGResearch and the National Retail Foundation, August 2007.

2.   T. Schadler, "Five-Year US Forecast of 14 Consumer Technologies," *Forrester Research,* September 6, 2006.

3.   T. Schadler; "College Explorer Report," *Harris Interactive and Alloy Media + Marketing,* August 2007 <http://www.harrisinteractive.com/news/newsletters/k12news/HI_TrendsTudes_2007_v06_i06.pdf>.

4.   "Back to College 2007."

5.   J. Crabtree, M. Nathan, and S. Roberts, "Mobile UK: Mobile Phones and Everyday Life," The Work Foundation, London, 2003.

6.   P. Wentzel, R. Lammeren, M. Molendijk, S. Bruin, A. Wagtendonk, "Using Mobile Technology to Enhance Students' Educational Experience," EDUCAUSE Center for Applied Research (ECAR), 2005.

7.   P. Wentzel, R. von Lammeren, M. Molendijk, S. de Bruin, and A. Wagtendonk, "Using Mobile Technology to Enhance Students Educational Experiences," Case Study 2, EDUCAUSE Center for Applied Research, 2005.

8.   "Mobile Subscriber Base Approaches One Billion in Asia-Pac," Frost and Sullivan Press Release, June 5, 2006.

9.   J. Jung and J. Leckenby, "Attitudes toward Mobile Advertising Acceptance and Behavior Intention: Comparison Study of Korea and US," 2007 American Academy of Advertising Asia-Pacific Annual Conference, May 31–June 2, 2007 <http://www.ciadvertising.org/

studies/reports/info_process/aaa_asia-pacific_2008_Jung&Leckenby.pdf>.

10. J. Lloyd, L. A. Dean, and D. L. Cooper, "Students' Technology Use and Its Effects on Peer Relationships, Academic Involvement, and Healthy Lifestyles," *NASPA Journal*, 44(3), 2007; A. Lenhart, M. Madden, and P. Hitlin, "Teens and Technology: Youth Are Leading the Transition to a Fully Wired and Mobile Nation," Pew Internet & American Life Project, Washington, DC, 2005; B. D. Arend, "New Patterns of Student Engagement," *About Campus*, July–August 2005.

11. L. M. Levine, "Campus-Wide Mobile Wireless: Mobility and Convergence," *Syllabus*, October 2002; R. McGhee and R. Kozma, "New Teacher and Student Roles in the Technology-Supported Classroom," paper presented at the annual meeting of the American Educational Research Association, Seattle, 2001; J. McKenzie, "The Unwired Classroom: Wireless Computers Come of Age," *Educational Technology*, 10(4), 2001.

12. C. Swett, "College Students' Use of Mobile Wireless-Internet Connections Becomes More Common," *Knight Rider Tribune Business News*, Washington, DC, October 2002.

13. R. Boggs, J. Smolek, and P. Arabasz, "Choosing the Right Wireless Network: A Technology Challenge for Higher Education," research bulletin, EDUCAUSE Center for Applied Research, June 11, 2002.

14. T. Wilen, Fall 2005, personal dialog with universities.

15. F. Maginnis, R. White, and C. Mckenna, "Customers on the Move: M-Commerce Demands a Business Object Broker Approach to EAI," *eAI Journal*, November–December 2000.

16. R. Boggs et al.; A. C. Galbus, "Are Wireless Computers a Cost-effective Alternative to Fixed Documenting and Reviewing Patient Cares?" Unpublished master's thesis, Cardinal Stritch University; 2001; A. Rzewnicki, "Rising Demand Lowers Cost, Increasing Usage of Wi-Fi," *Triangle Business Journal*, In Depth: Triangle Tech News, July 2004.

17. E. Tao, "Wireless Network Deployment and Its Impacts on Teaching and Learning—A Case Study of California State University Monterey Bay," *Proceedings of Syllabus*, San Jose Marriott, Stanford University, July 2003.

18. M. K. Shim and S. J. Shim, "Mobile Computing in Higher Education: Faculty Perceptions of Benefits and Barriers," *Journal of Educational Technology Systems*, 29(4), 2001.

19. C. Quinn, "mLearning: Mobile, Wireless, In-Your-Pocket Learning," *LineZine*, Fall 2000 <http://www.linezine.com/2.1/features/cqmmwiyp.htm>.

20. S. Wexler, B. Schlenker, J. Brown, D. Metcalf, C. Quinn, E. Thor, A. van Barneveld, and E. Wagner, "Mobile Learning: What It Is, Why It Matters, and How to Incorporate It into Your Learning Strategy," 360° Report, The eLearning Guild, July 2007.

21. "What is m-Learning?" Frequently Asked Questions, Centre for Distance Learning, University of London, retrieved March 24, 2008 <http://www.cde.london.ac.uk/support/faqs/faq2153.htm>.

22. L. Naismith, P. Lonsdale, G. Vavoula, and M. Sharples, "Literature Review in Mobile Technologies and Learning," © Futurelab 2006.

23. Ibid.

24. S. H. Kim, C. Mims, and K. P. Holmes, K.P, "An Introduction to Current Trends and Benefits of Mobile Wireless Technology Use in Higher Education," *AACE Journal*, 14(1), 2006.

25. J. McKenzie.

26. S. Yuen and P. K. Yuen, "PDAs as Educational Power Tools," *Tech Directions*, 62(9), 2003.

27. E. Klopfer, K. Squire, and H. Jenkins, "Environmental Detectives: PDAs as a Window into a Virtual Simulated World," *Proceedings of IEEE International Workshop on Wireless and Mobile Technologies in Education*, Vaxjo, Sweden, IEEE Computer Society, 2002.

28. F. Lehner, H. Nosekabel, and H. Lehmann, "Wireless e-Learning and Communication Environment: WELCOME at the University of Regensburg," *e-Service Journal*, 2(3), 2002; G. Cole, "The Classless Society," *Connectics*, June 2001; L. F. Motiwalla, "Mobile Learning: A Framework and Evaluation," *Computers and Education*, Vol. 49, 2007.

29. P. Wentzel et al., "Using Mobile Technology."

30. Y. Song, "Educational Uses of Handheld Devices: What Are the Consequences?" *Tech-Trends*, September/October 2007.

31. Ibid.

32. E. Morgen and B. Smith, "Student Use of PDAs at the UConn Health Center School of Medicine," Teaching and Learning with Mobile Technologies Event, NorthEast Regional Computing Program, January 25, 2008.

33. J. Trella and J. Swiatek-Kelley, "Extending Campus Resources to the Mobile Device," Teaching and Learning with Mobile Technologies Event, NorthEast Regional Computing Program, January 25, 2008.

34. D. Parry, "Teaching with Twitter," Video, *The Chronicle of Higher Education* Web site, retrieved March 24, 2008 <http://chronicle.com/media/video/v54/i25/twitter/?utm_source=at&utm_medium=en>.

35. "University of Cincinnati: University Increases Information Access and Quality of Life with Mobile Solution," Microsoft Case Studies, posted April 17, 2007, retrieved March 24, 2008 <http://www.microsoft.com/windowsmobile/business/success/education.mspx>.

36. "ClassInHand," ClassInHand page, Wake Forest University, retrieved March 24, 2008 <http://classinhand.wfu.edu/>.

37. "Empowering Learners: Mobile Learning and Teaching with PDAs," Case Studies, Joint Information Systems Committee, © Higher Education Funding Council for England (HEFCE) 2005 <http://www.elearning.ac.uk/innoprac/practitioner/resources/dewsbury.pdf>.

38. "Symbol Technologies Helps Unplug the Wires at Monash Medical Centre," ©2005 Symbol Technologies.

39. C. Houser and P. Thornton, "Japanese College Students' Typing Speed on Mobile Devices," *Proceedings, the 2nd IEEE International Workshop on Wireless and Mobile Technologies in Education*, 2004 <http://ieeexplore.ieee.org/xpl/freeabs_all.jsp?tp=&arnumber=1281353&isnumber=28620>.

40. Naismith et al., "Literature Review."

41. Song, "Educational Uses of Handheld devices."

42. Y. Cui and S. Bull, "Context and Learner Modelling for the Mobile Foreign Language Learner," *System*, 33(2), 2005; G. Gay and H. Hembrooke, *Activity-Centered Design: An Ecological Approach to Designing Smart Tools and Usable Systems*, Cambridge, MA: MIT Press, 2004.

43. M. Sharples, "The Design of Personal Mobile Technologies for Lifelong Learning," *Computers and Education*, 2000.

44. B. Patten, I. A. Sanchez, & B. Tangney, "Designing collaborative, constructionist and contextual applications for handheld devices," *Computers & Education*, 46(3), 294–308.

45. L. Naismith, P. Lonsdale, G. Vavoula, M. Sharples, "Literature Review in Mobile Tech-

nologies and Learning," *Futurelab Series* © 2006.

46. M. Rouan, "The Rise of Mobile Learning," Lecture, University Continuing Education Association Executive Leadership Academy Alumni Forum, July 10–11, 2008, San Francisco.

47. Lloyd et al., "Students' Technology Use."

48. S. Carlson, "With This Enrollment, a Toy Surprise: Colleges Give out iPods, Cellphones, and More for Educational Reasons, of Course," *The Chronicle for Higher Education*, September 17, 2004 <http://chronicle.com/free/v51/i04/04a02901.htm>.

49. Y. Kageyama, "Cellphone College Class Opens in Japan," *The Associated Press*, November 29, 2007.

50. C. Houser, P. Thornton, S. Yokoi, and T. Yasuda, "Learning on the Move: Vocabulary Study via Mobile Phone Email," *Enhancement of Quality Learning Through Information and Communication Technology*, 2001; P. Thornton and C. Houser, "Learning on the Move: Vocabulary Study via Email and Mobile Phone SMS," *Proceedings of EdMedia*, 2001.

Chapter 4

1. K. Squire and H. Jenkins, "Harnessing the Power of Games in Education," *Insight*, Vol. 3.

2. S. Jones et al., "Let the Games Begin; Gaming Technology and Entertainment among College Students," Pew Internet and American Life Project, Washington, DC, July 6, 2003.

3. "Media & Broadcasting Technology—Exploiting Opportunities in the Global Electronic Games Sector," Datamonitor Review Report, December 2006.

4. "FTTx—Experiences and Strategies—Filling the Pipe of the NGN," InfoCom report, November 2007 <http://www.researchandmarkets.com/reports/c79858>.

5. "Worldwide Online Gaming Community Reaches 217 Million People," *ComScore* Research, July 2007 <http://www.comscore.com/press/release.asp?press=1521>.

6. http://www.forrester.com/Research/Document/Excerpt/0,7211,43972,00.html

7. Datamonitor Review Report 2006.

8. "Worldwide Online Gaming Community Reaches 217 Million People."

9. Jones et al., "Let the Games Begin."

10. K. Squire and H. Jenkins, "Harnessing the Power of Games."

11. Ibid.

12. J. Gee, "High Score Education," *Wired*, Vol. 11, No. 5, May 2003.

13. J. Young, "Community College Uses a Video-Game Lab to Lure Students to Computer Courses," *The Chronicle of Higher Education,* December 14, 2007, Vol. 54, No. 16.

14. M. Prensky, "In Educational Games, Complexity Matters," *Educational Technology,* Vol. 45, No.4, July–August 2005.

15. K. Squire and H. Jenkins, "Harnessing the Power of Games in Education."

16. S. Rovner, "Video Game Aims to Engage Students," *Chemical and Engineering News*, American Chemical Society, April 10, 2006, Vol. 84, No. 15.

17. A. Baba, N. Hichibe, L. Shyba, and S. Tomiyasu, "Serious Game World Reports, Part II," Serious Games Summit Sessions, Game Developers Conference, February 2008, San Francisco.

18. R. Blunt, "Does Game-Based Learning Work?" The Interservice/Industry Training, Simulation & Education Conference (I/ITSEC), November 2007.

19. "Carnegie Mellon Collaborates with EA to Revolutionize and Reinvigorate Computer Science Education in the US," Alice Press Release, March 2006 <http://www.alice.org/index.php?page=sims_announcement/sims_announcement>.
20. Game Developers conference, http://www.gdconf.com/, San Francisco, February 19, 2008, Japan games market overview.
21. D. Oblinger, "Simulations, Games and Learning," *EDUCAUSE Quarterly*, May 2006, Vol. 29, No. 3.
22. Prensky, "Complexity Matters."
23. E. Marris, "Chemistry: The Video Game," *News at Nature.com*, March 31, 2006.
24. D. Daglow, A. Games, F. Lantz, and R. Wainess, panelists and E. Zimmerman, moderator, "The Paradox of Play: The Challenge of Measuring What Game Players Learn," Serious Games Summit Sessions, Game Developers Conference, February 2008, San Francisco.
25. N. Jennings and C. Collins, "Virtual or Virtually U: Educational Institutions in Second Life," *International Journal of Social Sciences*, Vol. 2, No. 3, 2008.
26. Ibid.
27. Ibid.

Chapter 5

1. L. Estabrook, E. Witt, and L. Rainie, "Information Searches That Solve Problems: How People Use the Internet, Libraries, and Government Agencies When They Need Help," Pew Internet and American Life Project, December 30, 2007 (www.pewInternet.org/pdfs/Pew_UI_LibrariesReport.pdf).
2. N. Cohen, "MIT Education in Taiwan, Minus the Degree," *The New York Times* Online, April 2, 2007 (www.nytimes.com/2007/04/02/technology/02link.html)
3. E. Lee, "Cal Offers Full Courses on YouTube—but Not for Credit," *San Francisco Chronicle*, October 4, 2007 (www.sfgate.com/cgi-bin/article.cgi?f=/c/a/2007/10/04/BUJ0SJ9JS. DTL).
4. M. Cutts, "Minty Fresh Indexing," www.mattcutts.com, August 7, 2007 (www.mattcutts.com/blog/minty-fresh-indexing).
5. W. Boswell, "Seek and Ye Shall Find: How to Search the Invisible," Lifehacker.com, September 30, 2005 (http://lifehacker.com/software/search-engines/special-seek-and-ye-shall-find-128317.php).
6. Ibid.
7. National Academies Press "About" page (www.nap.edu/about.html)
8. A. L. Foster, "Information Navigation 101," *The Chronicle of Higher Education*, March 9, 2007 (http://chronicle.com/weekly/v53/i27/27a03801.htm).
9. Ibid.
10. A. Frean, "White Bread for Young Minds," *The Times Online*, January 14, 2008 (http://technology.timesonline.co.uk/tol/news/tech_and_web/the_web/article3182091.ece).
11. A. L. Foster, "Information Navigation 101," *The Chronicle of Higher Education*, March 9, 2007 (http://chronicle.com/weekly/v53/i27/27a03801.htm).
12. "Information Literacy Competency Standards for Higher Education," The Association of College and Research Libraries, 2000 (www.ala.org/ala/acrl/acrlstandards/standards.pdf).
13. L. Estabrook, E. Witt, and L. Rainie, "Information Searches That Solve Problems: How

People Use the Internet, Libraries, and Government Agencies When They Need Help," Pew Internet and American Life Project, December 30, 2007 (www.pewInternet.org/pdfs/Pew_UI_LibrariesReport.pdf).

14. H. Goodall, "A New Wiki Collects IT Skills from Antiquity," *The Chronicle of Higher Education*, January 16, 2008 (http://chronicle.com/wiredcampus/article/2759/a-new-wiki-collects-it-skills-from-antiquity).

Chapter 6

1. Employment and Training Administration, US Department of Labor, "The President's High Growth Job Training Initiative," 2003 <http://www.doleta.gov/BRG/JobTrainInitiative/>.

2. D. E. Hecker, "Occupational Employment Projections to 2014," *Monthly Labor Review*, November 2005.

3. "2006 iSkills/ICT Literacy Assessment Preliminary Findings," US Educational Testing Service, 2006 <http://www.ets.org/Media/Products/ICT_Literacy/pdf/2006_Preliminary_Findings.pdf>.

4. "Information Literacy Competency Standards for Higher Education," The Association of College and Research Libraries, American Library Association, 2000 <http://www.ala.org/ala/acrl/acrlstandards/standards.pdf>.

5. "A Global Imperative: The Report of the 21st Century Literary Summit," New Media Consortium, 2005.

6. E. Daley, "Expanding the Concept of Literacy," *EDUCAUSE Review*, March/April 2003 <http://www.educause.edu/ir/library/pdf/erm0322.pdf>.

7. B. Bruce, "Diversity and Critical Social Engagement: How Changing Technologies Enable New Modes of Literacy in Changing Circumstances," *Adolescents and Literacies in a Digital World*, ed. D. E. Alvermann, NY: Peter Lang, 2002.

8. H. Jenkins, "Confronting the Challenges of Participatory Culture: Media Education for the 21st Century," MacArthur Foundation, 2006.

9. "iSkills."

10. A. Foster, "Information Navigation 101," *The Chronicle of Higher Education*, March 9, 2007.

11. E. Daley, "Expanding the Concept of Literacy," *EDUCAUSE Review*, March/April 2003.

12. "Information Literacy Competency Standards for Higher Education."

13. P. Thacker, "Testing for Technology Literacy," *Inside Higher Ed*, January 4, 2007 <http://www.insidehighered.com/news/2007/01/04/techtest>.

14. "Information Navigation 101."

15. A. Foster, "Educators Set Proficiency Level for Information-Literacy Tests," *The Chronicle of Higher Education*, February 27, 2008 <http://chronicle.com/wiredcampus/article/?id=2781>; R. J. Tannenbaum and Irvin R. Katz, "Setting Standards on the Core and Advanced iSkills Assessments," ETS RM-08-04, February 2008 <http://www.ets.org/Media/Research/pdf/RM-08-04.pdf>.

16. Jenkins, "Confronting the Challenges of Participatory Culture."

17. Ibid.

18. Ibid.

19. "Being Fluent with Information Technology," National Research Council, National Academy Press, Washington, DC, 1999 <http://books.nap.edu/catalog.php?record_id=6482#toc>.
20. Ibid.
21. Ibid.
22. J. K. Lippincott, "Student Content Creators: Convergence of Literacies," *EDUCAUSE Review*, Vol. 42, No. 6 November/December 2007 <http://connect.educause.edu/Library/EDUCAUSE+Review/StudentContentCreatorsCon/45230>.
23. Ibid.
24. A. H. Moore, "The New Economy, Technology and Learning Outcomes Assessment," *EDUCAUSE Quarterly*, Vol. 30, No. 3, 2007.
25. Lippincott, "Student Content Creators: Convergence of Literacies."
26. G. Daugenti, Conversation, December 23, 2007.

Chapter 7

1. S. Jones, "The Internet Goes to College," Pew Internet and American Life Project, September 15, 2002 <http://www.pewinternet.org/pdfs/PIP_College_Report.pdf>.
2. D. Nagel, "Research: College Students Use Internet for Education," *Campus Technology*, August 15, 2007 <http://campustechnology.com/articles/49702/>.
3. J. Boase, J. B. Horrigan, B. Wellman, and L. Rainie, "The Strength of Internet Ties," Pew Internet and American Life Project, January 25, 2006 <http://www.pewinternet.org/pdfs/PIP_Internet_ties.pdf>.
4. Ibid.
5. Ibid.
6. S. Jones, "The Internet Goes to College."
7. Ibid.
8. Ibid.
9. J. Lloyd, L. A. Dean, and D. L. Cooper, "Students' Technology Use and Its Effects on Peer Relationships, Academic Involvement, and Healthy Lifestyles," *NASPA Journal*, 44(3) <http://publications.naspa.org/naspajournal/vol44/iss3/art6>.
10. "Mindset List 2011," Beloit College <http://www.beloit.edu/~pubaff/mindset/2011.php>.
11. "Spending on Dorm Furnishings, Electronics Drives Back-to-College Sales Past $47 Billion," National Retail Foundation, August 14, 2007 <http://www.nrf.com/modules.php?name=News&op=viewlive&sp_id=354>.
12. M. Madden, "Online Video," Pew Internet & American Life Project, July 2007 <http://www.pewinternet.org/pdfs/PIP_Online_Video_2007.pdf>.
13. "Looking to Reach College Students—Look Online," Burst Media Online Insights, July 1, 2007 <http://www.burstmedia.com/assets/newsletter/items/2007_07_01.pdf>.
14. "Class of 2011 Heads Back to Campus Wielding More Connections, Concern and Consumer Clout Than Any Class Before Them," *Harris Interactive and Alloy Media + Marketing*, August 15 2007 <http://www.alloymarketing.com/investor_relations/news_releases/doc/amm_harris_collegeexplorer8_15_07FINAL.doc>.
15. P. McLean, "Apple Serving Up 1 Million Copies of iTunes Each Day," *AppleInsider*, June 12, 2007 <http://www.appleinsider.com/articles/07/06/12/apple_serving_up_1_million_

copies_of_itunes_each_day.html>.

16. T. Schadler, "Five-Year US Forecast of 14 Consumer Technologies," Forrester Research, September 6, 2006 <http://www.forrester.com/Research/Document/Excerpt/0,7211,40297,00.html>.

17. "Class of 2011," *Harris Interactive and Alloy Media + Marketing.*

18. Ibid.

19. Ibid.

20. Wilen, 2007 (www.ledtrends.com) "Gen V"

21. Ibid.

22. "Kidspoll: Are Kids Too Busy?" KidsHealth for Parents Web site, Nemours Foundation © 1995–2008, June 27, 2006 <http://www.kidshealth.org/research/kidspoll_busy.html>.

23. L. Porterfield, "Experts: Despite Their Energy, Kids Still at Risk of Burnout," CNN.com Education with Student News, September 2, 2006.

24. <http://www.cnn.com/2006/EDUCATION/08/30/overscheduled.kids/index.html>.

25. M. Prensky, "Digital Natives, Digital Immigrants," *On the Horizon,* NCB University Press, Vol. 9 No. 5, October 2001.

26. "Children Are Becoming Exposed to and Adopting Electronic Devices at Earlier Ages," The NPD Group, June 5, 2007 <http://www.npd.com/press/releases/press_070605.html>.

Chapter 8

1. S. Jones and C. Johnson-Yale, "Professors Online: The Internet's impact on college faculty," *First Monday,* Vol. 10, No. 9 (September 2005) <http://firstmonday.org/issues/issue10_9/jones/index.html>.

2. ARPANET definition, Searchnetworking.com definitions <http://searchnetworking.techtarget.com/sDefinition/0,,sid7_gci213782,00.html>.

3. Jones and Johnson-Yale, "Professors Online."

4. Ibid.

5. I. E. Allen and J. Seaman, "Online Nation: Five Years of Online Growth," *The Sloan Consortium,* October 2007 < http://www.sloan-c.org/publications/survey/pdf/online_nation.pdf>.

6. E. L. Ayers, "The Academic Culture and the IT Culture: Their Effect on Teaching and Scholarship," *EDUCAUSE Review,* Vol. 39, No. 6, November–December 2004 <http://www.educause.edu/ir/library/pdf/ERM0462.pdf>.

7. M. Ebner, "E-Learning–e-Learning 1.0 + Web 2.0?", Second International Conference on Availability, Reliability and Security (ARES'07), IEEE Computer Society, February 2007.

8. http://www.wfu.edu/technology/programs/stars/,,

9. http://its.psu.edu/newfaculty.html

10. http://www.educause.edu/ir/library/html/cem/cem99/cem994b.html

11. http://www.fdi.vt.edu/FDIprogram/Program_Summary.html

12. http://www.westminstercollege.edu/ftc/index.cfm?parent=658

13. http://www.bowdoin.edu/it/help/newfacfaqs.shtml

14. http://www.stlawu.edu/ctl/

15. D. W. Schaffer, R. Halverson, K. R. Squire, and J. P. Gee, "Video Games and the Future of Learning," Wisconsin Center for Education Research, University of Wisconsin Madison

School of Education, June 2005 <https://www.wcer.wisc.edu/publications/workingPapers/Working_Paper_No_2005_4.pdf>

16. S. Jones and M. Madden, "The Internet Goes to College," Pew Internet and American Life, September 15, 2002 <http://www.pewinternet.org/pdfs/PIP_College_Report.pdf>.
17. B. L. Hawkins and J. A. Rudy, "Fiscal Year 2006 Summary Report," EDUCAUSE Core Data Service, September 2007 <http://www.educause.edu/apps/coredata/reports/2006>.
18. T. Wilen, September 12, 2007, U.K.
19. "The Horizon Report 2007 Edition," The New Media Consortium and the EDUCAUSE Learning Initiative, 2007 <http://www.nmc.org/pdf/2007_Horizon_Report.pdf>.

Chapter 9

1. "The Faculty Room—Statistics," Disabilities, Opportunities, Internetworking and Technology (DO-IT) Department Page, University of Washington <http://www.washington.edu/doit/Faculty/Rights/Background/statistics.html>.
2. L. Horn and J. Berktold, "Students with Disabilities in Postsecondary Education: A Profile of Preparation, Participation and Outcomes," National Center for Education Statistics, 1999.
3. S. Burgstahler, "Making Distance Learning Accessible to Everyone," DO-IT, University of Washington, 2006.
4. J. Nelson, J. Dodd, and D. Smith, "Faculty Willingness to Accommodate Students with Learning Disabilities: A Comparison Among Academic Divisions," *Journal of Learning Disabilities*, Vol. 23, No. 3, 1990.
5. L. Lewis and E. Farris, "An Institutional Perspective on Students with Disabilities in Postsecondary Education," National Center for Education Statistics, U.S. Department of Education, August 1999.
6. Proloquo main Web site <http://www.assistiveware.com/proloquo.php>.
7. J. Williams, "Buying an Assistive Technology Product," National Organization on Disability, November 2005 <http://www.nod.org>.
8. L. Briggs, "Bloomsburg U Tailors Online Learning to the Deaf," *Campus Technology*, November 2007 <http://campustechnology.com/articles/56259/
9. "What Is Sorenson VRS?" Sorenson VRS Web site accessed March 23, 2008 <http://www.sorensonvrs.com/what/index.php>.
10. C. Chong and S. Booth, "Buying a Computer," *Braille Monitor*, Vol. 46, No. 11, December 2003.
11. "Links to Software and Hardware Resources," Assistive Technology for Computers and Printed Material Web site, accessed March 21, 2008 <http://kpope.com/assistech/index.php>.
12. J. Williams, "MP3 Technology Advances Options for Readers with Disabilities," National Organization on Disability, June 10, 2004 <http://www.nod.org>.
13. J. Williams, "The Optical Braille Reader (O. B. R.) Expands Communications Opportunities for Blind People," *National Organization on Disability E-Newsletter*, April 10, 2002 <http://www.nod.org>.
14. "ViewPlus to Incorporate Text-to-Speech Technology from Wizzard Software in New Chameleon Product Line," Wizzard Press Release, June 9, 2004.

15. J. Williams, "Voice Mate—An Ideal Electronic Organizer for People with Disabilities," *National Organization on Disability E-Newsletter*, June 5, 2002 <http://www.nod.org>.

16. J. Williams, "Corda's Software Enhance Career Opportunities for People with Disabilities," at508.com, October 2001 <http://www.at508.com/articles/jw_010.cfm>.

17. "Links to Software and Hardware Resources," Assistive Technology for Computers and Printed Material Web site, accessed March 21, 2008 <http://kpope.com/assistech/index.php>.

18. Ibid.

19. Ibid.

20. J. Williams, "Review of Dolphin's SuperNova Pen," National Organization on Disability, September 15, 2005 <http://www.nod.org>.

21. "Links to Software and Hardware Resources," Assistive Technology for Computers and Printed Material Web site, accessed March 21, 2008 <http://kpope.com/assistech/index.php>.

22. Ibid.

23. Ibid.

24. A. Taylor, S. Booth, and M. Tindell, "Deaf-Blind Communication Devices," *Braille Monitor*, October 2006.

25. J. Williams, " Lomak Is an Innovation in Empowerment for People with Disabilities," National Organization on Disability, March 16, 2006 <http://www.nod.org/index.cfm?fuseaction=Feature.showFeature&FeatureID=1582>.

26. "Links to Software and Hardware Resources," Assistive Technology for Computers and Printed Material Web site, accessed March 21, 2008 <http://kpope.com/assistech/index.php>.

27. Ibid.

28. Ibid.

29. J. L. Levine and M. A. Schappert, "A Mouse Adapter for People with Hand Tremor," *IBM Systems Journal,* Vol. 44, No. 3, 2005.

30. www.naturalpoint.com.smartnav/product.

31. J. Williams, "ATIA Conference Showcases Technologies for People with Disabilities", National Organization on Disability ENewsletter, February 16, 2006 www.nod.org.

32. T. Floyd, "Website Makes Gaming Accessible for Everyone," kotaku.com, March 5, 2008 <http://kotaku.com/364074/website-makes-gaming-accessible-for-everyone>.

33. Ibid.

34. J. Williams, "People with Disabilities Put Cell Phones to Good Use," National Organization on Disability, May 16, 2005 <http://www.nod.org>.

Chapter 10

1. J. Boase, J. Horrigan, B. Wellman, and L. Rainie, "The Strength of Internet Ties," Pew Internet and American Life Project, Washington, DC, January 25, 2006.

2. J. Dobson, "Purdue Professors Create Chemistry-Focused Serious Game," Serious Game Source, Jason Dobson, April 2007 <http://seriousgamesource.com/item.php?story=13384>.

3. L. Gomes, "Will All of Us Get Our 15 Minutes on a YouTube Video?" *Wall Street Journal,*

August 30, 2006 <http://online.wsj.com/public/article/SB115689298168048904–5wWyr-Swyn6RfVfz9NwLk774VUWc_20070829.html>.

4. "Statistics," Press Room, Facebook.com, retrieved March 31, 2008 <http://www.facebook.com/press/info.php?statistics>.

5. D. Sifry, "State of the Live Web, April 2007," Sifry's Alerts, Sifry.com, April 5, 2007 <http://www.sifry.com/alerts/archives/000493.html>.

Chapter 11

1. J. Pirani, "Supporting E-Learning in Higher education," EDUCAUSE Center for Applied Research, Vol. 2, July 2003 <http://www.educause.edu/ir/library/pdf/ERS0303/ecm0303.pdf>.

2. V. Sehgal, "Worldwide Online Population Forecast, 2006 to 2011: Emerging Economies Catalyze Future Growth," *Jupiter Research*, June 2007.

3. United Nations Educational, Scientific and Cultural Organization (UNESCO), 2003; United Nations, 2005; IDP Education Australia, 2002; Cisco IBSG, 2007.

4. N. Glakas, "Trends, Policies and Issues Reauthorization—2003," National Council of Higher Education Loan Programs, January 2003.

5. E. Zito, "The Online Learning Lowdown" *Online Degrees Magazine*, Fall/Winter 2007

6. I. E. Allen and J. Seaman, "Online Nation: Five Years of Growth in Online Learning," The Sloan Consortium and Babson Survey Research Group, October 2007.

7. http://www.open.ac.uk/; http://www.athabascau.ca/; http://university.phoenix.edu/; http://www.itesm.edu; http://www.ouhk.edu.hk.

8. T. Snyder, "Learn & Earn: The Key to Unlocking Financial Success," *Online Degree Magazine,* Fall/Winter 2007.

9. "In a Global Workforce, Does an MBA Still Carry Clout?" Knowledge@Emory, September 14, 2006 <http://knowledge.emory.edu/article.cfm?articleid=989>.

10. Ibid.

11. L. A. Karoly and C. W. A. Panis, "The 21st Century at Work: Forces Shaping the Future Workforce and Workplace in the United States," RAND Corporation, 2004 <http://www.rand.org/pubs/monographs/2004/RAND_MG164.pdf>.

12. http://scpd.stanford.edu/scpd/about/

13. http://exlweb.csun.edu/dl/; http://www.fuqua.duke.edu/mba/executive/cc/distance.html

14. J. B. Horrigan and A. Smith, "Home Broadband Adoption 2007," Pew Internet & American Life Project, June 2007 <http://www.pewinternet.org/pdfs/PIP_Broadband%202007.pdf>.

15. R. Musyoka, "What's behind the Explosive Growth in Distance Learning?" Friends of Vista Inc., July 2005 <http://www.friendsofvista.org/articles/article3975.html>.

16. Ibid.

17. Allen and Seaman, "Online Nation."

18. M. Williams, K. Paprock, and B. Covington, *Distance Learning: The Essential Guide*, Sage Publications, 1999.

19. E. Kesim and E. Agaoglu, "A Paradigm Shift in Distance Education: Web 2.0 and Social Software," *Turkish Online Journal of Distance Education*, Vol. 8, No. 3, July 2007 <http://tojde.anadolu.edu.tr/tojde27/pdf/article_4.pdf>

20. M. Weller, C. Pegler, and R. Mason, "Use of Innovative Technologies on an e-Learning Course," *The Internet and Higher Education*, Vol. 8, No. 1.

21. J. D. Spiceland and C. P. Hawkins, "The Impact on Learning of an Asynchronous Active Learning Course Format," *Journal of Asynchronous Learning Networks*, Vol. 6, No. 1, July 2002 <http://www.sloan-c.org/publications/jaln/v6n1/pdf/v6n1_spiceland.pdf>.

22. http://ocwconsortium.org/

23. http://istpub.berkeley.edu:4201/bcc/Fall2007/1114.html.

24. http://youtube.com/; http://www.itunes.com; http://www.bigthink.com.

25. L. A. Annetta, M. R. Murray, S. G. Laird, S. C. Bohr, and J. C. Park, "Serious Games: Incorporating Games in the Classroom," *EDUCAUSE Quarterly*, Vol. 29, No. 3, 2006.

26. L. A. Annetta, M. Klesath, and S. Holmes, "V-Learning: How Gaming and Avatars Are Engaging Online Students," February 17, 2008 <http://www.distance-educator.com/highereducation/modules.php?op=modload&name=News&file=article&sid=15763>.

27. "Portable Professor: Distance Learning in Your Pocket," © 2005 Military.com, <http://www.military.com/soldiertech/0,14632,Soldiertech_PocketED,,00.html>.

28. "Two Groups Funded for Innovative Learning Initiatives," College of Engineering University of Wisconsin-Madison, News and Events, August 29, 2005 <http://homepages.cae.wisc.edu/~blanchar/mepp/handhelds.html>.

29. B. Black, "Universities Still Confronted by Student Plagiarism," *Concordia's Thursday Report*, January 24, 2002 <http://ctr.concordia.ca/2001–02/Jan_24/01-Plagiarism/index.shtml>.

30. D. Muha, "Cheating: When Students Cheat," *Rutgers Focus*, March 17, 2000 <http://ur.rutgers.edu/focus/article/Cheating/88/>.

31. Ibid.

32. .A P. Kellogg, "Students Plagiarize Less Than Many Think, a New Study Finds," *The Chronicle of Higher Education*, Information Technology, February 1, 2002 <http://chronicle.com/free/2002/02/2002020101t.htm>.

33. L. S. Hamlin and W. T. Ryan, "Probing for Plagiarism in the Virtual Classroom," *Campus Technology*, April 29, 2003 <http://campustechnology.com/articles/39378_3/>.

34. A. L. Foster and B. Read, "Community-College Professors Grapple with Web Trends," *The Chronicle of Higher Education*, November 3, 2006 <http://chronicle.com/weekly/v53/i11/11a03101.htm>.

35. Hamlin and Ryan, "Probing for Plagiarism."

36. http://www.coastal.edu/library/presentations/mills5.html

37. http://www.turnitin.com

38. R. Salado, online program director, conversation February 2004.

39. http://www.plagiarism.com

40. Hamlin and Ryan, "Probing for Plagiarism."

41. L. Shyles, "Authenticating, Identifying, and Monitoring Learners in the Virtual Classroom: Academic Integrity in Distance Learning," Education Resources Information Center, November 2002.

42. "Cracking Down on Cyber Cheating," eLearners.com, July 31, 2007 <http://community.elearners.com/blogs/penn_foster_college_blog/archive/2007/07/31/Cracking-Down-on-Cyber_2D00_Cheating.aspx>.

43. Hamlin and Ryan, "Probing for Plagiarism."

Chapter 12

1.   P. Abramson, "2006 College Construction Report," *College Planning and Management*, February 2006 <http://www2.peterli.com/global/pdfs/CPMConstruction2006.pdf>.
2.   B. Sinclair, "Commons 2.0: Library Spaces Designed for Collaborative Learning, *EDUCAUSE Quarterly*, Vol. 30, No. 4, 2007.
3.   A. L. Bishop, R. K. Dinkins, and J. L. Dominick, "Programming Handheld Devices to Enhanced Learning," *EDUCAUSE Quarterly*, No. 1, 2003 <http://www.educause.edu/ir/library/pdf/eqm0318.pdf>.
4.   "Target PC Initiative Wins HP Grant," SMUHub e-newsletter, Singapore Management University, January 2005 <http://www.smu.edu.sg/news_room/smuhub/jan2005/microsite/CorBuzz_05_Tablet.html>.
5.   L. Estabrook, E. Witts, and L. Rainie, "Information Searches That Solve Problems: How People Use the Internet, Libraries and Government Agencies When They Need Help," Pew Internet and American Life Project and the Graduate School of Library and Information Science, University of Urbana at Urbana-Champaign, December 30, 2007.
6.   "Libraries: How They Stack Up," A Report from OCLC Online Computer Library Center, 2003 <http://www5.oclc.org/downloads/community/librariesstackup.pdf >.
7.   Ibid.
8.   Ibid.
9.   Ibid.
10. Ibid.
11. Ibid.
12. The concept has been inspired by multipurpose buildings and environments I have visited including but not limited to Stanford University Clark Center, MIT's Stata Center, the Time Warner Building, New York City, Monash University Library, Stanford Wallenberg Hall, Las Vegas multipurpose retail hotels and malls, Magnificent Mile's building 900 Michigan Ave, Georgetown neighborhood, Washington, DC, Stanford Shopping Mall, California, Lincoln Road, South Beach Miami, Hyatt Hotel underground mall Beijing, the city of Düsseldorf, Harrods London, Republic Polytechnic, Lied Library UNLV, City of Delft, Cisco Systems workplace of the future, Cisco Systems Executive Briefing center, The Gap retail stores, Sephora retail stores, One Cleveland Ohio, Second Life islands, Murdoch University Library Archipelago in Second Life, HP Pavilion arena San Jose, Whole Foods NYC, Equinox Health Clubs, Starbucks, airports at Singapore, San Francisco, and Bangkok, The Blue Hotel, Woolloomooloo Bay, Australia, Albertsons Grocery Jackson Hole, Wyoming, The Tech Museum of Innovation (San Jose), The Field Museum (Chicago), Exploratorium ,San Francisco, National Taiwan Normal University Library, The Laundry Bar, South Beach Miami, Bites on Wheels South Beach Miami, Loyola Marymount University (Santa Monica), Work loft apartments (San Francisco), Wake Forest College mobility, Dartmouth College wireless, Bryant University's IP-enabled campus, UCLA, Erasmus, Seton Hall, Centre Pompidou France, Telnor, Norway.

Chapter 13

1.   Cuban, L. (1986). *Teachers and Machines: The Classroom Use of Technology since 1920*. New York: Teachers College Press). Cuban, L. (2001). *Oversold and Underused*. Cambridge, MA:

Harvard University Press.

2. Cuban, L. (2001). *Oversold and Underused*. Cambridge, MA: Harvard University Press.

3. Cuban, L. (1986). *Teachers and Machines: The Classroom Use of Technology since 1920*. New York: Teachers College Press.

4. Tyack, D. B., & Cuban, L. (1995). *Tinkering toward Utopia: A Century of Public School Reform*. Cambridge, MA: Harvard University Press.

5. Noble, D. (1999). Digital Diploma Mills: Rehearsal for the Revolution. Paper presented at the Digital Diploma Mills Conference ,

6. Postman (1992). *Technopoly: The Surrender of Culture to Technology*. New York: Knopf. Postman (1995) *The End of Education: Redefining the Value of School*. New York: Knopf.

7. Selwyn, N. (2007). The Use of Computer Technology in University Teaching and Learning: A Critical Perspective. *Journal of Computer Assisted Learning, 23*(2), 83–94.

8. Williams, D. (2007). *US Broadband Forecast, 2007 to 2012*. Jupiter Research: http://www.jupiterresearch.com/bin/item.pl/research:concept/59/id=99229/.

9. Budde, P. (2008). *2008 USA Telecoms, Wireless, and Broadband*. Paul Budde Communication Ltd: http://www.budde.com.au/buddereports/4498/2008_USA_-_Telecoms_Wireless_and_Broadband.aspx.

10. IPSOS Insight (2007). *The Face of the Web*.

11. Sharma, D. (2005). Broadband Penetration to Surge by 2010, *CNET News*: CNET News.

12. Salaway, G., & Caruso, J. (2007). *The ECAR Study of Undergraduate Students and Information Technology, 2007*. Boulder: EDUCAUSE Center for Applied Research.

13. Prensky, M. (2006). *Don't Bother Me Mom—I'm Learning!* St. Paul, MN: Paragon House.

14. Mitchell, R. (2008). Harvard to Collect, Disseminate Scholarly Articles for Faculty, *Harvard University Gazette Online* (p. 1). Cambridge, MA: Harvard University Press.

15. Last, J. (2007). Google and Its Enemies, *The Weekly Standard* 13. Washington, DC: Weekly Standard.

16. Postman, N. (1995). *The End of Education: Redefining the Value of School*. New York: Knopf.

17. Salaway, G., & Caruso, J. (2007). *The ECAR Study of Undergraduate Students and Information Technology, 2007*. Boulder: EDUCAUSE Center for Applied Research.

18. Madden, M. (2007). *Online Video*. Washington, DC: Pew/Internet & American Life Project.

19. Prensky, M. (2006). *Don't Bother Me Mom—I'm Learning!* St. Paul, MN: Paragon House.

20. Prensky, M. (2001). *Digital Natives, Digital Immigrants*. From *On the Horizon, 9*(5).

21. Prensky, M. (2001). *Digital Natives, Digital Immigrants*. From *On the Horizon, 9*(5).

22. Wesch, M. (2008). Human Futures for Technology and Education, EDUCAUSE Learning Initiative. San Antonio, TX: EDUCAUSE.

23. McLuhan, M., & Fiore, Q. (1967). *The Medium Is the Massage*. New York: Random House.

24. Clegg S., Hudson A. & Steel J. (2003). The Emperor's New Clothes. *British Journal of Sociology of Education* 24, 39–53

25. Tyack, D. B., & Cuban, L. (1995). *Tinkering toward Utopia: A Century of Public School Reform*. Cambridge, MA: Harvard University Press; Graham, P. (1995). Battleships and Schools. *Daedalus, 124*(4), 43–47; Oliver, D. W. (1976). *Education and Community*. Berkeley: McCutchan Publishing Corporation.

26. Cevetello, J. P. (2001). *Together Alone: A Multi-Method Case Examination of on Online Asynchronous Learning Network*. Cambridge, MA: Harvard University Press.

27. Tyack, D. B., & Cuban, L. (1995). *Tinkering toward Utopia: A Century of Public School Reform*. Cambridge, MA: Harvard University Press.
28. Tyack, D. B., & Cuban, L. (1995). *Tinkering toward Utopia: A Century of Public School Reform*. Cambridge, MA: Harvard University Press; Ravitz, D., & Vinovskis, M. (1995). Learning from the Past: What History Teaches Us about School Reform. *Journal of American History, 82*(3), 1293–1294.
29. Salaway, G., & Caruso, J. (2007). *The ECAR Study of Undergraduate Students and Information Technology, 2007*. Boulder: EDUCAUSE Center for Applied Research. "
30. Cuban, L. (1986). *Teachers and Machines: The Classroom Use of Technology since 1920*. New York: Teachers College Press.
31. Postman, N. (1995). *The End of Education: Redefining the Value of School*. New York: Knopf.
32. Postman, N. (1995). *The End of Education: Redefining the Value of School*. New York: Knopf.
33. Allen, I. E., & Seaman, J. (2006). *Making the Grade: Online Education in the United States*. Needham, MA: Sloan Consortium.
34. Synder, T. (2007). *Digest of Education Statistics*. Washington, DC: National Center for Education Statistics, U.S. Department of Education.
35. Gerald, D., & Hussar, W. (2002). Projections of Education Statistics to 2012. U.S. Department of Education, National Center for Education Statistics.
36. Goldberg, C. (2001). Auditing Classes at MIT, On the Web and Free. *New York Times*: April 4, 2001.
37. Pacey, A. (1995). *The Culture of Technology*. Cambridge, MA: MIT Press.
38. McLuhan, M. (1964). *Understanding Media: The Extensions of Man*. New York: American Library.
39. Zemsky, R. M. (2004). *Thwarted Innovation: What Happened to E-Learning and Why*. Philadelphia, PA: University of Pennsylvania Press.
40. Cuban, L. (2006). Cuban Op-Ed: The Laptop Revolution Has No Clothes. *Education Week, 26*(8), 29.
41. Hahn, K. (2008). Talk about Talking about New Models of Scholarly Communication. *Journal of Electronic Publishing, 11*(1).
42. Nelson, M. (2008). *E-books in Higher Education: Nearing the End of the Era of Hype*. Accessed from http://connect.educause.edu/Library/EDUCAUSE+Review/EBooksinHigherEducationNe/46314?time=1211898596.
43. Ediger, J. (2007). Apple Executive Briefing. Cupertino, CA.
44. Jensen, M. (2007). The New Metrics of Scholarly Authority. *Chronicle of Higher Education*, 53(41), B6.
45. Hahn, K. (2008). Talk about Talking about New Models of Scholarly Communication. *Journal of Electronic Publishing*, 11(1).
46. Tapscott, D., & Williams, A. (2006). *Wikinomics: How Mass Collaboration Changes Everything*. New York: Portfolio.
47. Salaway, G., & Caruso, J. (2007). *The ECAR Study of Undergraduate Students and Information Technology, 2007*. Boulder: EDUCAUSE Center for Applied Research.
48. Ball, C., & Moeller, R. (2007). Re-Inventing the Possibilities: Academic Literacy & New Media, *Fibreculture Journal*. 10
49. Van Note Chism, N. (2006). Challenging Traditional Assumptions and Rethinking Learning Spaces. In D. Oblinger (Ed.), *Learning Spaces*. Boulder: EDUCAUSE.
50. Graetz, K. (2006). The Psychology of Learning Environments. In D. Oblinger (Ed.), *Learn-*

ing Spaces. Boulder: EDUCAUSE.

51. Cevetello, J. P. (2001). *Together Alone: A Multi-Method Case Examination of on Online Asynchronous Learning Network.* Cambridge, MA: Harvard University Press.

52. Brown, J. S., & Adler, R. P. (2008). Minds on Fire: Open Education, the Long Tail, and Learning 2.0. *EDUCAUSE Review, 43*(1), 16–32.

53. Hahn, K. (2008). Talk about Talking about New Models of Scholarly Communication. *Journal of Electronic Publishing, 11*(1).

54. Young, J. (2008). A Future without Courses, *The Wired Campus: Chronicle of Higher Education.*

Chapter 14

1. http://www.digitalcenter.org/pdf/2008-Digital-Future-Report-Final-Release.pdf
2. According to the Pew Internet & American Life project; Lenhardt and Madden, 2005
3. Adler, 1982
4. Erickson quote (presumably from the panel).
5. Arthur W. Chickering and Zelda F. Gamson's *Seven Principles for Good Practice in Undergraduate Education.*
6. "The Way People Learn," http://www.nap.edu/catalog.php?record_id=6160
7. (*Educom Review* September/October 1998 www.educause.edu/ir/library/html/erm/erm98/erm9853.html)
8. in the *AAHE Bulletin* (October, pp. 3–6)
9. http://www.tltgroup.org/programs/seven.html
10. http://web.archive.org/web/20040105092358/csf.colorado.edu/gpe/gpe95a/index.html
11. http://mediatedcultures.net/worldsim.htm
12. http://www.youtube.com/watch?v=dGCJ46vyR9o
13. http://com.bradley.edu/faculty/lamoureux/website2/slstuff.html
14. http://honolulu.hawaii.edu/intranet/committees/FacDevCom/guidebk/teachtip/7princip.htm
15. http://www.nytimes.com/2003/11/09/jobs/26jmar.html
16. http://www.news.com/Silicon-Graphics-Unveils-Cosmo/2100-1023_3-279022.html
17. http://video.csupomona.edu/streaming/daf/daf_index.html
18. www.digitalstorytelling.org
19. www.melbourne2051.com
20. http://icohere.com
21. http://eluminate.net
22. digent.rit.edu
23. www.pageflakes.com/cnhs/14568889
24. http://web.mit.edu/edtech/casestudies/teal.html
25. http://web.mit.edu/smcs/icampus/2005/mit-Teal1-220k.asx, http://web.mit.edu/edtech/casestudies/pdf/teal1.pdf
26. http://www.disinterest.org/resource/imaginary-realities/HISTOR~1.HTM
27. N. Jennings & C. Collings (2008). Virtual or Virtually U: Education Institutions in Second Life. *International Journal of Social Sciences* 3 (2), pp. 180-186.http://wp.nmc.org/mrpixel/

28.   http://jcmc.indiana.edu/vol1/issue4/rafaeli.html

Conclusion

1.   M. Castells, *The Rise of the Network Society*, Wiley-Blackwell, 2nd edition, January 15, 2000; *The Network Society: A Cross-cultural Prospective*, Edward Elgar Publication, July 30, 2005; *The Network Society; from Knowledge to Policy*, Center for Transatlantic Relations, Washington, DC, 2006.
2.   Demiray, U. (2005). Defining Distance Education. In A. Isman, M. Barkan, and U. Demiray (eds.) *Distance Education: The Winds of Change*. Ankara: PEGMA Publications.
3.   E. Kesim and E. Agaoglu, "A Paradigm Shift in Distance Education: Web 2.0 and Social Software," *Turkish Online Journal of Distance Education*, Vol. 8, No. 3, Article 4, July 2007.
4.   Y. Punnie and M. Cabrera, *The Future of ICT and Learning in the Knowledge Society*, Report on a Joint DG JRC-DG EAC Workshop, Seville, European Commission Joint Research Center, 2006.
5.   J. Q. Anderson, "The Future of the Internet II," Pew Internet and American Life Project, Elon University, September 24, 2006.
6.   C. Jones, Carolyn, "Teleworking: The Quiet Revolution," 2005 Update, Gartner Research, ID Number: G00122284 2005.

About the Authors

Dr. Tracey Wilen-Daugenti

Director Higher Education
Cisco Internet Business Solutions Group

As IBSG Higher Education Lead, Dr. Tracey Wilen-Daugenti guides public sector organizations in innovation and Internet excellence to help post secondary education institutions achieve their goals.

Before joining IBSG, Dr. Wilen-Daugenti held various positions at Cisco in the areas of business development, marketing, and operations. Prior to Cisco, she held executive posts at Hewlett-Packard and Apple Computer.

Dr. Wilen-Daugenti was recognized in 1995 as a notable, modern academic researcher on the topic of business women. She has authored eight books on women and international business, and has published a number of higher-education papers, including "Top Trends in Higher Education, 2007–2008," "Top Trends in Higher Education, 2008–2009," "21st Century Learning Environments: Next-Generation Strategies in Higher Education," and "Dual-Mode Phones and Mobility in Tertiary Institutions." Her latest book is *edu Technology and Learning Environments in Higher Education.*

A frequent contributor to the media, Dr. Wilen-Daugenti has appeared on *CNN, ABC, CBS,* and has been quoted in *The Wall Street Journal* and the *Los Angeles Times.* She is also a speaker for key universities and business groups, and was recently named "San Francisco Woman of the Year," by Globalwomen.biz, for her outreach efforts in the fields of academia, women's research, and technology.

Dr. Wilen-Daugenti holds an MBA and a Doctorate in international business, and has been a visiting scholar at Stanford University researching topics in higher education and an adjunct professor of graduate and doctoral programs for a number of San Francisco Bay Area universities. She is a member of the Grammy Music Foundation, International Game Developers Association, and EDUCAUSE.

Forward Through a Rearview Mirror: What the History of Technology in Higher Education Tells Us About Its Future

By Joseph Cevetello, EdD
Loyola Marymount University

Joseph Cevetello is Senior Director of Information Technology and Director of Academic Technology at Loyola Marymount University. In this role he provides strategic leadership and vision in support of online learning infrastructure, policy and faculty integration of technology in their teaching and research.

Dr. Cevetello received his masters and his doctorate from the Graduate School of Education at Harvard University. His research and teaching interests encompass how online learning technologies affect adult learner and teacher interaction/collaboration, how media influence student and faculty perspectives of learning and their roles, and how the use of technology impacts organizational effectiveness, communication, and change.

Prior to joining LMU, Joseph was a consultant to a number of higher-education institutions and organizations including the University of Chicago, Harvard University, The Massachusetts Institute of Technology, The Austrian National Bank, and the World Bank.

Learning 2.0: Re-Visiting the 7 Principles

By Lev S. Gonick, PhD
Case Western Reserve University

Lev Gonick is Vice President and CIO at Case Western Reserve University in Cleveland, Ohio. He is co-chair of the CIO Executive Council's higher education committee. Gonick is also the founder of OneCleveland, now known as OneCommunity, the award-winning project to create a connected community throughout Northeast Ohio through high speed wired and wireless network connectivity. Additionally, Dr. Gonick served as president of the board of the New Media Consortium (2005–2007) and is the Chair of the NMC's 2008 Horizon Report on emerging technology trends impacting the academy.

In 2007, he and Case Western Reserve University were recognized with a ComputerWorld Laureate for launching the Cleveland 2.0 project to leverage technology to address community priorities. In 2006, he was recognized by ComputerWorld as a Premier 100 IT leader and honored in the same year by CIO magazine with a CIO 100 Award.

Title: Increase of Credible Content on the web and proper evaluation

Title: Adaptive and Assistive Technology for use in Higher Education

By Patricia D. Wilen, PhD

Patricia Wilen is a New York State Licensed Psychologist who moved to the Bay area to engage in research on technological innovations in education. She holds a Ph.D. in Psychology from Hofstra University in New York and an M.S. and B.A. from the City University of New York. Dr. Wilen worked for the New York State Department of Cooperative Educational Services for 25 years and also maintained a private practice in psychotherapy. She was co-author of *Asia For Women in Business (95)*, and a contributor to *China for Business Women (07)*. An active world traveler, Dr. Wilen is particularly interested in educational issues in all areas of the world. She and her husband live in Pleasanton, CA.

Title: Glossary

By Alva Grace R. McKee

Alva Grace R. McKee is currently a student at UC Berkeley in Molecular and Cell Biology with a minor in Classical Civilizations. She has presented at workshops designed to encourage school-age girls to pursue a career in the sciences, helped write review materials for takers of the Test of English as a Foreign Language (TOEFL), volunteered for the Red Cross and Habitat for Humanity, and tutored underserved K-12 schoolchildren in the East Bay as well as students at her local community college. She has a passion for education and the sciences.

Figures and drawings:

Anne Mueller website: http://www.hueq3.com/index.php